WORLD BANK TECHNICAL PAPER NO. 527

World Bank/European Commission Programme on Private Participation in Mediterranean Infrastructure

Transport Policies for the Euro-Mediterranean Free-Trade Area

An Agenda for Multimodal Transport Reform in the Southern Mediterranean

Daniel Müller-Jentsch

The World Bank
Washington, D.C.

1 2 3 4 04 03 02

ISBN: 0-8213-5198-2
ISSN: 0253-7494

Daniel Müller-Jentsch is an Economist for the Brussels-based World Bank/European Commission Programme on Private Participation in Mediterranean Infrastructure.

Library of Congress Cataloging-in-Publication Data.

Müller-Jentsch, Daniel, 1969-
Transport policies for the Euro-Mediterranean free-trade area : an agenda for multimodal transport reform in the southern Mediterranean / Daniel Müller-Jentsch.
p. cm. — (World Bank technical paper ; no. 527)
Includes bibliographical references.
ISBN 0-8213-5198-2
1. Transportation and state—Mediterranean Region. 2. Free Trade—Mediterranean Region. I. Title. II. Series.

HE267.7.M85 2002
388'.0918'2—dc21

2002031141

CONTENTS

Boxes

Chapter 1: Transport Logistics and Multimodal Transport

Chapter 2: Air Transport

Chapter 3: Maritime Transport

Chapter 4: Land-Based Transport and Other Sector Issues

Diagrams

Tables

FOREWORD

This is the second regional sector study published by the joint World Bank - European Commission Programme on Private Participation in Mediterranean Infrastructure (PPMI). It has been produced as an analytical basis for the work of the Euro-Mediterranean Transport Forum, as well as for a large regional technical assistance project for transport policy reforms that the European Commission has prepared with assistance from PPMI. This project should be launched towards the end of 2002. The study seeks to map out key policy issues that need to be addressed to successfully implement transport sector reforms across the Mediterranean. The proposals made do not necessarily represent the official views of the European Commission or of the World Bank, but are meant as a contribution to the ongoing reform debates in the region. Given the complexity of the subject matter, the document is designed in a modular fashion. Modal chapters, thematic sections, text boxes, footnotes and bibliography with further reading, and cross-references should allow readers to find specific information more easily.

The key proposal developed throughout this study is that the Euro-Mediterranean free-trade area – to be completed by around 2010 – should be complemented by a *common transport space* between the European Union and its Mediterranean Partners. The guiding principle of transport policies at the national and regional level should be the creation of such a common transport space. This involves the removal of legal, regulatory, and institutional barriers in the sector, as well as the removal of physical infrastructure bottlenecks. The study argues that the European Single Market for transport and its extension to the accession countries can provide some useful lessons for this process. By providing an overview of global and regional reform trends, this report should also facilitate the dissemination of international best practice.

Most southern Mediterranean countries have begun to modernize their transport sectors. This is a welcome development, but much work remains to be done, if transport is to fulfill its critical role as a facilitator for trade, tourism, and foreign direct investment throughout the region. Moving reforms into a higher gear will require a concerted effort on behalf of governments, donors, and the private sector. While this study can contribute to a broader and more structured debate between these parties, reform efforts by policy makers will be needed to move from strategy to action. The overhaul of the policy framework in the transport sector will also require technical assistance from the donor community. Given the complexity of the policy issues involved, an essential ingredient for all reform initiatives will be rigorous analysis and state-of-the-art expertise.

Since no single donor can provide all the required funding and expertise, close donor coordination is essential. This regional study and the joint World Bank - European Commission Programme that produced it are testimony of the potential for more systematic cooperation across institutional boundaries. The reform agenda outlined in this document can only be implemented if all parties play their respective roles and work together hand-in-hand.

Emmanuel Forestier
Director
Finance, Private Sector and Infrastructure
Middle East and North Africa Region
World Bank

ACKNOWLEDGMENTS

This study was compiled during a three-year period under the supervision of first Pierre Guislain, and then Elisabetta Capannelli in their capacity as PPMI Program Manager. Draft versions of the document were sent for comment to EuropeAid and DG Energy and Transport from the European Commission, as well as the transport ministries of the twelve Mediterranean Partner governments. Given the scarcity of statistics and literature on transport policies in the southern Mediterranean, the personal knowledge of some seasoned sector experts was indispensable. Particular thanks go to Michel Loir, who repeatedly shared his expertise. Help on the compilation of statistics came from CESD Roma. On specific themes, the author drew on the know-how of Honoré Paelinck, Mark Juhel, and Wolfgang Elsner (ports); René Fennes and Carlos Berospe (EU aviation); Kamal Shehadi (Mashrek countries); Salim Balaa (customs); Karim Jacques-Budin (rail); Ismail Mobarak (Suez Canal); and Jürgen Lohmeyer (post). The help of Manuela Chiapparino in data analysis and background research, as well as the assistance of Henriette Mampuya on presentation and formatting, was also much appreciated. At the initial stages of the drafting process, important conceptual inputs came from Pierre Guislain – the eminence grise on PPI in the Mediterranean region.

Besides acknowledging these direct contributions, I would like to take the completion of this study as an opportunity to thank three people to whom I am grateful in a deeper sense. Foremost, I would like to thank my parents, who instilled me with the curiosity, intellectual rigor, and optimistic determination needed to tackle a project as challenging as this regional study. Moreover, I would like to express my gratitude to Richard Dills, who was my teacher in an advanced course on English literature during a high school exchange year in a remote part of the American West Coast. He had a remarkable ability for teaching the beauty of language, the power of ideas, and the art of essay writing. Unfortunately, I came to use these skills only for the mundane task of economic analysis. It seems to remain the privilege of a selected few to change the world through poetry.

ABSTRACT

This study argues that the 15 EU countries and their 12 Mediterranean Partners should complement their Euro-Mediterranean free-trade area for industrial goods (to be completed by around 2010) with a common transport space. This would require the removal of policy-induced frictions in the region's multimodal transport system in order to facilitate the flow of goods, people, and investments within this emerging trade block. The purpose of the report is to identify the bottlenecks and inefficiencies that currently exist and to map out the reforms in the legal, regulatory, and institutional framework that should be implemented to address them. This includes both national and cross-border policy measures in the various modes (air, maritime, and land-based transport) as well as in transport logistics. The study compares sector performance and sector policies within the concerned countries and it benchmarks these against international best practice. It draws on policy lessons from other developing regions, such as Latin America and Eastern Europe and assesses the extent to which the policy framework of the EU Single Market in the transport sector could provide guidance for the creation of a common transport space throughout the Mediterranean region.

The joint World Bank – European Commission Programme on Private Participation in Mediterranean Infrastructure (PPMI) was launched in 1997 and is located in Brussels. Its mandate is to promote infrastructure sector reform and provide technical expertise in this important and complex area of economic policy. PPMI assists countries in the Middle East and North Africa in the design and implementation of policies in the infrastructure sectors (telecommunications, transport, energy, water). Activities focus on the introduction of competition, the modernization of regulatory frameworks, and the creation of an environment conducive to private participation. PPMI carries out research, provides direct policy advice to governments, and helps its parent institutions prepare technical assistance projects in the infrastructure sectors.

Abbreviations and Acronyms

AA	Association Agreement
AACO	Arab Air Carriers Organization
ACI	Airport Council International
AEA	Association of European Airlines
AMU	Arab Maghreb Union
ASA	air service agreement
ATC	air traffic control
BA	British Airways
BOT	build-operate-transfer concession
BPO	Baltic Ports Organization
CAA	Civil Aviation Authority
CEE	Central and Eastern Europe
CEECs	Central and Eastern European Countries
CEN	Centre Européen de Normalisation
CFMU	Central Flow Management Unit
CIF	cost, insurance, freight
CIS	Commonwealth of Independent States
DG Relex	Directorate General for External Relations
DG TREN	Directorate General for Energy and Transport
DPA	Dubai Port Authority
EBRD	European Bank for Reconstruction and Development
ECAA	European Civil Aviation Area
ECAC	European Civil Aviation Conference
ECMT	European Conference of Ministers of Transport
EDI	electronic data interchange
EFTA	European Free-Trade Association
EIB	European Investment Bank
EMP	Euro-Mediterranean Partnership
ESC	European Shipper's Council
EU	European Union
FAA	Federal Aviation Administration
FDI	foreign direct investment
FIATA	International Federation of Freight Forwarders
FOB	free on board

FTA	free-trade area
GAFTA	Greater Arab Free-Trade Area
GATS	General Agreement on Trade in Services
GATT	General Agreement on Trade and Tariffs
GDP	gross domestic product
GNSS	Global Navigation Satellite Systems
GPS	Global Positioning System
GTMO	Groupe de Transport de la Meditérranée
IATA	International Air Transport Association
ICAO	International Civil Aviation Organization
ICC	International Chamber of Commerce
ICT	information and communication technology
IECC	International Express Carriers' Conference
IMO	International Maritime Organization
ISO	International Organization for Standardization
IT	information technology
JIT	just-in-time
MDF	Mediterranean Development Forum
MEA	Middle Eastern Airline
MEDA	Mésure d'Accompagnement
MEED	Middle Eastern Economic Digest
MENA	Middle East and North Africa
MP	Mediterranean Partner
NAFTA	North American Free-Trade Area
O&M	operations and maintenance
ODEP	Office d'Exploitation des Ports
OECD	Organization for Economic Co-operation and Development
OMMP	Office de la Marine Marchande et des Ports
ONT	Office National des Transports
OPNT	Office des Ports Nationaux Tunisien
PPI	private participation in infrastructure
PPMI	Programme for Private Participation in Mediterranean Infrastructure
RAM	Royal Air Moroc
RAS	risk analysis and selectivity
RPK	revenue-passenger-kilometer
RJ	Royal Jordanian
RoRo	roll-on, roll-off
SAS	Scandinavian Airlines Systems

SICA	Central American Integration System
SOE	state-owned enterprise
STAM	Société Tunisienne d'Acconage et de Manutention
TA	technical assistance
TCAA	Trans-Atlantic Common Aviation Area
TEU	twenty-food equivalent unit
TEN	Trans-European Network
TINA	Transport and Infrastructure Needs Assessment
TMA	Trans Mediterranean Airways
UIC	International Union of Railways
UK	United Kingdom
UN	United Nations
UNCITRAL	United Nations Commission on International Trade Law
UNCTAD	United Nations Conference on Trade and Development
UNDP	United Nations Development Programme
US	United States
VAT	value-added tax
WCO	World Customs Organization
WTO	World Trade Organization

EXECUTIVE SUMMARY

A central pillar of the Euro-Mediterranean Partnership (EMP) between the 15 Member States of the European Union (EU) and their twelve Mediterranean Partners (MPs) is the creation of a free-trade area (FTA) during the coming decade. If the economic benefits of this FTA are to be maximized, non-tariff barriers will also have to be removed – particularly all frictions and inefficiencies in the regional transport network. The FTA should therefore be complemented by a 'common transport space' throughout the Euro-Mediterranean region.

Economic development, trade, tourism, and personal travel in the emerging Euro-Mediterranean free trade area require a smoothly functioning multimodal transport system. More efficient transport would permit the southern Mediterranean countries to increase exports, attract more foreign direct investment, and participate in increasingly complex cross-border supply chains. Since the 1995 Barcelona Conference, where transport was identified as a priority issue, a broad consensus has developed that transport reform should be an integral part of economic adjustment at the national level as well as intergovernmental cooperation at the regional level. The objective of this study is to identify the range of transport policy reforms that would be needed to create a common transport space that spans the two sides of the Mediterranean Sea.

The multimodal transport network includes air transport (chapter 2), maritime transport (chapter 3), land-based modes (chapter 4), as well as intermodal logistics services (chapter 1). Many of the pressing bottlenecks and frictions in the Euro-Mediterranean transport system are policy-induced, rather than due to lack in physical infrastructure. What traders, investors, tourists, and business travelers ultimately care about are the cost, flexibility, and reliability of transport services provided on the basis of the physical infrastructure. These parameters are primarily determined by the way the transport sector is organized. This insight has induced governments worldwide to privatize transport companies, introduce competition in port services and air traffic, modernize regulatory frameworks, and remove bureaucratic frictions.

Several EMP policy documents emphasize the importance of implementing such policy reforms in the Mediterranean region. According to a Commission communication on transport in the Euro-Mediterranean region, for example, 'software' measures "should be given priority over 'hardware' measures. Many transport bottlenecks [...] have their principle causes in 'software' rather than 'hardware' problems." The 1997 Lisbon Declaration of Euro-Mediterranean transport policy makers demanded that an evaluation of "alternative solutions to the given transport problem should be made, especially where operational and organizational changes (including private participation) offer viable alternatives to capital-intensive and infrastructure solutions."

In several southern Mediterranean countries transport reforms are now underway, but a range of economic and efficiency indicators suggest that much remains to be done. Benchmarking of macroeconomic freight costs against best practice suggests that the potential economic benefits of comprehensive transport reforms in the Maghreb and Mashrek countries could be as high as € 3 to 5 billion per year. There are still southern Mediterranean ports where it takes longer to obtain customs clearance for a container than to ship it all the way from Hong Kong. The Lebanese government has sunk $ 450 million into a loss-making airline, while Jordan's flag carrier accumulated debt of more than $ 850 million, or around 10 percent of the country's GDP. Before recent reforms, the total economic costs imposed by port inefficiencies in Egypt were estimated to be as high as $ 2 billion annually, and in Algeria private sector sources calculated that the costs of customs inefficiencies in the port of Algiers alone amount to $ 200 million – the equivalent of 14,000 social housing units each year.

On the northern shore of the Mediterranean, the European Union has created a Single Market for transport, which comprises 15 nations and 376 million inhabitants. Air transport for both passengers and cargo has been fully liberalized, the majority of flag carriers and many key airports have been privatized, regulations for ground handling and airport charges have or will be strengthened, air traffic control is being reorganized to create a Single European Sky, and agreement has been reached with ten EU accession candidates to create a European Civil Aviation Area. Road freight has been fully competitive for about a decade, border controls have been abolished, and a vibrant logistics industry is rapidly consolidating across borders. The EU's strict competition and state aid rules have repeatedly been applied throughout the sector and the Commission has drafted new legislation to introduce competition in port services. In rail transport, a pan-European route network, comprising 50,000 kilometers of track, will be opened to private freight train operators. By the time the Euro-Mediterranean FTA is completed around 2010, the European Single Market for transport is expected to be fully liberalized, privatized, and integrated across national borders. With 13 official accession candidates in the process of adopting EU rules and regulations, this market will include 20 to 30 countries with 400 to 500 million consumers.

Transport flows in the region are characterized by some general patterns. First, the majority of cross-border traffic flows through maritime and air chains, especially in the countries of North Africa. Second, traffic tends to be heavily concentrated on few key ports, airports, and land-corridors. Third, about 50 percent of MP trade is conducted with the EU and South-South trade is limited to 5 percent of the total. One policy implication is that reforms and investments should be concentrated on a network of priority ports and airports, as well as a backbone network of roads and railroads. Another key implication is that maritime and air chains deserve specific attention.

Chapter 1: Transport Logistics and Multimodal Transport

A variety of technical innovations have transformed the global logistics industry beyond recognition. Unitized cargo, and especially containers, dramatically reduced the costs and time needed for modal transfer and thus door-to-door transport. Information technology permits the real-time tracking of shipments, satellite-based fleet management, electronic data interchange between the multiple parties involved in trade transaction, or a matching of demand and supply through online market places. Sophisticated port equipment and modern container vessels that can carry 6,000 containers are turning the shipping industry into a high-tech business.

At the same time, the third-party logistics industry is evolving rapidly. Freight forwarders have long acted as intermediaries that bundle different transport services and handle paper work on behalf of their clients. Increasingly, integrators offer all transport services in-house, reducing what can be up to 40 different steps in a transport chain to as few as a dozen. Express carriers in particular have perfected this business to offer overnight, time-definite delivery across the world. Additional value-added logistics services include warehousing, reverse logistics, or light assembly. As the boundaries between freight forwarders, integrators, carriers, and even postal operators blur, the race is on to be among the few dominant players in a consolidating industry.

This logistics revolution has been driven by the explosive expansion of global trade as well as the transformation of the way goods are manufactured and distributed. Trends like global sourcing, just-in-time production, ever shorter product- and time-to-market cycles, and the outsourcing of individual production stages have created 'a global conveyor belt'. Supply-chain management permits extended supply and distribution networks to be organized as 'virtual companies'. The increasing sophistication of these systems and the elimination of buffer stock have allowed leading companies to reduce total logistics costs by 50 percent in less than a decade.

These changes in global goods and transport markets have profound implications for the integration of developing countries in the international economy. As individual production stages are becoming geographically footloose and supply-chains ever more sensitive to transport-related disruptions, access to state-of-the-art transport services is a key determinant for the competitiveness of individual firms and entire countries. Tunisia, for instance, recently lost a bid for a factory by a German car part manufacturer for logistics reasons. A $ 12 million investment and 1,700 jobs went to Romania instead, because the one day time saving in each direction was vital for an industry reducing order-to-delivery cycles from nine to six days. Transport users no longer 'move goods but manage flows' and transport policies need to reflect these realities.

Southern Mediterranean countries are currently poorly integrated in international supply chains and comprehensive transport sector reforms are required to avoid further marginalization. Many of the state-owned ports, shipping lines, airports, airlines, and logistics companies that dominate transport markets in the region have found it difficult to adapt to the changing needs of their clients. More private sector participation, competitive dynamics, and regulatory reforms are needed to provide a framework for the development of a modern logistics industry. Modal interfaces, port hinterland connections, and logistics-related banking and insurance services need to be improved while documentation requirements and red tape ought to be minimized.

Many of the most severe bottlenecks stem from cumbersome border-related controls, especially customs. In Egypt, around 1,500 tariff lines are subject to product standards and depending on the product category, different forms must be submitted to several agencies. In Jordan, 51,000 import transactions were subjected to tests by the standards institute in one year, even though only 65 (or 0.1 percent) failed the tests. It is not uncommon for cargo imported through ports to require five to ten days for customs clearance. In countries like Morocco or Lebanon, customs reforms have worked wonders and most MPs have now started to tackle border-related frictions.

While most transport sector reforms will have to take place at the national level, cross-border cooperation will also be needed. Priorities should be a harmonization of customs procedures and product standards, juxtaposed controls at border crossings, and coordinated facilitation measures along main land corridors. A large number of international conventions to facilitate cross-border trade and transport exist, which the MPs could ratify and implement. Of 16 key United Nation transport facilitation conventions, for example, Italy ratified 16 and France 15 – compared to only 4 in the case of Algeria and 5 in the case of Tunisia. Donor funding for physical infrastructure should focus on a network of key ports and airports, as well as a backbone network of roads and railroads. Moreover, it could be made conditional on complementary policy reforms.

Chapter 2: Air Transport

In the multimodal transport system of the region, air transport plays a critical role for the transport of passengers (including tourists) and high value-added, time-sensitive goods. In terms of weight, only 1 percent of trade between the two sides of the Mediterranean is being conducted by air, but in terms of value it is around 15 percent. While a mere five million people arrive in the MPs by sea each year, the figure for air transport is more than 40 million. With tourism receipts in the twelve MPs amounting to more than $ 20 billion annually, cheap and efficient air transport is vital.

One important reform challenge is the restructuring and eventual privatization of airlines. Some MP flag carriers, such as Tunis Air or Royal Air Moroc, are well managed, but most still under-perform. Load factors of virtually all MP airlines, for instance, were below the world average, often by 10 to 20 percent. The comprehensive restructuring of Royal Jordanian, which for many years incurred heavy financial losses, provides general lessons for other countries. Regarding privatization, state-ownership in MP flag carriers still averages 95 percent, while virtually all Latin American and most European flag carriers are now in private hands. An example for how regulatory reform can induce even state-owned airlines to excel is Emirate Airlines. Operating in the open skies environment of Dubai, without subsidies or protection, Emirates has won more than 150 quality awards and makes profits of about $ 100 million per year.

The liberalization of licensing rules and traffic rights will be needed to foster competition and greater private participation in air transport. Several MPs have started to dismantle the exclusivity rights granted to flag carriers and issued licenses to private operators. Most of these, however, remain niche players and the incumbents continue to influence sector policies. In Egypt, the tourism industry has long complained about the grip of EgyptAir on the market and a special aviation minister was recently appointed to oversee reforms. In Morocco, express carrier DHL lost an important contract after it was refused regulatory permission to operate a larger aircraft. One market segment where liberalization is far advanced in the southern Mediterranean is charter traffic. While this is a good start, MPs should follow the EU example and remove regulatory distinctions between scheduled and non-scheduled services, by liberalizing the latter.

Market access, frequencies, and many other important parameters in cross-border traffic continue to be governed by bilateral air service agreements (ASAs) between governments. Several MPs have started to relax the provisions in the ASAs they negotiate in an effort to increase flexibility and competition. The most far-reaching reforms to date took place in Lebanon, which recently adopted an open skies regime. Inside the EU Single Market, all ASAs have been abolished, and on behalf of the 15 EU countries the Commission recently negotiated the creation of a European Civil Aviation Area with ten accession candidates. This will liberalize air traffic rights and oblige all signatories to generally adopt EU rules and regulations in the air transport market.

While liberal amendments to existing ASAs should be a short-term priority for MPs, the eventual transition to open skies regimes and a regional civil aviation area would be desirable. The positive effects of such liberalization are well documented. Between 1997 and 1998, six Latin American countries that entered into open skies agreements with the United States saw traffic levels rise by an average of 21 percent, while other markets in the region barely grew. A Commission report found that ticket prices on routes with two operators were 5 to 17 percent cheaper, and with three operators prices were 10 to 24 percent lower than on monopoly routes.

Other items on the regulatory reform agenda in the air transport market are the liberalization of ground handling, transparent regulation of airport fees and slot allocation, as well as the reform of air traffic control. Costs related to airports and air traffic control can account for up to a quarter of airline expenses. Evidence shows that transparent regulation of monopolistic activities and the introduction of competition in ground handling can reduce these costs significantly. The EU has formally liberalized ground handling, but competitive dynamics have been slow to unfold. With draft legislation on the regulation of airport charges blocked by some EU member states, the Commission relied on general competition rules to counter anticompetitive abuses. In air traffic control, the work of Eurocontrol and the planned creation of a Single European Sky could provide guidance for cross-border coordination in the Euro-Mediterranean.

One policy area in air transport where reforms are gathering considerable momentum in the southern Mediterranean is airport privatization. Egypt has successfully issued several private concessions for secondary airports and is contemplating private participation for a new terminal in Cairo. The privatizations of the airports in Algiers, Beirut, Cyprus, and Malta are planned or under preparation, while Tunisia would like to see a private investor build a new $ 400 million airport. To date, however, none of the major airports in the MPs has actually been privatized and before such disposals occur, adequate regulatory regimes ought to be put in place.

Chapter 3: Maritime Transport

Especially in North Africa, the majority of cross-border transport flows through ports. Ports are a major bottleneck in maritime chains and streamlining their operations is an obvious reform priority. As entry points into a country, ports are not only the place where cargo changes modes, but also the place where it 'hits the administration'. The transfer and clearance of goods through ports can involve up to 50 documents. Goods change hands several times and with at least half a dozen parties involved, multiple transfers of ownership titles, insurance certificates, letters of credit, invoices, customs forms, and administrative documents are inevitable.

While the complexity of port operations has always created frictions, current sector structures are increasingly at odds with rapidly changing technical and economic requirements, such as containerization or the demand for just-in-time delivery. Most ports in the MPs continue to be managed by public port authorities, with ill-defined incentive frameworks and insufficient accountability. Exclusivity rights, unregulated monopolies, collusive practices, and labor problems hamper competition and undermine efficiency. These problems plague ports worldwide, but reforms in the MPs are lagging behind regions such as Latin America or Europe. The Baltic Sea, where port reforms and maritime trade play an important role in regional integration between the EU and transition countries, could be an interesting precedent for the Mediterranean.

In accordance with international best practice, a key priority will be a separation of regulatory and commercial functions through the creation of landlord ports, especially in large ports. This implies a three-tier institutional structure: the government remains in charge of sector policy and planning, autonomous port authorities manage and regulate ports, while private companies provide commercial services. The landlord port model is becoming the norm in the EU and a survey found that 88 of the world's 100 largest ports have adopted this operating structure. In the MPs, landlord ports basically do not yet exist. For smaller ports, the tool port model, with the port authority owning the equipment and renting it to private operators, is more appropriate.

For modern container terminals and certain bulk cargo terminals, vertical integration of port management and service provision is needed for operational efficiency. In these cases concessions should be given to private operators, with a competitive tender and transparent regulation preventing the extraction of monopoly rents. Egypt, for example, has issued concessions for a container terminal in East Port Said, for a petroleum terminal in Alexandria, and for a port in a new industrial zone at the southern end of the Suez Canal. In East Port Said alone, private investment commitments amount to $ 480 million. Morocco has granted a 20-year concession for a coal terminal to a private power plant operator and has long toyed with plans for a private container terminal in Tangier. In 1999, Lebanon issued a concession for a container terminal in Beirut, but the investor subsequently pulled out. To date, none of the large existing ports in the southern Mediterranean has been privatized.

Competition between ports can also induce efficiency improvements, but it requires overlapping hinterlands. Several MP ports, especially in the Middle East, would be well placed to serve catchment areas in neighboring countries. In practice, however, regulatory restrictions, and especially the disruptions caused by controls at land borders, prevent this from happening. In Egypt, one of the few MPs where several large domestic ports share a potentially contested hinterland, state-ownership and decreed prices restrict competition. This contrasts with Europe where a customs union, the removal of border controls, and efficient hinterland connections bring ports from different countries into direct competition with each other.

An important reform item in maritime transport, facilitated by the introduction of landlord ports, is the introduction of private participation and competition in port services. A wide range of services is being provided to ships and cargo and many of them lend themselves to such reforms. There is no economic justification for public sector involvement or exclusivity rights in services, such as general cargo handling, warehousing, bunkering, banking, and insurance services or for restrictions to the operation of shipping agents and freight forwarders on port premises. Ideally, the role of the port authority should be to issue licenses to private operators and to create a level playing field for competition. Exceptions are pilotage, tug services, port security, and health services for which public provision, or at least strict but transparent regulation, is required.

While port reforms are the most pressing issue in maritime transport, the shipping market also deserves some attention by policy makers. Generally, the shipping industry is highly international and competitive. Different cargoes – such as dry and liquid bulk, general cargo, or containers – constitute specific market segments as they involve different types of terminals and vessels. General cargo traffic, especially container and RoRo (roll-on, roll-off) traffic plays a key role for the flow of manufactured and high value-added goods. An enabling policy framework for these trades, as well as for transshipment activities, should be ensured.

Chapter 4: Land-Based Transport and Other Sector Issues

Efficient hinterland connections for ports and airports, as well as smooth traffic flows along a backbone network of roads and railroads are priorities in land-based transport. As far as regional cooperation is concerned, the identification of physical and policy-induced bottlenecks along these corridors and a coordination of facilitation measures are obvious priorities. With land-borders a major source of disruptions, a streamlining of procedures, juxtaposed controls, adequate staffing and physical facilities are needed.

Roads account for the vast majority of land-based freight transport and the effective regulation of the trucking industry is an important policy issue. In most MPs, the industry is dominated by the private sector and quite competitive, but further deregulation of prices and market access would enhance efficiency. In cross-border haulage, a harmonization of standards for equipment and personnel, as well as the liberalization of cabotage and rights of establishment would be desirable from an economic point of view. In fact, all these policies were key elements of road freight reform in the EU since the late 1980s. Overloaded trucks do significant damage to roads, and a violation of safety and environmental rules creates negative externalities. As in maritime and air traffic, modern and strictly enforced technical, environmental, and safety regulations are thus called for.

In rail freight, the restructuring of state-owned companies tends to be the policy measure with the largest efficiency effect. In this mode, opportunities for the introduction of private participation and competition are more limited. Morocco has implemented a comprehensive and successful restructuring program in recent years that other MPs should be looking at. Most MP railway companies lack modern commercial management and many are incurring heavy losses. Overstaffing and the outsourcing of maintenance work to the private sector are other issues to be addressed. The facilitation of equipment and personnel transfer at border crossings, and the opening of key routes to private freight operators could also yield significant benefits.

Customs reform is one of the items on the policy agenda for which the payoff in terms of transport facilitation is highest. In this regard, the Lebanese experience with customs reforms can provide some useful lessons. With the help of donor assistance, the government streamlined procedures from 13 to 4 steps, and reduced the number of forms from 26 to 1. A tariff reform simplified the nomenclature and brought it in line with international standards. A computer system was rolled out to permit electronic data entry and processing and to collect more reliable and real-time statistics. All border-related rules were summarized in one table and all checks are to be performed at the same time. In the first two years of reforms, the number of shipments cleared without inspection quadrupled from 10 to 40 percent, the average tariff rate collected remained constant, and clearance times declined from six to four days.

The wide range of mode-specific, intermodal, national, and cross-border reform measures discussed in this study address bottlenecks and frictions in the regional transport system. Together they would amount to the creation of a common transport space, in complementarity to the Euro-Mediterranean FTA. A far-reaching package of economic and transport sector reforms in Mexico allowed this country to reap the full benefits from its participation in the North American Free Trade Area. Another precedent for the catalytic role the transport sector can play in the process of regional integration is the gradual extension of the EU Single Market for transport to the accession candidates of Eastern and Central Europe. This report argues that a large pool of international experience and best practice exists to guide the decisions of policy makers and the assistance of donors in the Euro-Mediterranean region.

With most of the Association Agreements now signed, the implementation of the free-trade area and the reform of the transport system are moving center stage. There are encouraging signs of reform in several Mediterranean Partners, but much remains to be done. The ultimate objective of the transport system is to provide fast, reliable, and flexible transport services at low cost. This requires an enabling policy environment to allow for the seamless integration of different modes into a multimodal system, effective competition between service providers, the elimination of bureaucratic frictions, and greater private sector participation. The reform agenda for the transport sector is clear. It is now up to governments and donors to effectively implement it.

Chapter 1

Transport Logistics and Multimodal Transport

Chapter 1

Transport Logistics and Multimodal Transport

1.1 The Euro-Mediterranean Partnership and Transport Reform

The aim of the Euro-Mediterranean Partnership (EMP) between the 15 European Union (EU) member states and their 12 Mediterranean Partners (MPs) is to establish a region of peace and prosperity around the Mediterranean Sea.[1] The EU has a population of 376 million, compared to 235 million in the MPs. GDP figures are € 8.5 trillion and € 0.6 trillion, respectively. In 1999, the EU exported a total of € 80 billion to the MPs and imported € 53 billion.[2] More than half the total GDP and trade figures for the 12 MPs, however, are accounted for by Turkey and Israel. The cornerstones of the partnership are bilateral Association Agreements (AA) between the EU and each of the MPs; a multilateral free-trade area (FTA) to be completed around 2010; and financial assistance in support of social and economic adjustment (the MEDA budget line), administered by the European Commission. The partnership was launched at the 1995 Barcelona Conference and the sum of initiatives it comprises is referred to as the Barcelona Process.

The Maghreb and Mashrek countries are becoming increasingly sidelined in the global economy and significant reform efforts will be needed to reverse that trend. The share of the Middle East and North Africa (MENA) in world trade, including the oil-rich Gulf countries, is a mere 2.5 percent while its share in global foreign direct investment (FDI) is stagnating at 1 percent. Growth in merchandise trade during the past decade was the lowest of all world regions (6.5 percent) and with the neighboring EU it was even lower (3.6 percent).[3] The net inflow of FDI was equivalent to 0.1 percent of GDP, compared to an average of 2.0 percent for all developing countries (20 times as much). The share of the largest Arab MP (Egypt) in world exports fell from an already low 0.17 percent in 1983-86 to 0.07 percent in 1993-96, whereas that of much smaller Chile rose from 0.21 to 0.28 percent during the same period.[4] Only 2 percent of European FDI goes to the MPs.[5]

The average per capita income in the MPs is only one-tenth of that in the EU, and even lower in the eight Arab MPs. The Commission estimates that even under a very optimistic growth scenario, it would take 40 years to halve this income gap.[6] Many economies in the region risk becoming marginalized as the globalization of goods and capital markets accelerates. While other developing economies are successfully advancing on the ladder of dynamic comparative advantage, towards human capital and technology-intensive goods, many MPs remain specialized in raw material exports and labor intensive, low-skilled manufactures.

---

[1] The MPs include the *Maghreb* (Morocco, Algeria, Tunisia), the *Mashrek* (Jordan, Lebanon, Syria, Egypt, Israel, West Bank and Gaza), and the EU accession candidates (Turkey, Cyprus, Malta). The Middle East and North Africa (MENA), as defined by the World Bank, includes the Arab peninsula but excludes Turkey, Cyprus, and Malta.

[2] Eurostat. 2001. *Euro-Mediterranean Statistics 1/2001*. These figures are for 1999.

[3] OECD. 2001. *The Development Dimensions of Trade*. These figures are for the period 1987-1997.

[4] World Bank Institute and Mediterranean Development Forum. 2000. *Trade Policy Developments in the Middle East and North Africa*. Chapter 1 by M. Nabli and A. De Kleine (FDI) and chapter 5 by A. Refaat (trade).

[5] (1) Eurostat. 1999. *EU Direct Investment Yearbook 1999*. (2) Financial Times (15 November 2000).

[6] This is under the assumption that annual per capita growth is 5 percent in the MPs and 1 percent in the EU.

The Euro-Mediterranean free-trade area provides an opportunity for economic growth, which the Mediterranean Partners must seize. Even though the FTA does not cover all sectors (agriculture and services are excluded), trade and deeper economic integration could become key drivers of development throughout the southern Mediterranean. For this to happen, however, the MPs will have to comprehensively modernize their economic and social structures to prepare their industry for the competition and opportunities associated with free trade. As the precedents of Mexico and the Central and Eastern European Countries (CEECs) show, regional integration needs to be complemented by domestic reforms if the full economic benefits are to be reaped.

Box 1.1 EU Institutions and EU Legislation

The European Union is a supranational organization, which means that its 15 member states have partly ceded national sovereignty to multilateral EU institutions. The European Commission, as the executive branch of the EU, prepares EU legislation in the form of regulations (legally binding upon their entry into force) and directives (general principles to be transposed into national law by member states). The corpus of EU law is referred to as the *acquis communautaire* and comprises about 80,000 pages.[7] The Commission also manages the EU's € 90 billion per year budget. Approximately 10 percent of this budget is earmarked for assistance to non-EU countries, including the MEDA program for the southern Mediterranean. The Directorate General for External Relations (DG Relex) is in charge of the policy dialogue with the MPs and the programming of the financial assistance. Europe Aid is the project implementation unit for all regions outside the EU. The Directorate General Transport and Energy (DG TREN) is in charge of transport policies. The Commission is politically controlled by the Council of Ministers (representatives of member state governments) and increasingly by the European Parliament (directly elected representatives). The European Investment Bank (EIB) is the EU's long-term financing institution and provides loans in support of EU policies. In 2002, EU governments decided to expand the EIB mandate with regard to the MPs.

Note: Legislative documents and background information can be found on the EU web-site (www.europa.eu.int).

At the national level, transport sector reform will be an integral part of the process of economic adjustment in the MPs. The efficiency of transport logistics is an important determinant of the commercial success of individual firms and the international competitiveness of entire countries. The division of labor between companies is becoming ever more sophisticated as a result of business trends such as lean manufacturing, just-in-time production, and reduced time-to-market cycles. At the same time, production is becoming increasingly dispersed geographically due to trade and capital market liberalization, cross-border mergers, and advances in information technology. Insufficient access to efficient logistics will make it more and more difficult for countries to successfully participate in global trade and investment flows.

At the regional level, transport reforms are an important facilitator for trade and economic integration. As long as cross-border transport remains more costly, time-consuming, or unreliable than domestic transport, it will discourage and distort the flow of goods and people throughout the Euro-Mediterranean. To remove these non-tariff barriers, the ultimate objective of policy makers should be the creation of a 'common transport space' in complementarity to the free-trade area. In the EU, the convergence of transport policies and the integration of transport networks has already created a common transport space (see box 1.2 and box 1.12) which is no longer a mere patchwork of national systems, but functionally integrated. With Cyprus, Malta, and Turkey being EU accession candidates and Israel a high-income country, the eight Arab MPs of the Maghreb and Mashrek constitute a sub-group facing distinct reform challenges. These countries will thus be the main focus of this study.

[7] The Economist (17 November 2001).

The Euro-Mediterranean Free-Trade Area

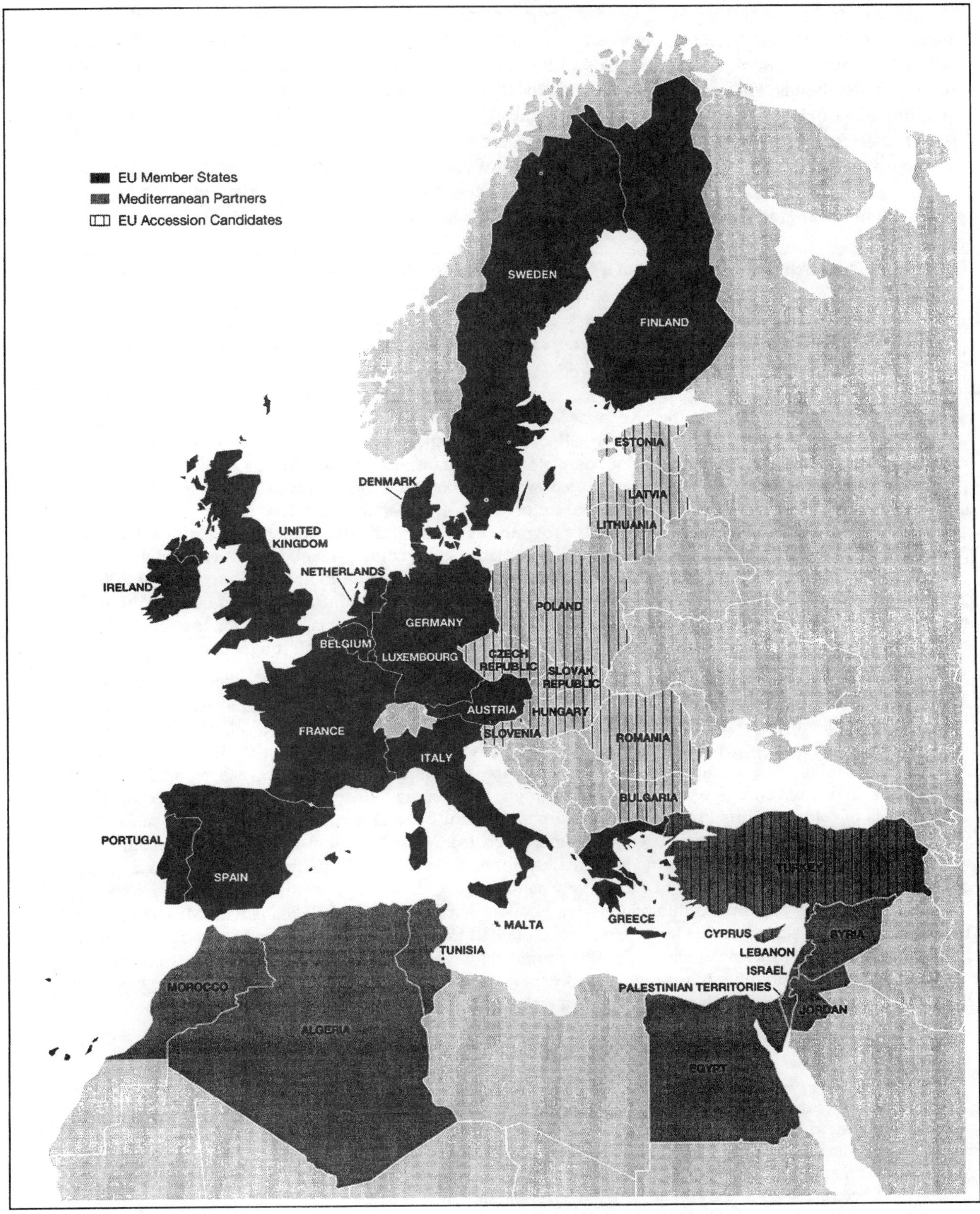

Although transport logistics requires physical infrastructure, it is ultimately the cost, reliability, and flexibility of transport and logistics services provided on the basis of this infrastructure, that matter to users. Many of the logistics bottlenecks in the region are policy-induced. State-owned companies and monopolies are shielded from the discipline of market forces and ill-suited to meet increasingly complex client needs. Opaque regulation, bureaucratic border controls, as well as outdated laws and institutional structures create further inefficiencies. Policy makers in the southern Mediterranean should therefore concentrate on the reform of their legal, regulatory, and institutional sector framework. As the experience of Central and Eastern Europe shows, market dynamics will ensure the effective provision of transport and logistics services, once governments provide for a favorable policy environment (see box 1.9).

Box 1.2 EU Instruments in Support of Transport Sector Reform

A number of policy instruments designed for the implementation of the Euro-Mediterranean Partnership are available to support transport sector reform in the southern Mediterranean. The most important instrument is the MEDA budget line, which provides grant money in the magnitude of about € 1 billion per year to fund projects in support of economic adjustment. Ninety percent of funds are earmarked for national projects in the eight poorest MPs: the Arab countries of the Maghreb and Mashrek. Ten percent are set aside for regional projects.[8] In the 5 years of MEDA I (1995 to 2000), however, less than 1 percent of the almost € 5 billion MEDA commitments were allocated to transport sector reform. Exceptions were a small customs project in Tunisia, which was not completed, and a transport component in a public sector reform program for Lebanon. A regional maritime project was also identified, but its focus was on technical issues such as port dredging and navigation, not on sector policy. As part of its effort to increase support to transport reform under the ongoing MEDA II program, the Commission is preparing a regional transport policy project. Since most reforms will have to take place at the country-level, however, several national MEDA projects in the transport sector have been included in the National Indicative Programs for 2002 to 2004. While most of these are technical assistance (TA) projects, sector adjustment programs could also be used to support the reform process. The World Bank also provides technical assistance for transport reforms to several MP governments; references to several ongoing projects can be found throughout this publication.

Another useful instrument in support of transport sector reform could be the Euro-Mediterranean Transport Forum. Since its creation in 1998, senior sector officials from the EU and the MPs have met three times (March 1999, November 2000, July 2001). Besides such annual meetings, however, there have been few tangible results. A work program was drafted, but it is rather a general list of issues to be addressed than a specific action plan. The Commission, which holds the secretariat of the forum, has recognized these deficiencies and wants to turn the Transport Forum into an instrument for policy dialogue and the coordination of reform efforts in the region.[9] It also wants to use the regional MEDA project to support the work of the Forum. EIB loans could become another mechanism to support transport sector restructuring. To date, however, EIB loans in the sector have mainly funded physical infrastructure and have gone almost exclusively to state-owned entities. In future, they could be linked more systematically to policy reforms by including TA components for institutional capacity building or by bundling EIB loans with MEDA projects. In early 2002, discussions were underway to expand the EIB mandate for the southern Mediterranean region. In summary, a range of complementary EMP instruments to support transport sector reform are available. The challenge over the coming years will be to deploy them more systematically, to unlock the synergies between them, and to improve donor coordination (see box 4.5).

[8] As EU-accession candidates Cyprus, Malta, and Turkey are committed to full adoption of the EU acquis. Turkey already has a customs union with the EU. Euro-Mediterranean Association Agreements (AAs), in which both sides primarily commit themselves to gradual trade liberalization, have entered into force in the case of Tunisia, Morocco, Israel, and the Palestinian Authority (an interim agreement). The AAs for Jordan, Egypt, Lebanon, and Algeria have been signed. The agreement between Syria and the EU is still under negotiation.

[9] European Commission. 2001. *Communication on Enhancing Euro-Mediterranean Cooperation in Transport and Energy*.

Sector reform should generally precede new infrastructure investments for several reasons. First, policy reforms increase the efficiency with which existing infrastructure is being used and can often achieve the same effect as physical capacity expansion, but at a much lower cost. Second, the exact nature of new infrastructure requirements will depend on the way the sector is organized and thus on policy reforms. Third, driven by competitive pressure and the profit motive, private investors tend to be more efficient in planning and implementing investments – as long as governments provide adequate incentives through a transparent and competitive sector framework. The focus of this study is therefore on policy reforms. References to physical infrastructure bottlenecks can be found in box 1.8, section 2.12, section 3.5, and box 4.1.

The Barcelona Declaration acknowledges the importance of transport sector reform. The EMP founding document states that "the participants decided to facilitate the progressive establishment of this free-trade area through [...] the pursuit and the development of policies based on the principles of market economy and the integration of their economies [...]; the adjustment and modernization of their economic and social structures, giving priority to the promotion and development of the private sector [...] and to the establishment of an appropriate institutional and regulatory framework for a market economy." It stresses "the importance of creating an environment conducive to investment" and identifies transport as one of the priorities for cooperation. "Efficient interoperable transport links between the EU and its Mediterranean partners, and among the partners themselves, as well as free access to the market for services in international maritime transport, are essential for the development of trade patterns and the smooth operation of the Euro-Mediterranean Partnership. [...] Cooperation will focus on the development of an efficient Trans-Mediterranean multimodal combined sea and air transport system, through the improvement and modernization of ports and airports, the suppression of unwarranted restrictions [and a] simplification of procedures."

Box 1.3 The EU Single Market for Transport

The policy framework of the EU Single Market for transport comprises dozens of sector-specific directives and regulations, as well as cross-sectoral rules such as competition policy or the right of establishment. Key elements of the transport acquis are discussed throughout this study – including the liberalization package for air transport (box 2.5), a directive on groundhandling in airports (box 2.11), measures to introduce competition in road freight (box 4.2), or competition and state aid policy (section 4.6). In some parts of the transport market, particularly in air and road transport, reforms are largely complete. In others, especially in rail transport, liberalization is less advanced. In most of areas of transport policy, however, individual member states have gone considerably beyond EU reform requirements. In September 2001, the Commission published A White Paper on Transport.[10] It develops a sector vision for 2010 and proposes an action plan to address 'second generation' reform issues.

With all of these developments underway, transport markets across the EU should be fully liberalized, privatized, and integrated across borders by the time the Euro-Mediterranean FTA is completed. In the coming years, the European Union and thus its Single Market for transport is also supposed to be extended eastwards to a group of up to the ten EU accession candidates in Central and Eastern Europe (see box 1.9) as well as southwards to the accession candidates Turkey, Cyprus, and Malta. The EU acquis could also be used to guide and harmonize transport reforms in the remaining MPs of the Maghreb and Mashrek. This way, it could provide a policy framework for a common transport space across the Mediterranean region and allow for the de facto extension of the EU Single Market for transport to the South.

[10] European Commission. 2001. *White Paper – European Transport Policies for 2010.*

1.2 Transport Flows and Transport Costs in the Southern Mediterranean

Transport flows in the region reflect underlying social, economic, and trade patterns.[11] With a total GDP of € 243 billion, the Maghreb and Mashrek economies are very small by international standards – Belgium alone, with only ten million inhabitants, has a GDP of € 246 billion. This translates into very small trade flows – exports of € 44 billion for the eight Arab MPs compare to the € 42 billion of Sweden (nine million people) or to the € 39 billion of Israel (six million people).[12] Those countries with the largest economies are usually also the largest traders. Since most southern Mediterranean countries have negative current account balances, their cross-border transport flows tend to be strongly biased towards imports – except for countries with large commodity exports like Algeria (petrochemicals) or Morocco (phosphate). With little intra-regional trade taking place, traffic flows between the Maghreb and Mashrek countries are very small. Those countries with large tourism sectors (e.g. Tunisia, Morocco, Egypt) have over-proportionate air transport volumes and commodity exporters have over-proportionate outbound flows in maritime transport (e.g. Algeria, Morocco, Jordan). Sections 2.2 and 3.2 provide more detailed statistics with regard to maritime and air transport.

A number of regional patterns in the modal mix can be identified. Most cross-border trade, particularly in the Maghreb, is sea or airborne. The land-based modes, road and rail, are primarily used for domestic transport and for the land-legs of maritime and air transport chains. In terms of weight and value, the majority of imports and exports are shipped by sea, except for some Mashrek countries where road transport plays a larger role. The share of air transport is higher in value terms since products with a low weight-to-value ratio tend to be carried by plane. Seaborne trade between the EU and its Mediterranean partners (including Turkey, Cyprus, and Malta) accounted for 83 percent of the 1997 total in terms of weight, but for only 53 percent in terms of value. Cross-border flows of passengers in the region, however, are predominantly by air. In 2000, the Maghreb and Mashrek countries recorded 40 million passengers by air, but only 5.5 million by sea. For tourism – of critical importance for several economies in the region – the gap between the two modes is even larger.

Table 1.1 Trade Statistics (2000)

Country	Imports (m €)	EU share (%)	Exports (m €)	EU share (%)
Algeria	9,982	58	21,232	63
Egypt	15,146	34	5,105	40
Lebanon*	5,825	46	635	24
Jordan	4,923	33	1,651	3
Morocco	12,469	58	8,034	74
Syria*	827	30	748	65
Tunisia	9,275	72	6,330	80
WB & G*[1]	2,440	16	349	0
Total / Av.	**60,887**	**49**	**44,084**	**62**
Israel	38,777	43	33,991	27
Turkey	58,773	49	29,719	53

Source: Eurostat. * *1999 figures* [1] *West Bank and Gaza*

Some important observations with regard to the direction of transport flows in the Maghreb and Mashrek can be made. First, the majority of MP trade takes place with the European Union, particularly in the case of the Maghreb. As table 1.1 shows, the EU share in imports averages 49 percent and ranges from 30 to 72 percent. Exports are even more strongly oriented towards the EU,

[11] Unless otherwise stated, all statistics in this section have been taken from the MED-Trans Database of Eurostat.
[12] World Bank. 2001. *World Development Indicators 2001.*

amounting to around two-thirds of the total in the Maghreb and between 24 and 65 percent in the Mashrek (with Jordan a notable exception). These percentages are likely to increase further as a result of the FTA. The combined share of the twelve MPs in total EU trade is much smaller, accounting for a mere 6 percent of imports and 9 percent of exports.[13] Second, one of the most lamented structural features of trade flows in the region is the negligible role of South-South trade, which accounts for a mere 5 percent of the total.[14] This is partly a reflection of similarities in economic endowments and thus little potential for trade driven by comparative advantage. But it is also a consequence of government-imposed impediments, such as red tape and the closure of land borders. Third, cargo flows in the MPs tend to be lopsided, with imports generally exceeding exports by a significant margin. In Egyptian ports, for example, three times as much general cargo was discharged than loaded in 2000, and across all cargo categories the ration between imports and exports was more than 4:1. In Jordanian airports, the ration was 2:1.[15] Another structural pattern is the heavy concentration of traffic flows in a small number of key ports and airports per country. These central nodes in the intermodal system of the region should thus be the focus of policy reforms and infrastructure investments. The Euro-Mediterranean partners should consider identifying a network of priority ports and airports for the purpose of reform and targeted infrastructure investments.

Table 1.2 Freight Costs for Imports (2000)

Country	**Imports** ($ billion)	**Freight Costs** ($ million)	(%)
Algeria	10.0	1,144	11.4
Egypt	21.7	2,620	12.1
Lebanon	6.2	657	10.6
Jordan	4.5	574	12.8
Morocco	12.4	1,776	14.3
Syria	5.3	687	13.0
Tunisia	8.6	627	7.3
Total / Av.	68.7	8,085	11.8
Israel	36.8	2,993	8.1
Turkey	54.5	2,556	4.7
Chile	16.7	1,004	6.0

Source: UNCTAD

In addition to the flow statistics discussed so far, the analysis of transport costs yields insights into reform needs and policy priorities. Calculating transport-related costs for an economy, however, is a complex task. The most common macro-economic approach is to compare national accounts. "An ad valorem measurement of the cost of international transport and insurance can be obtained by comparing CIF [cost, insurance, freight] and FOB [free on board] values of trade. The volume of exports and their FOB values [i.e. total cost at point of export] are listed in the exporting country's statistics. The same product is entered in the partner's import statistics in volume and CIF value [i.e. total cost at point of entry]. The difference between the CIF and FOB values as a fraction of the FOB value, gives an indication of the ad valorem freight and insurance costs. The bi-directional approach makes it possible to estimate, by country and product, comparable indicators of transport costs, referred to as freight factors. Because export and import statistics are available at a very disaggregated level [...], freight factors for a given country can be calculated by product and

[13] Eurostat. 2000. *Euro-Mediterranean Statistics 2/2000.*

[14] This European Commission estimate for trade between the twelve MPs is confirmed by another figure: In 1997, only 3.1 percent of exports from members in the Arab Maghreb Union (UMA) – Tunisia, Morocco, Algeria, Libya, and Mauritania – were to other UMA members. (World Bank. 1999. *World Development Indicators 1999*).

[15] In 2000, Egypt's main ports registered 9.8 million tons of imports and 3.2 million tons of exports in the general cargo category. For all cargo types, the figures were 37.2 million tons and 8.6 million tons respectively. In 2000, Jordan's airports unloaded 17,400 tons of air freight, while loading a mere 8,900 tons.

destination. These data constitute the 'ad valorem transport cost profile' of a country. [...] Comparing profiles [between years and across countries, makes it possible] to identify products or transport chains with potential bottlenecks or restrictions."[16] A drawback of this methodology is that transaction records often differ between countries.

Nonetheless, this macroeconomic indicator for transport sector efficiency illustrates the large potential gains from sector reforms. Table 1.2 provides freight cost estimates for imports of the Maghreb and Mashrek countries, as calculated by the United Nations Conference on Trade and Development (UNCTAD). Despite certain inconsistencies in the data, two patterns indicate that there is considerable scope for a reduction in transport costs. First, freight costs within the region vary considerably, ranging from 4.7 percent of import value in Turkey, to 14.3 percent in Morocco. Second, with an average of 11.8 percent the Arab MPs have higher costs than Turkey (4.7 percent) and Israel (8.1 percent), as well as international best practice benchmarks. Even in Chile, a developing and geographically more isolated country, freight costs were only 6.0 percent of total import value. Throughout the region, transport costs and delays for exports tend to be lower than those for imports. Two reasons for this asymmetry are that the majority of trade enforcement procedures, like customs, are geared towards imports and that lop-sided trade flows result in spare capacity and lower freight rates on outbound traffic. Nonetheless, the large variance between freight costs within the region and the gap with best practice countries suggest that the eight Arab MPs could save freight costs of up to 2-4 percent of their trade value if transport systems were more efficient.

These direct freight costs are likely to underestimate the true economic costs of transport sector inefficiency. First, expensive and unreliable transport actually reduces the overall level of trade for which these costs are estimated, creating a deadweight loss for the economy.[17] Second, logistic considerations are an important determinant for the location of foreign direct investment, particularly in trade-intensive industries. Thus transport inefficiencies impose additional economic costs by reducing FDI flows to a country. Third, delays and unreliable transport logistics impose indirect costs on users which are not captured by these indicators (frictions in the supply chain force firms to keep higher stocks, delays can lead to penalties and the loss of contracts, etc.). Fourth, these macro-estimates are for freight only and do not include excess costs in passenger transport. Finally, these statistics do not account for the open and hidden subsidies to the sector – a cost borne by taxpayers. If these and other factors are taken into account, the above-mentioned figures would be considerably higher. Under the cautious assumption that the total economic cost of transport inefficiencies are equivalent to 3-5 percent of the trade value, an overhaul of transport systems could lead to economic gains for the eight Arab MPs of the Maghreb and Mashrek in the magnitude of € 3-5 billion per year.[18]

---

[16] World Bank. 1996. *Logistical Constraints on International Trade in the Maghreb*. FOB and CIF are INCOTERMS (see section 1.7).

[17] *The economic costs of transport frictions are economically equivalent to unrealized gains from trade.* Reductions of tariffs and non-tariff barriers both reduce the price of traded goods, thus increasing the demand for imports and exports (trade creation effect). Trade increases economic welfare because it allows countries to specialize on production according to their comparative advantage and because economies of scale can be reaped as markets are integrated. The latter is particularly important for the region, since most MP economies are relatively small. The combined GDP of the three Maghreb countries, for instance, is smaller than that of Portugal. Besides these static effects, increased trade also has important dynamic effects on economic efficiency. It increases competition (exposure to foreign competitors) and permits knowledge spill-overs associated with the physical flow of goods, investments, and people. The elasticity of exports and imports with regard to transport costs (the higher the costs, the lower the trade volume) determines the deadweight loss imposed by transport inefficiencies.

[18] With total exports of the eight Arab MPs amounting to € 44 billion and imports to € 61 billion, 3 percent of total trade (€ 105 billion) would be € 3.2 billion and 5 percent € 5.3 billion.

Box 1.4 The North American Free-Trade Area and Transport Reform in Mexico

The North American Free-Trade Area (NAFTA)[19] between the United States, Canada, and Mexico entered into force in 1994. Mexico, as the only emerging economy in this regional trade block, implemented wide-ranging economic reforms to increase its competitiveness. An integral part of this adjustment process was comprehensive transport reform. In the mid-1980s, the entire sector was government controlled, while monopolistic structures and red tape undermined efficiency. In 1989, trucking was liberalized and legal restrictions on multimodal operations were removed.[20] Between 1989 and 1994 one of the largest toll road programs ever implemented doubled the toll road network to 10,000 kilometers. While about $ 13 billion were invested by the private sector, poor planning and a currency devaluation forced the government to bail out half of the 53 concessionaires.[21] Regulatory reforms in ports started in 1993 and port privatization in 1995. Airline privatization and air transport liberalization were tackled between 1991 and 1996.[22] In the late 1990s, controlling stakes in three groups of airports were sold to strategic investors and the remaining equity is being floated on the stock exchange.[23] The rail network was divided into four concessions and the two northern sections were awarded to US-Mexican consortia to facilitate cross-border traffic. A central government department was created to coordinate policies across modes. An independent competition authority has repeatedly ruled on transport sector cases.[24] The Mexican Transport Institute was set up to provide independent research. Despite a decade of successful adjustment, Mexico has also encountered a number of difficulties and is still fine-tuning sector policies.

At the regional level, several NAFTA working groups deal with transport and trade-related issues. The International Border Clearance Planning and Deployment Committee, for example, was created to streamline trade procedures at border crossings, while the Land Transportation Standards Subcommittee is harmonizing rules for road and rail traffic. Cross-border liberalization measures under NAFTA include the elimination of market access restrictions for bus services, the liberalization of foreign ownership rules for port infrastructure and services, as well as provisions for access to the railway network.[25] The liberalization of cross-border trucking services, long delayed due to safety concerns and political lobbying, is still being debated. In air transport, cross-border traffic was deregulated in 1991 and further liberalized in 1999.

As a result of national and regional reforms, efficiency and private investment in the sector grew dramatically. According to World Bank estimates, the cost savings from customs reforms, for instance, were more than $ 2 billion in the first year alone (1989). Thanks to NAFTA and radical economic reforms, Mexico's trade more than tripled from $ 82 billion in 1990 to $ 279 billion in 1999. At 15 percent, annual growth was thrice the global average and made Mexico the seventh largest trading nation in the world.[26] Manufactured goods now represent the majority of exports, replacing petroleum products as the main export item. Foreign direct investment between 1994 and 2000 amounted to $ 85 billion. Seventy-five percent of Mexico's exports go to the United States and 60 percent of FDI comes from there.[27] The government estimates that half of the average 5.1 percent economic growth achieved over the four years to 2000 can be attributed to increased exports. To maintain the reform momentum, the government is pursuing further trade liberalization. In 2000, Mexico signed a far-reaching free-trade agreement with the EU (giving it privileged access to both EU and US markets), as well as with Israel and four of its Central American neighbors. In the meantime, discussions between 34 countries of the Western Hemisphere are under way to create the Free-Trade Area of the Americas, with around 800 million consumers.

---

[19] In this publication, the acronym NAFTA refers to the North American Free-Trade Area.

[20] Lakshmanan, T. and William Anderson. 2001. "Transport and Trade in the North American Free Trade Agreement." In *Integration of Transport and Trade Facilitation*. World Bank.

[21] Ruster, Jeff. 1997. "A Retrospective on the Mexican Toll Road Program." World Bank Viewpoint Series 125.

[22] Reuters Business Briefing (20 April 2001).

[23] Oxford Analytica (28 March 2001).

[24] Based on a constitutional principle that prohibits private sector monopolies, the Federal Competition Commission ruled in 2000 that the conglomerate created after the state took over the two bankrupt airlines Aeromexico and Mexicana would have to be privatized in separate units. (Oxford Analytica, 28 March 2001).

[25] University of Texas. 1998. *Multimodal Transport in the United States, Western Europe, and Latin America*.

[26] The Mission of Mexico to the EU. 2000. *The Mexico-EU Free-Trade Agreement*.

[27] Financial Times Deutschland (28 March 2001).

Sector case studies support these macro-economic calculations of transport costs. Before recent port reforms, a study on the Egyptian port sector estimated the direct and indirect economic costs imposed by port inefficiencies to be up to $ 2 billion per year. This total comprised higher freight rates ($ 100 million); excess cargo handling costs ($ 200 million); investments costs that could be saved through improved container handling productivity ($ 50 million); customs clearance delays (e.g. $ 60 million of costs to shippers); higher handling and modal transfer costs due to low containerization rates (several hundred million dollars); and subsidies to loss-making transport companies. For the same country, another study estimated the overall economic costs imposed by a cumbersome enforcement of product standards at borders to exceed 1 percent of GDP due to "higher import costs, lower exports, reduced product variety and availability, reduced access to best available technology, and the waste of government resources expended on duplicative and unnecessary activities."[28] For the three Maghreb countries, a 1996 World Bank study found the excess costs of transport frictions borne by traders to be around $ 200 million per year. Freight costs were "five times higher than those in the European Union and twice as high as those in developing countries."[29] In Jordan, the state-owned airline Royal Jordanian accumulated debts of $ 850 million, equivalent to 10 percent of the country's GDP. In Syria, transport deficiencies increased the costs of fruit and vegetables exported to Europe by 20 percent.[30]

1.3 Transport Logistics and Supply-Chain Management

Transport logistics is concerned with the management and optimization of transport flows. Given the increasingly sophisticated division of labor in the global economy, different stages of the supply chain are often spatially separated, both within a country and between countries. The flow of goods from raw material to the final consumer via intermediate products thus involves a sequence of transactions.[31] To add to the complexity, four different items flow through supply chains. Besides the actual goods, legal titles, cash, and information all have to be transferred with a minimum of friction. Due to trends like global sourcing, foreign direct investment, and trade liberalization, the transport sector is generally growing considerably faster than underlying GDP. "In the 1980s and 1990s, the growth of international trade was twice that of the increase in global production."[32] A significant amount of trade takes place between subsidiaries of multinational companies. It has been estimated that intra-company trade, particularly common among developed countries, accounts for 35 to 40 percent of total trade.

[28] A study of Nathan Associated, cited in: Kheir-El-Din, Hanaa. 2000. "Enforcement of Product Standards as Barriers to Trade: The Case of Egypt." In Bernard Hoekman and Hanaa Kheir-El-Din, eds., *Trade Developments in the Middle East and North Africa*. Mediterranean Development Forum and World Bank Institute.

[29] Amiot, François and Ovadia Salama. 1996. "Logistical Constraints on International Trade in the Maghreb." World Bank. This study provides a comprehensive review of different methodologies to estimate logistics costs.

[30] World Bank. 2000. *Syria – A Preliminary Assessment of Transport Costs for Export Development* (not published).

[31] The sequence of production processes is also referred to as the 'value chain' since each stage creates additional added value. An interesting example of the complexity of an international supply chain ('global conveyor belt') can be found in "A Survey of Global Manufacturing" (The Economist, 20 June 1998): "A team of researchers from the Cardiff Business School found that the chain of actions required to make [a cola] can – starting at the Bauxite mine in Australia, and passing through the various smelting and rolling processes to the manufacture of the can itself, printing its label, filling it with the cola drink and getting it into somebody's refrigerator – took no less than 319 days. [...] But, even so, only three hours of that time was spent in doing something that actually added value. The rest was spent in storage and transport; as many as 14 storage lots and warehouses were involved."

[32] Holland International Distribution Council. 1998. *World Wide Logistics – The Future of Supply Chain Services*. Phillip Hastings, eds. The estimate on intra-company comes from UNCTAD.

Transport logistics increases economic welfare. Speed, flexibility, and reliability are service characteristics that add real value to users. If they are unable to deliver on time, manufacturers may be forced to pay contract fines or risk losing orders. Slow or unpredictable delivery induces customers to hold costly buffer-stocks. Inflexibility and long lead times delay the response to new market opportunities and rapidly changing demand patterns. Poorly performed transport services increase the proportion of cargo that is damaged or lost. Much of the added value of logistics arises from the fact that transport services are not a homogenous commodity but a highly differentiated product. Some of the main parameters defining a particular transport service are the routing (origin and destination); the timing (date, transit time); the technical characteristics of the shipment (cargo type, size, fragility); and the flexibility of the service (lead time, frequency). By matching supply and demand along these dimensions, logistics services increase the efficiency of resource allocation.

The past decades have witnessed an accelerating logistics revolution. Driving forces have been the introduction of containers in the 1960s and 1970s; the global adoption of lean manufacturing and just-in-time (JIT) techniques in the 1980s; supply-chain management and the wide-spread introduction of information technology for advanced logistics in the 1990s; and most recently, the emergence of the internet. Supply-chain management, a concept that became popular in the late 1980s, marked a culmination of the logistics revolution. Its objective is to integrate a company's supply and distribution functions with its other business processes, while linking the company's internal processes with those of its suppliers (upstream) and consumers (downstream). Real-time information about market demand is fed down the supply-chain from retailers, to manufacturers, and then first and second tier suppliers, where it triggers just-in-time production and supply. Ideally, all parts of the supply chain should operate as one integrated system ('extended enterprises' or 'virtual companies') and processes should be demand-driven (products are 'pulled' through the supply chain) instead of supply-driven ('pushed'). By shifting the emphasis from moving products to managing flows, supply-chain management permits a significant reduction in lead-times and the need for expensive buffer-stocks.

Improved logistics can considerably increase the competitiveness of firms. "The top companies have reduced logistics costs – administration, inventory, warehousing and transport – to 7.5 percent of revenues in 1998 from 14.3 percent in 1987," that is, by half in just one decade.[33] One of the most prominent examples is Dell Computers, which became the second biggest PC manufacturer in the United States by perfecting its supply-chain management through a build-to-order system. Consumers can order a computer with customized specifications through the company's web-site and call centers. Information about the parts needed for assembly is automatically passed on to suppliers. Within a week a tailor-made computer is home-delivered to the client (mass customization). Another case in point is supermarkets, whose bar-code data from the point of sale automatically trigger replenishment orders from suppliers. An example of reverse logistics is Philips, which "offers every customer with a broken cellular phone a replacement within 24 hours, anywhere in the world. Express delivery company DHL is employed to deliver the new phone and pick up the damaged unit at the same time. [Information is] communicated to DHL using EDI [electronic data interchange] and the two companies' own IT networks."[34]

[33] Financial Times (1 December 1998). Supply-chain management integrates such diverse intra-firm processes as manufacturing, inventory management, distribution, and sales. Since many of these processes are interdependent and based on the same sets of information, their integration considerably increases efficiency. Supply-chain management can be defined as "the integration of the flow of materials, documents, information and finance."

[34] Holland International Distribution Council. 1998. *Worldwide Logistics – The Future of Supply Chain Services.*

These transformations taking place within firms and industries have broader economic repercussions for developing countries. Industrial restructuring is transcending national boundaries and "many of the stages of production have become locationally footloose. Developing countries have been able to enter global manufacturing chains without either the basis of a strong local market for the final products or a strong initial technological capability. By the same token, however, the location of such activities has become more volatile and the struggle to maintain position more competitive. Logistical excellence is, thus, the essential counterpart to production process efficiency for developing as well as developed countries."[35] An example of global sourcing in the textile sector (important for several of the MPs) is Donna Karan International, one of the world's leading fashion design houses. It "does not actually own any production facilities but sources products from some 500 leading contractors. [...] In 1997, Donna Karan sourced 52 percent of its raw materials and finished goods from Asia, 22 percent from the US and 26 percent from Europe."[36]

There is one particularly important aspect of the 'slicing-up' of the production process and the outward-processing trade (OPT) that it generates. OPT mainly takes place in sophisticated manufacturing industries and entails significant foreign direct investment and spillover effects. "The spillover effects of production sharing processes include the diffusion and absorption of new and improved production technologies, management and labor skills, and information about markets." It thus permits "a catching-up with best practice in the world economy" as well as "strengthening know-how and skills of both firms and labor." Equally important are the effects on flows of foreign direct investments: "The globalization of production structures takes place through investments abroad, which in turn stimulates trade. It is thus unsurprising to find that the same non-OECD countries that were able to attract the bulk of FDI were the ones that participated most vigorously in production sharing arrangements, and which experienced the most dramatic increases in their shares in world trade."[37] A concrete example for the links between outward-processing trade, foreign investments, and transport logistics is given in box 1.6.

The southern Mediterranean is still poorly integrated in international supply chains, except for a few markets (e.g. textiles) and countries (e.g. Tunisia, Israel). This deficiency is reflected by the limited volume of trade in manufactured and intermediate goods in the trade accounts of many Maghreb and Mashrek countries. The "region's economies, with few and limited exceptions, are under-represented in manufacturing relative to economies with similar economic characteristics."[38] Extreme cases are Algeria and Syria, where 96 percent and 86 percent of exports to Europe are petrochemicals.[39] Even more worrisome, some countries are falling still further behind. "Between 1990 and 1998, Egypt's merchandise exports declined from 15 percent of GDP to merely 6.2 percent and their share in total world merchandise exports declined from 0.15 percent in 1990 to 0.1 percent in 1998."[40] The free-trade area with Europe provides a unique opportunity for these countries to increase exports, attract more FDI, and benefit from important knowledge spillovers that are transmitted through supply chains. In order to support the new operational structures of manufacturers and retailers and in order to encourage multinational companies to extend their supply chains towards the MPs, logistics and transport systems will have to become far more flexible, reliable, and sophisticated. An example of the trading potential, which efficient transport

[35] K. Gwilliam in: OECD Trilog. 1998. *Public Policy Issues in Global Freight Logistics – Conference Proceedings*.
[36] This and other supply-chain case studies can be found in: Holland International Distribution Council. 1998. *Worldwide Logistics – The Future of Supply Chain Services*. (*www.hidc.nl*).
[37] OECD. 2001. *The Development Dimension of Trade*.
[38] Petri, Peter. 1997. "Trade Strategies for the Southern Mediterranean." OECD Technical Paper Series 127.
[39] Handoussa, Heba and Jean-Louis Reiffers. 2001. *The Evolution and Structure of Trade and Investment Between the EU and its Mediterranean Partners*. FEMISE Research Network.
[40] World Bank. 2001. *Egypt Country Assistance Strategy* (not published).

can unlock, between the two sides of the Mediterranean (i.e. its market-creating role) are North Sea shrimps, which are trucked to Morocco and back for labor-intensive (and thus job-creating) peeling.

Box 1.5 The Transport of Mediterranean Cut-Flowers to EU Markets

Cut-flowers are highly fragile and provide an illustrative example for the complex logistics requirements of perishable goods. Their transport requires a closed cool-chain with special refrigerated equipment and careful handling at every stage. Such chains can comprise up to a dozen stages (e.g. farm, truck, airport, plane, airport, truck, flower auction, repackaging, truck, shop). Only one unintended temperature increase of 5-10 °C in this entire chain – for example during customs control or airport groundhandling – can dramatically reduce the shelf-life of the flowers. Holland is the main distribution hub for cut-flowers in Europe. The six Dutch flower auctions have a total turnover of € 2.3 billion per year and Aalsmeer is the largest auction with a total of 7,000 registered sellers and 1,300 buyers. Imported flowers account for about 20 percent of the Dutch market. In 2000, Israel was the largest exporter (€ 160 million), followed by Kenya, Zimbabwe, and Spain. All MPs taken together (excluding Israel) accounted for a negligible € 5 million. However, some MPs ship cut-flowers via countries other than Holland (e.g. Morocco via France). Flowers are auctioned under the name of the grower and only growers who manage to build a reputation for consistently high quality have a chance to stay in business. For such a reputation, flawless logistics are essential. In fact, industry participants cite logistics inefficiencies as one of the reasons why many MPs barely participate in the trade of cut-flowers.

The journey of a batch of cut-flowers from Israel to Switzerland, for example, looks as follows. Flower exports used to be the monopoly of the Israeli flower board until the market was liberalized in the late 1990s. The flower board was turned into a statutory organization in charge of overseeing the development of the market. Private companies now compete for business and there are four big exporters specialized in cut-flower logistics. The exporter ensures transport to the airport, the passage through export controls, which have been streamlined to accommodate these trades, and hires plane capacity from an airline. During the season, three to four cargo jumbos with cut-flowers leave Israel each day. The Dutch airline KLM is one of the carriers that have developed specific expertise in flower transport. Since ramphandling tends to be one of the weakest links in the chain, KLM prefers to organize the handling itself or to cooperate closely with specialized fresh cargo handlers. Customs at Amsterdam airport are also specifically equipped to deal with cut-flower shipments. The company Traffic, one of the freight agents operating from Aalsmeer, specializes in managing the outbound transport chain to Switzerland. After the daily 6 a.m. auction, Traffic consolidates individual orders into complete shipments and sends four to five trucks to Switzerland. Customs documents are faxed or emailed to the Swiss authorities, so clearance can take place while the truck is on the road. At Traffic's Basle distribution center, the flowers are reloaded to smaller trucks for the final leg of their journey. They are delivered to the shops by 8 a.m. the next morning, only 48 hours after they were harvested in Israel.

Sources: Bloemenbureau Holland, Flower Auctioning Aalsmeer, KLM, and Traffic.

1.4 A Systems Approach to Transport

Manufacturers, retailers, and logistics companies are increasingly managing supply chains as integrated systems. Policy makers should also adopt a systems approach to transport. The defining characteristics of a system are the interdependencies between its elements, which make the whole more than the sum of its parts. Compared to a piecemeal approach to individual modes, (air)ports, or routes, a systems perspective of transport yields additional insights. It takes into account interdependencies, linkages, and trade-offs between the individual components of the transport system. This section, as well as the following ones on multimodal transport and logistics intermediaries, looks at some analytical and policy implications of such an approach.

Examples of concepts derived from a systems approach to transport are networks externalities, bottlenecks, modal nodes, multimodal corridors, and hub-and-spoke patterns. Network externalities are a special form of scale economies that arise when the addition of further connections or participants to a network increases the value or reduces the costs for existing ones. Transport sector examples of network externalities are airlines or shipping companies that can offer customers interconnections to additional routes or the extension of the railway network into a port, which increases the value of the existing rail tracks to users. Certain structural features of the transport sector are a consequence of the economies of scale arising from network externalities, including airline alliances, liner conferences, the emergence of mega carriers for container shipment, and the existence of specialized logistics intermediaries.[41]

Another important concept associated with a systems approach is that of transport bottlenecks. In order to prioritize policy reforms and investments, policy makers need to identify those parts of a transport chain where delays and excess costs arise. An important characteristic of multimodal transport systems is the existence of modal nodes, such as ports, airports, and railway stations, where cargo and passengers are being transferred from one mode to another. These nodes are often important bottlenecks and a natural focus of policy reform. Since a modal transfer in these nodes requires the handling of goods, ports and airports also tend to be well-suited as locations for the provision of value-added logistics services and the nucleus of logistics clusters (see also the Panama Canal case study in section 4.7). Another concept derived from a systems approach to transport is that of transport corridors. Since the majority of trade in the Euro-Mediterranean region moves through a small number of modal or multimodal corridors, policy reforms and infrastructure investments should be particularly geared at removing bottlenecks along these corridors.

Diagram 1.1 The Competition Effect of Hub-and-Spoke

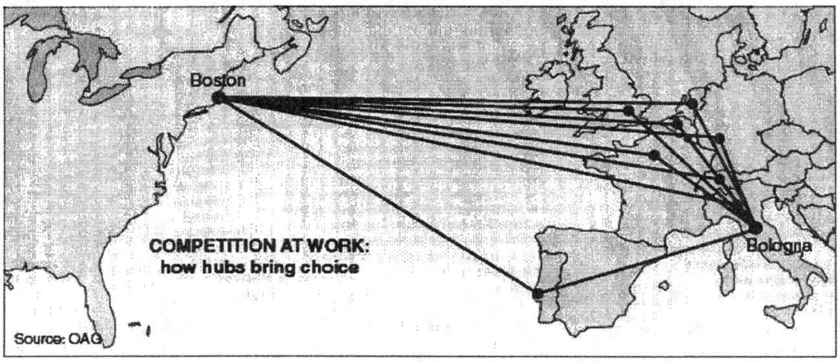

Source: Association of European Airlines (1998).

Hub-and-spoke patterns in logistics networks are another feature of transport systems. Such indirect routings via central transfer points permit higher traffic frequencies and capacity utilization (efficiency effect). The United Kingdom Civil Aviation Authority, for instance, has calculated that pure point-to-point traffic on UK-US routes would support only about half the current flight frequency on trans-Atlantic routes. Another benefit of hub-and-spoke structures is that they increase the competition between transport operators with different hubs (competition effect). Diagram 1.1, taken from the Yearbook of the Association of European Airlines, demonstrates this effect for the case of a passenger flying from Boston to Bologna. "Each of the world's major airlines has constructed a portfolio of routes radiating from its home country [...] inevitably, these networks overlap, as each of the major airlines will tend to serve the same set of destinations from their respective hubs [...] the Bologna-Boston passenger has a choice of single-carrier services over eight different European hubs, with eight airlines all competing for the business [...]. So while the

[41] Besides network externalities, there are several other sources of scale economies in the transport sector, including expensive information technology systems (i.e. high fixed but relatively low marginal costs) and the knowledge-intensity of the industry (i.e. once best practice has been developed, for instance in port or airport management, it can be spread over a larger number of units).

number of carriers on a given route may be restricted to one, two, or three, the choice in a given market is likely to be much wider."[42]

A number of market structure and policy issues are associated with hub-and-spoke patterns. First, hub-and-spoke structures are more important for cargo traffic than for passenger traffic. The main reason is that most passengers prefer direct flights without the transfer inconvenience and the risk of missed connections or delays. Second, for efficient regional hub-and-spoke structures to emerge in air transport, the liberalization of cross-border traffic rights will be needed. As discussed in section 2.6, traffic rights for airlines are currently granted on the basis of bilateral air service agreements between countries, making the optimization of international route networks difficult. The creation of a common air transport space through a multilateral liberalization of air traffic rights across the Euro-Mediterranean region would thus be desirable. Third, hub functions tend to be geographically mobile and thus countries are competing to attract them. Although certain ports and airports have a natural predisposition to become hubs (those with a central location or a large traffic-generating hinterland), liberal sector policies and modern infrastructure are mechanisms through which countries can attract hub functions.

Thanks to the interdependencies between its elements, the multimodal system is more than the sum of its parts. However, this fundamental strength is also its Achilles heel. As a consequence of the complex coordination needs and interdependencies between its constituent parts, the system is very sensitive to any hiccups in the transport chain. Since a chain is only as strong as its weakest link, good policies and state-of-the-art management in all parts of the system are needed. Even small inefficiencies and frictions can have important knock-on and multiplier effects in subsequent stages of the transport chain. In many of the Maghreb and Mashrek countries, for instance, customs clearance in ports can take several days and sometimes up to three weeks. The unpredictability of customs clearance makes it difficult to optimize the subsequent hinterland transportation of goods, manage inventories, and plan production activities. Banking and insurance services provide another example. Physical transactions in the transport chain imply frequent changes of ownership title and corresponding payments; cargo insurance further adds to the administrative complexity of logistic chains. Since inefficiencies in the provision of such transport-related service can be very disruptive, comprehensive transport reforms will also have to address these issues.

Many policy reforms needed to render the overall transport system more efficient are mode-specific and are discussed in chapters 2 to 4. Nonetheless, MP governments should take a holistic intermodal approach and develop comprehensive transport strategies for their countries. At the policy-level, cross-sectoral expertise and effective institutional structures are needed. Transport policies in many of the MPs tend to be ad hoc and decision making remains fragmented. Multiple agencies with overlapping responsibilities are a common problem, while sector policy and planning capacities at the ministry-level tend to be weak. In Algeria, for instance, three ministries – Transport, Public Works, and Finance (customs) – plus a dozen modal institutions are involved in sector management.[43] Moreover, to integrate transport policies with wider trade and tourism strategies, cooperation between the ministries of transport on the one hand and the ministries of trade and tourism on the other should be strengthened.[44] The case studies on the Panama Canal and on Mexico provide examples for comprehensive transport sector reforms.

---

[42] Association of European Airlines. 1999. *Yearbook 1999*.

[43] World Bank. 1999. *Algérie – Note sur la Strategie des Transports* (not published).

[44] An interesting example is Spain, a country with an important tourism industry, where the Ministry of Tourism was given responsibility for air transport in an attempt to accelerate reforms that had been blocked by vested interests.

Box 1.6 The Logistics Needs of a German Car Part Manufacturer in Tunisia

As the subsidiary of a large German car part supplier, Leoni Tunisie S.A. produces cable and electronic components for DaimlerChrysler and other European car manufacturers. It was established 25 years ago, employs 2,400 employees (including 170 in research and development), and invests about € 3.5 million in facilities and training each year. The just-in-time supply chains in the car industry put extremely high demands on logistics systems. Leoni has outsourced all logistics needs to a international forwarder, which has a local subsidiary in Tunisia. As an example of the long-term relationship with its logistics provider, Leoni has developed a tailor-made stacking system that is specifically fitted to the trucks of the forwarder and permits for a capacity utilization between 95 and 98 percent.

A full production and logistics cycle lasts about nine days and looks as follows. Raw materials and intermediate products are sourced from across Europe, Asia, and the United States. They are consolidated at Leoni's headquarters in Germany and shipped to about a dozen different factory locations in various countries. Seven trucks leave Germany for Tunisia each week. The trailers are cleared and sealed by German customs on the firm's premises, where they are picked up by the logistics provider. The forwarder drives the trailers to Genoa or Marseilles (2-2.5 days for the land-leg), places them without driver on RoRo ferries (20-24 hours for the sea-leg), picks them up at Radès port, and delivers them to the factory in Sousse (2-3 hours for the land-leg). The next day the finished components have been assembled and are cleared by a Tunisian customs officer on the premises before they are sent on their return journey. Eight trucks with 320-350 tons of finished products leave Tunisia each week. The company considers the chain both efficient and reliable. As a major exporter, Leoni has off-shore status in terms of tariffs and customs, and receives favorable treatment in Tunisia's ports – privileges many smaller exporters do not enjoy.

Nonetheless, the just-in-time demands of the industry are so high that they are now posing a threat to Tunisia as a production base. Instead of the current cycle of nine days, clients increasingly demand cycles of six days. Internal production processes have been streamlined so far (incoming orders are produced within 24 hours) that any additional time savings must come from logistics. Leoni Tunisie recently lost a company-internal competition for a completely new factory with 1,700 jobs and € 12 million investment to Leoni's Romanian subsidiary. The reasons were not wages or the investment environment – where the company regards Tunisia as very competitive – but primarily Eastern Europe's logistics advantage. The land journey between Romania and Germany takes one day less in each direction, saving € 1,000 per trailer-load. According to the CEO of Leoni Tunisie, who also sits on the board of the Tunisian-German Chamber of Commerce (TGCC), Tunisia will need cheaper and better air cargo connections or high-speed ferries to Europe if it wants to remain competitive in time-sensitive industries. Representing 270 German manufacturers who produce in Tunisia, TGCC plans a logistics workshop with the government to explore options for further reducing travel times between Tunisia and the European markets.

Source: Leoni Tunisie S.A.

1.5 Modal Mix and Multimodal Transport

One of the basic implications of a systems approach to transport is the need to create multimodal networks through the seamless integration and efficient coordination of individual modes. In an intermodal transport system, individual modes are interconnected through network nodes, like ports and airports. Cargo and passengers flow through transport chains, that is through sequences of modal legs. Relative to unimodal transport, multimodal transport has decisive advantages. Since it permits greater route and mode flexibility, it increases customer choice without a direct need to increase the stock of physical infrastructure. It also unlocks network externalities between modes. Moreover, it increases intermodal competition, and thus provides incentives for managers and investors to improve services, reduce costs and cut prices. Intermodal competition can be particularly effective for cargo, where routing is more flexible than for passengers.

Finally, with different modes having clearly defined competitive advantages, an effective division of labor between modes can considerably increase efficiency. Air, sea, and rail have an advantage for long-haul cargo. Sea and rail are better placed to transport bulk freight. Air transport is the preferred option for goods with a high value-to-weight/volume ratio (e.g. electronics, textiles) and those where speed is of the essence (e.g. perishable products like cut-flowers or fruit). Trucking has a door-to-door advantage and plays a vital role in the first and last leg of a journey. Rail freight can be more efficient for long-distance journeys. "Logistics parameters including annual movement volume, shipment size, number of shipments between each origin and destination (i.e. the transportation density), length of haul and the characteristics of the goods themselves determine the comparative advantage of one transport mode versus another."[45] Cross-border trade in the Mediterranean region flows primarily through multimodal maritime and air transport chains, especially in North Africa. By definition, maritime and air transport can only deliver goods and passengers between ports and airports. To provide the door-to-door service that customers demand, effective integration with land-based modes is needed.

The containerization of cargo is one of the main drivers of increased intermodal transport. Like other forms of unitized cargo (e.g. pallets, trailers), it can dramatically reduce the delays and handling costs associated with modal transfer and thus increases the efficiency of multimodal chains (door-to-door advantage). Containerization requires specific infrastructure and equipment (e.g. container vessels and container terminals). Intermodal nodes, such as ports and main railroad stations, need to be equipped with container cranes and container storage facilities. International standardization of sizes and technical specifications for containers and equipment is a precondition for universal interoperability. The last years have witnessed an explosive growth in containerization world-wide. It is estimated that 15 million containers exist and that containers account for "about 90 percent of the world's traded cargo by volume."[46] The capacity of the world containership fleet almost tripled from 1.3 million TEU (twenty-foot equivalent units) to 3.6 million TEU between 1988 and 1996.[47] Containerization is particularly important for maritime chains. Despite recent growth, containerization rates in most MPs are still low by international standards. Another means of multimodal transport – which plays an important role in trade between the Maghreb, Spain, and France – are trucks shipped by RoRo ferries (roll-on, roll-off).

In addition to mode-specific transport reforms, some multimodal policy issues arise. Economic efficiency requires that the role and market share of individual modes (the modal mix) be determined by their respective comparative advantage. Ensuring an optimal modal mix as well as effective modal competition will require the creation of a level playing field between different modes. One priority is the removal of open and hidden subsidies as well as monopoly rents in order to ensure that users pay the full economic costs for each of the modes. Other distortions to competition and relative performance also need to be addressed. For instance, an important reason why railways in many countries find it so difficult to compete with trucks for long-haul traffic, is that the former are dominated by state-owned monopolies without a commercial culture. The trucking industry, on the other hand, benefits from the dynamics of private participation and competition.

Besides ensuring intermodal competition, policy makers in the Maghreb and Mashrek countries should facilitate multimodal transport by removing regulatory and physical barriers. Company statutes, licensing regimes, and laws should not preclude the creation of multimodal transport operators. There ought to be no unnecessary restrictions to the use of multimodal bills of lading (contracts of carriage comprising different modal components), compatible with the international

[45] World Bank. 1997. *Brazil – Multimodal Freight Transport: Selected Regulatory Issues.*
[46] The Economist (6 April 2002).
[47] OECD. 1999. *Discussion Document on Regulatory Reform in International Maritime Transport.*

documentation standards set by the International Chamber of Commerce (ICC). Liability rules should be harmonized across modes and between countries, while transport insurance markets should be liberalized (some countries maintain requirements to use domestic insurance companies). Load units and technical specifications for multimodal equipment ought to be standardized to facilitate interoperability. The development of a dynamic third-party logistics industry should be encouraged. A level playing field should be established by removing discrimination between public and private operators or between domestic and foreign operators. The introduction of private participation and competition in the individual modes would help to foster a commercial culture in the transport sector and thus induce transport companies to seek efficiency gains and meet client needs by adopting multimodal strategies.

Box 1.7 Commission Communication on Intermodality

A 1997 European Commission communication on intermodality defines the main principles for multimodal transport policies in the EU. It states that, "intermodality is an essential component of the European Union's Common Transport Policy [and] provides the policy tool for a systems approach to transport in view of integrating the different modes into one coherent transport system. [...] The main challenge will lie with the market, namely to organize seamless and customer-oriented door-to-door transport services [...]. The role of the Commission and the EU member states is to define the framework in which the market can operate. The rules and conditions must be such that they create a level playing field for all operators and that they foster innovation [...] whilst favoring competition between transport operators. [...] Intermodality is, therefore, complementary to other EU transport policies such as liberalization of transport markets, developing the TENs [Trans-European Networks] and the promotion of fair and efficient pricing. [...] Taxes and charges are currently set in very different ways across different modes [and] modal choices are distorted, due to different cost coverage ratios and the use of different bases of cost imputation. [...] Operators [...] should not find themselves unduly disadvantaged by competitors who enjoy state aids. [...] A key element will be the scrutiny and regulation of any abuse of dominant positions by carriers and operators [...] which carry heavy fines under EC law. [...] In order to identify best practices in intermodal transport, the Commission will support [...] the development of methodologies for benchmarking in transport policy and intermodality."

Source: European Commission (1997a).

The reform of ports, as key nodes in multimodal cargo chains, should be high on the agenda. In cases where the lack of intermodal facilities and missing link infrastructure creates physical barriers between modes, governments should provide incentives for private investors to fill these gaps. One particular obstacle for more efficient multimodal transport is the relatively low containerization rates of general cargo in most Maghreb and Mashrek countries (see section 3.10). The reform of port operations and customs procedures would encourage higher containerization rates. In some countries all containers formally have to be unpacked for clearance, giving officials a considerable leverage to extract bribes from clients that want to avoid the associated delays. As successful precedents show, private investments in container terminals is another important policy instrument (section 3.5), as are better multimodal hinterland connections (section 4.1). Since problems vary from one country to another, multimodal bottlenecks and reform priorities will need to be analyzed on a country-by-country basis. As discussed before, MP governments should consider developing multimodal sector strategies and develop effective policy structures that cut across modes.

Box 1.8 Financing Multimodal and Missing-Link Infrastructure

The removal of legal, regulatory, and institutional bottlenecks should be the main policy priority for the transport sector in most MPs. However, infrastructure investments will also be needed to address capacity constraints, a lack of intermodal equipment, and missing link infrastructure. To the extent possible, the financing of new and the rehabilitation of existing infrastructure should be left to the private sector. Policy makers have a range of policy instruments at their disposal (see section 3.5) to encourage private participation in infrastructure (PPI). In most MPs, the public sector has a track record of underinvestment and insufficient maintenance of transport infrastructure, as well as poor planning and execution of investment projects. The Algerian port of Jen Jen, for instance, was constructed at the cost of about half a billion dollars, but has been virtually unused since its inauguration in 1991. In Egypt, the port of Damietta stood idle for five years following its completion in 1985. Many of the state-owned ports in the MPs lack modern infrastructure and equipment to accommodate large container vessels. Poor planning and under-funding have long delayed the required expansion of the airports in Cairo and Algiers.

In most of the transport sector, the role of governments should be confined to the provision of a transparent and stable regulatory framework, including commercial incentives for private investors. Market dynamics will then determine what type of infrastructure is needed and whether the risk-return ratio of a particular project justifies the necessary investments. Private investors also tend to be better at planning and operating infrastructure in view of minimizing costs. According to a 1998 Commission Communication concerning the Euro-Mediterranean Transport Partnership, 'software' measures (i.e. policy reforms) "should be given priority over 'hardware' measures" (i.e. physical infrastructure investments) since "many transport bottlenecks have their principle cause in 'software' rather than 'hardware.'"[48] In the EU, policy reforms were also given priority over infrastructure investments. Only after a common transport market had largely been completed (see box 1.3) did the Commission and the EIB start to systematically address physical bottlenecks, particularly in land-based transport, through the Trans-European-Networks initiative (see box 4.1).

Chapters 2 to 4 provide a large spectrum of successful examples for privatizations, concessions, and other forms of PPI – both in the region and beyond. They also contain references to possible future projects in which PPI could be mobilized. Examples are the new container ports in East Port Said (Egypt) and possibly Tangiers (Morocco); the new airport terminals in Algiers and Cairo; or railway-concessions. Possible investment projects in the western Mediterranean, identified in a 1997 study commissioned by the Groupe de Transport de la Meditérranée Occidentale (GTMO), include a railway connection to the Moroccan port of Nador, the installation of EDI systems in major ports (e.g. Radés, Algiers), and sections of the trans-Maghreb highway. A 1996 study, commissioned by the Israeli government in the context of the Oslo peace process, proposed several infrastructure projects for transport corridors in the Middle East, including the completion of the Mediterranean Coastal Highway to Egypt; the restoration of the coastal railway route between the two countries; road and railway connections between the port of Haifa and Jordan; and an extension of the Israeli railway network to Jordan's Red Sea port of Aqaba.[49]

1.6 The Third-Party Logistics Industry

Third-party logistics intermediaries play an important role in the integration of different transport modes into a multimodal network. They consolidate small shipments into single loads of standard size and match shipments with available transportation capacity. They combine different legs of multimodal chains under a single bill of lading, offer door-to-door transport packages, and handle documentation and administrative formalities on behalf of their clients. Originally, most firms used to organize their transport requirements in-house and interfaced directly with transport providers such as carriers, terminal operators, or warehouse operators . As the complexity of

[48] European Commission. 1998. *Communication Concerning the Euro-Mediterranean Partnership in the Transport Sector*.
[49] Government of Israel. 1996. *Programs for Regional Cooperation 1997* (draft, November 1996).

logistics needs increased, however, and firms began to focus on their core competencies, the trend to outsource logistics services to specialized intermediaries gathered pace. In the United States, "the industry has grown from just $ 6 billion in 1991 to $ 40 billion but is still underdeveloped compared to Europe, where roughly 30 percent of corporate logistics is outsourced. [...] Recent studies [...] have indicated that companies using third-party logistics providers have reduced their overall logistics costs by up to 10 percent."[50] Seventy-eight percent of European and 58 percent of US companies surveyed were using third-party logistics providers.[51] The emergence of a fast-growing third-party logistics industry over the past couple of decades has been a key feature of the overall logistics revolution.

The management-intensity and IT-intensity of logistics systems, as well as the significant scale economies of the business, have led to the emergence of a specialized logistics industry. A variety of players act as middlemen between shippers and carriers. The most important are freight forwarders and express carriers, who both offer a door-to-door service and act as a one-stop-shop for their clients. Freight forwarders package transport services from different carriers according to customers' needs: they collect freight from shippers; handle paperwork, customs procedures, and payments; and deliver the goods to consignees. Since they maintain long-term relationships with carriers and consolidate shipments (retail intermediaries), they can negotiate better prices than their individual customers. The "freight forwarding industry handled 60 million shipments across the world in 1996 and generated combined annual revenues of $ 42-48 billion."[52] Forwarders vary in size and the range of services they offer.

Freight forwarders have been around for centuries. Integrators, who integrate the functions of modal carriers, freight forwarders, and customs brokers have emerged more recently. Perhaps the most important of them, express carriers (e.g. DHL, UPS, or Federal Express) only came into existence a couple of decades ago, in the wake of air cargo liberalization in the United States. "Under earlier regulations, cost minimizing and speed maximizing networks were difficult to build and operate, because of the many technical and route design constraints surrounding carriers."[53] Express carriers use proprietary infrastructure (i.e. their own transport equipment, storage facilities, and IT systems) to offer door-to-door services. This permits closer coordination between different elements of the multimodal chain and a more efficient management of information. The results are lower costs, higher speed, and greater reliability (e.g. real-time tracking of goods, time-definite and overnight delivery). A study by Cargo 2000, a grouping of International Air Transport Association (IATA) airlines, concluded that transport "delays were mostly the result of the 40 different steps involved in forwarder-airline chains, compared to only 11 steps in integrated carriers." The capital-intensive nature of the industry has led to market consolidation – with the four largest express carriers accounting for 90 percent of the global market.[54]

The boundaries between different categories of logistics service providers are blurring increasingly as different market segments converge and the industry consolidates. Across Europe, for instance, the recent years have seen a wave of mergers and acquisitions. A handful of large third-party logistics companies have emerged that offer standardized services for multinational companies

---

[50] "Survey of Supply Chain Management." Financial Times (17 June 1999).

[51] Holland International Distribution Council. 1998. *Worldwide Logistics – The Future of Supply Chain Services*.

[52] "The top 20 [air cargo] forwarders, including AEI (Air Express International), Schenker, Kuehne&Nagel, Panalpina, Airborne Express, Burlington etc. handle nearly half of the total forwarding traffic." (OECD. 1999. *Regulatory Reform in International Air Cargo Transportation*).

[53] OECD. 1999. *Regulatory Reform in International Air Cargo Transportation*.

[54] OECD. 1999. *Regulatory Reform in International Air Cargo Transportation*. The main companies were DHL (40 percent market share), Federal Express (21 percent), UPS (15 percent), and TNT (12 percent).

across the European Single Market. As discussed in section 4.5, postal service companies are also trying to transform themselves into full-blown logistics providers. Large maritime and air cargo carriers (e.g. Lufthansa Cargo) are already offering full service packages to their customers, thus competing with integrators and freight forwarders. An important reason for consolidation are clients demanding comprehensive door-to-door solutions (one-stop-shop). Increasingly, companies outsource their entire logistics and supply-chain management functions and appoint single logistics providers or lead logistics providers (who bundle the services of subcontractors), from whom they receive comprehensive solutions for their logistics and supply-chain management problems.

Another driver of consolidation is the economies of scale in the logistics industry. They arise from high fixed costs (e.g. IT systems, proprietary infrastructure, brands), network economies, and learning economies. "Express carriers often need to develop their own airport and terminal infrastructure, to guarantee access at will, swiftness, reliability, and cost efficiency. Advances in bar-code traceability, automated handling and computer controlled dispatching also necessitate such proprietary solutions. As a result, 'ground' investments are becoming a major cost factor for freight carriers. Contrary to aircraft, these investments are not versatile (they are 'sunk' and have no alternative uses) and can be cost-effective only under long-term network planning. [...] The 'smooth management' of the cascade of interactions in the cargo transportation chain is also an important productivity factor [since] transportation mobilizes a large number of players and operations – including those involved in handling, carriage, customs clearance, storage, surface transportation, etc."[55]

Companies are not only outsourcing their logistics functions and supply-chain management, but also related stages of the value chain. As a result, the third-party logistics industry is increasingly offering value-added logistics services. Transport services are merely one component in such comprehensive logistics packages and the transport chain is increasingly becoming a production chain. Examples are warehousing, inventory and spare-part management, or even light assembly. Postponement, where products are customized at the end of the delivery chain for particular markets and customers, is another facet of supply-chain re-engineering. Increasingly, the final configuration of products, in-transit-assembly of components, and breakdown of container loads into smaller consignments for JIT delivery is taking place in transportation hubs close to the market. In the other direction, consolidation and inventory management centers are pooling supplies within a sourcing region before exporting them to the manufacturing base. The natural locations for the clustering of such functions are gateway ports and airports. These modal transfer points "are no longer simply a place for cargo exchange but are a functional element in the dynamic logistics chains through which commodities and goods flow."[56] For such a transformation to occur, however, a favorable regulatory environment, adequate infrastructure, and space are needed (e.g. dry ports, distriparks, or free-zones).

MP governments should create an enabling environment for the third-party logistics industry. No studies on logistics intermediaries in the region seem to exist and more research would be needed in order to make detailed policy recommendations. Anecdotal evidence, however, suggests a few areas for reforms. All restrictions on the right of establishment and market entry for logistics providers (e.g. licensing regimes, rules on foreign ownership) create an artificial segmentation of the industry and should thus be removed. This can include a lifting of restrictions for shipping companies and freight forwarders to operate in ports but also postal service liberalization (see section 4.5). Any restrictions to contracting freedom and pricing freedom (e.g. decreed prices for services) should be

---

[55] OECD. 1999. *Regulatory Reform in International Air Cargo Transportation.*

[56] Juhel, Marc. 1998. *Globalization, Privatization, and Restructuring of Ports*. World Bank.

abolished. State-owned logistics companies should be privatized to introduce modern management and private investments. The legal framework should provide transparent and easily enforceable rules concerning such issues as custodial responsibility, loss and damage claims, and agency liability for completing the terms of buy/sell transactions. Largely due to remaining legal restrictions and the complexity of doing business in the southern Mediterranean, many international logistics companies tend to use domestic firms for their operations in the MPs instead of expanding their own networks to these countries. This undermines the efficiency of operations, reduces competition, and hampers the transfer of international know-how and best practice to the logistics industry of the MPs.

There are also success stories in the third-party logistics industry of the MP countries. Jordan-based Aramex International, for example, offers a comprehensive range of transport services, including express delivery, freight forwarding, and catalogue services. Founded in 1982, it was the first company from an Arab country to be listed on the Nasdaq stock exchange in the United States. It has an annual turnover of around $ 100 million, operates 80 offices in 31 countries, and maintains regional hubs in Amman and Dubai. Part of a global six-member alliance of regional logistics companies, Aramex focuses on service provision in the Arab countries. It claims to be the second largest express company in the region, after DHL.[57]

The experience of the Central and Eastern European Countries (CEECs) shows to what extent the third-party logistics industry can be a catalyst for regional integration (see box 1.9). The situation in the CEECs differs in some respects from that in the Maghreb and Mashrek countries: living standards are higher; EU accession will require the CEECs to fully adopt the acquis communautaire; and due to the land connections to the EU, land modes account for the majority of cross-border transport. Nonetheless, the extension of the EU transport space to the enlargement candidates provides some useful lessons. First, a free-trade area should be complemented by a harmonization of the policy framework in the transport sector to remove non-tariff barriers to trade. Second, many of the rules for the EU Single Market for transport are well-suited to guide policy reforms in the MPs: they are largely in line with international best practice and would help to harmonize the sector framework across the region. Third, private companies can be expected to build a common transport space, if governments provide an enabling policy environment and adequate market incentives through liberalization, privatization, and cross-border harmonization.

Box 1.9 EU Enlargement and the Expansion of EU Transport Markets to the East

In the 1990s, the CEECs have successfully integrated their economies with those of the EU though trade liberalization, far-reaching economic reforms, and substantial foreign direct investment. At the end of the 1980s, most of the CEECs traded primarily with other socialist economies. A decade later, most CEECs had redirected two-thirds of their trade to the EU.[58] They are quickly integrating into international supply chains, as many companies have already "become part of intra-product division of labor organized around the EU."[59] By the time the Euro-Mediterranean FTA is completed, up to ten of the CEECs are expected to have joined the EU.[60] This would expand the Single Market for transport from 15 countries with a total population of 376 million, to 20-25 countries with 400-450 million inhabitants. The main accession requirement is the adoption of the acquis communautaire, including that in the transport sector. Although a favorable policy framework is a necessary precondition for the eastern expansion of the European transport

[57] Arab World Online (26 September 1997) (*www.awo.net*) and Aramex website (*www.aramex.com*).

[58] Piazolo, Daniel. 2001. *The Integration Process Between Eastern and Western Europe*. Springer.

[59] Kaninski, Batolomiej and Francis Ng. 2001. *Trade and Production Fragmentation – Central European Economies in EU Networks of Production and Marketing*. World Bank.

[60] Ten CEE countries (Poland, Hungary, Czech Republic, Slovakia, Slovenia, Estonia, Latvia, Lithuania, Romania, and Bulgaria) have started accession negotiations, as had the EU's southern neighbors and Cyprus and Malta.

space, it can only become a reality if private carriers and logistics companies expand their services to the accession countries beyond current EU borders. This is illustrated by the following examples:

- In the 1990s, DHL, a leading international express carriers, expanded heavily across the CEECs. Before, "legislation only allowed DHL to operate via government-appointed agents or through joint ventures. But after the fall of communism (and as the law allowed), DHL quickly established wholly owned subsidiaries throughout the region, and it has continued to grow. Today DHL has 160 offices and over 3,000 staff throughout Eastern and Central Europe. [...] DHL has invested nearly $ 100 million in the region since 1989. Half of that has gone into developing facilities and a proper working infrastructure; the other half has been invested in aircraft, vehicles, staff training, and state-of-the-art computer technology. DHL is linking up all its offices in the region with a combination of leased lines, satellite links, and dial-up facilities. DHL has also invested heavily in its airport facilities where shipments are handled and sorted by their destinations. Many such facilities – known as 'gateways' – have been opened, [including] in Budapest, Bucharest, Katowice, and Gdansk. DHL already uses its own flights to connect most of the countries with its international network. This system of connections is being expanded extensively over the next two years. [...] The company invests 7 percent of its revenue in staff training; 99 percent of its 3,000 employees in the region are local."[61]
- There are also plenty of examples of the eastern expansion of more specialized niche providers. "Emery Worldwide, the US-based global logistics operator, included both Hungary and the Czech Republic among 20 European countries covered by a recently-launched, second-day, time-definite pick-up and delivery service for heavyweight shipments. [...] Intercontainer-Interfrigo (ICF), a Swiss-based pan-European combined transport and temperature-controlled network provider [...] has also been involved in running a series of banana block trains between Antwerp and the Czech capital, Prague, and transporting deep-frozen meat from Spain to Russia in cooperation with TransRail, the freight forwarding agency of Russian and other CIS railways."
- "Coupled with a marked expansion in the type of freight services being operated between Western and Central/Eastern Europe at present is a noticeable acceleration in the pace of modern logistics facilities development within the latter region. [...] In Hungary, for example, a consortium of 10 companies from six European countries" is building a very large combined distribution and logistics center near Budapest, which will be connected to the country's main highways, the rail network, and Central Europe's main waterway, the Danube river. The center opened in 2001 and will eventually cover a total of 100 hectares. "Leading locally-based logistics service providers in countries such as Poland and Hungary are also stepping up development of their facilities. In Poland, for example, nationally-based operator Raben Logistics recently opened a new $ 4 million, 12,000 m^2 groupage terminal at its Gadki distribution center, near Poznan."[62]
- The German company Eurokai operates container terminals in Hamburg and Bremen and provides regular train services not only to key cities in southern Germany but all the way to Hungary. For these hinterland connections it uses its own trains, which it is permitted to operate on public tracks (see also section 4.3). It is now planning similar hinterland connections from its Italian container terminals of Giao Tauro and La Spezia to cities in Central Europe.[63]
- In November 1999, a partial privatization enabled Swissair to acquire 38 percent of the Polish flag carrier LOT for $ 184 million – 10 percent directly and the rest through a capital increase used for balance-sheet restructuring and fleet expansion. LOT was to be closely integrated into the Swissair-led Qualiflyer group and Warsaw was to become a regional hub for the alliance and its 'gateway to the east.'[64] LOT not only benefited from code sharing and network integration but also from the transfer of know-how from its strategic partners. With the restructuring of Swissair and Sabena (both airlines filed for bankruptcy but continued operations under new names) in the wake of the September 11, 2001, however, the future of this partnership was unclear at the time of writing.

---

[61] World Bank. April 1999. *Transition*.

[62] This and the previous bullet: Financial Times (9 December 1999). Information on the Budapest logistics center also from a supplement by the Hungarian government in The Economist (9 March 2002).

[63] Financial Times Deutschland (15 June 2001).

[64] Financial Times (19 November 1999).

1.7 Information Technology for Transport Logistics

Transport logistics is a highly information-intensive business. The effective processing and exchange of information is a prerequisite for a smooth physical flow of goods. Transport is a very heterogeneous product and the matching of differentiated supply with demand requires the accurate transfer and processing of large amounts of information. The same holds for the tracking of shipments and the efficient repositioning of mobile equipment like trailers or containers. Since transport is a 'perishable' product (unused capacity on a plane or ship cannot be sold once the trip has been made), an efficient use of capacity requires rapid and preferably real-time information flows.

Moreover, transport systems involve a multitude of physical, legal, and financial transactions between various parties including senders (shippers) and recipients (consignees), carriers and forwarders, banks and insurance companies, or customs and port authorities. Business trends like JIT and supply-chain management require an ever closer integration of logistics with other business processes. As a consequence, the effective exchange of information, payments, and documents across both national and institutional boundaries, is essential. Traditionally, most trade and transport related transactions have been paper-based, involving such documents as bills of lading, letters of credit, customs forms, invoices, or insurance certificates.[65] Such systems not only entail repeated entry of the same information by multiple parties, but are also much slower and more erratic than the electronic transmission of data. Inefficiencies in the banking system or in the physical transfer of documents often obstruct the flow of goods. According to the United Nations "$ 420 billion, or 7 percent of the $ 6,000 billion value of international trade each year, is swallowed up by the cost of administering paper-based systems."[66]

The processing and exchange of information is facilitated by a variety of information and communication technology (ICT) tools. Specialized logistics ICT includes inventory and warehouse management systems; route optimization programs; tracing and tracking software; and satellite-based fleet-management systems. At the same time, most large companies are installing Enterprise Resource Planning (ERP) systems throughout their organizations. ERP replaces formerly proprietary and self-standing programs for individual business processes (e.g. purchasing and billing, inventory and manufacturing, planning and scheduling, finance and personnel) and integrates them into a unified system.[67] Increasingly, these intra-firm IT systems (closed networks)

---

[65] The *bill of lading (BoL)* is a title of ownership and "the document issued by a carrier to a shipper acknowledging receipt of goods, and stating the point of pick-up and delivery, value declared for carriage, freight charges and terms and conditions of transport." (Ollivier, G. and P. Taborga. 1999. "Development of Trade Support Services." World Bank ECSIN Working Paper Series 12.) The International Federation of Freight Forwarders Associations has developed a standard BoL for Multimodal Transport based on ICC and UNCTAD rules.
The *letter of credit* (or documentary credit) enables "the seller to be sure that his goods could not pass to the buyer until due payment had been made, while the buyer knows that his money would not pass to the seller until the goods were safely in hand." (Raven, John. 2000. *Trade and Transport Facilitation*. World Bank and IECC.) Using the letter of credit, banks have traditionally acted as intermediaries in such transactions where buyers and payers are spatially separated by authorizing the release of goods in return for payment. The ICC, which has defined international standards for such documents, however, is working on an electronic alternative to reduce delays and frictions associated with payment systems (e.g. inefficient banks, delays in the physical transfer of the document). It is also setting up a web-site for online training and advise on drawing up letters of credit (*www.dcprofessional.com*). "Because of drafting errors, an estimated two-thirds of all letters of credit are rejected when first presented, holding up payment until the mistakes are ironed out." (Financial Times, 31 August 2000).
INCOTERMS, as formulated by the ICC (*www.iccwbo.org*), define the rights and obligations of buyers and sellers in cross-border sales contracts. Another industry body promoting standard trading conditions and offering uniform forwarding documents is the International Federation of Freight Forwarders Associations (FIATA, *www.fiata.org*).
[66] Financial Times (23 August 1999).
[67] These include financial and payroll data, management information systems, manufacturing and inventory

are being connected to those of suppliers and customers (open networks) in order to ensure the efficient flow of information up and down the supply chain.

The traditional ICT interface between the internal networks of firms with those of their business partners has been electronic data interchange (EDI). These are proprietary systems based on a common network infrastructure and codification standards permitting members of an EDI community to electronically exchange information with each other. Recently, however, EDI is being eclipsed by web-based applications. The internet has several advantages over traditional EDI systems. Instead of relying on proprietary technology, which locks suppliers and customers together, it is flexible and in principle open to everyone. It is also considerably easier and cheaper to use and it permits to extend the supply chain all the way down to the final consumer.[68] In September 1999, Bolero, an electronic system for transmitting trade documents, was launched. It is a joint venture between the international banking and logistics communities and provides a system for the online exchange of bills of lading, customs forms, letters of credit, and insurance certificates. Given the value and sensitivity of such documents, Bolero wants to act as a trusted third party linking shipping companies, banks, and forwarders through a common web-site.[69] Other internet initiatives that could transform the logistics industry include global market places for container cargo (e.g. GoCargo) and air freight (e.g. Global Freight Exchange).[70]

The virtual integration of Euro-Mediterranean supply chains through modern ICT could play an important catalytic role for the economic integration within the emerging FTA. So far, however, the southern Mediterranean countries have largely missed out on these developments and risk falling further behind. An important impediment to the increased use of modern ICT in the transport sector of many MPs is the lack of competition and the lack of commercial management in state-owned enterprises (SOEs). Throughout the region, state-owned airlines, airports, and ports have failed to introduce state-of-the-art information technology compatible with the systems employed by their clients. This not only reduces their own efficiency, but also disrupts the system-wide flow of information and thus the operations of other players in the industry. Many SOEs are not even ready to introduce these systems, since outdated institutional structures and cumbersome working procedures are incompatible with such modern process technologies. Commercialization and privatization of SOEs, preferably with involvement of foreign strategic partners, could bring the needed restructuring, training, and investments. The liberalization of transport markets would provide companies with the necessary incentives to adopt modern technologies to keep up with competitors and provide the services clients demand.

In addition to the privatization of transport companies and the liberalization of transport services, governments could considerably facilitate the efficient use of modern logistics technology if the public administration, and particularly customs authorities, would adopt internet-based EDI to interact with their customers. Since government agencies require the submission of large amounts of data on consignments and transactions, they should permit their clients to do so electronically through ICT systems that are compatible with those used by the private sector. In maritime transport, for instance, the electronic exchange of information between shipping lines and their agents via EDI is already the norm. Ideally, detailed information on consignments would be channeled electronically from the producer (the shipper) to the final destination (the recipient) with copies to ship's agents and handling operators (stevedores). The same information should be sent

records, purchasing and customer-related information.

[68] The Economist (26 June 1999).

[69] Financial Times (23 August 1999). The Bolero web-site is (*www.bolero.net*).

[70] For a discussion of electronic transfer of trade documents see also: United Nations. 1998. *Review of Maritime Transport 1998*. The web-sites are GoCargo (*www.gocargo.com*) and Global Freight Exchange (*www.gf-x.com*).

via electronic manifest to customs for clearance, while electronic declaration and payment of import duty should be feasible via the same system. The MPs should also ratify the International Convention for the Unification of Certain Rules for International Carriage by Air, which permits for electronic air waybills (see section 2.7). An interesting example of the facilitating role the public administration can play is Thailand. The government recently passed a law obliging companies to process their import-export documentation online "in order to encourage e-commerce in cross-border supply-chains."[71]

At the regional level, the Euro-Mediterranean Partners could eventually consider the installation of a common IT network to track cargo. In the southern African trade block Comesa, for instance, the UN Conference on Trade and Development (UNCTAD), sponsored by the EU, installed the Advanced Cargo Information System (ACIS). "ACIS allows computers at ports, railway stations, and road checkpoints to talk directly to their customers, saying what cargo is in which container, where it has reached, and helping to find the most efficient way of moving it one step further. Eventually, the system should enable a trader anywhere in the world to track a consignment stage-by-stage [...] with only a laptop and an internet connection."[72] The installation of such a system, however, should go hand-in-hand with institutional and procedural reforms as well as with close involvement of the user community and private investors.

1.8 Cross-Border Logistics: The Domestic Reform Agenda

In transport logistics, at least two sets of cross-border issues arise. The first are reforms that each country has to address domestically (discussed in this section). National borders separate two jurisdictions and any cross-border transport thus implies a trade transaction. This entails trade-related controls (e.g. standards, immigration), taxes and charges (e.g. customs duties), as well as the associated administrative procedures and red tape. Borders tend to introduce considerable delays, costs, and uncertainties into international transport and supply chains. Therefore, trade facilitation (the reduction and streamlining of these trade-related procedures) also entails transport facilitation. The second set of policy issues relates to reforms that require bilateral or regional coordination (see section 1.9). Examples are bilateral air traffic agreements granting airlines access to international routes, multilateral management of trade corridors, or the effective interconnection of railway systems between neighboring countries.

Throughout the Euro-Mediterranean region, some of the worst transport bottlenecks are located at national borders. This is partly due to the fact that borders often coincide with a change of modes (i.e. ports and airports are the key entry points into most MPs). However, it is primarily a consequence of the costs and administrative frictions associated with a transfer of goods between jurisdictions. Most trade-enforcement measures and formalities are geared towards imports to ensure compliance with safety and health standards to raise revenues for the treasury, but also as a means to protect domestic companies. Throughout the region, most tariffs (import taxes based on the cost of the commodity at the port of entry) will eventually have to be removed in preparation for the Euro-Mediterranean FTA. The MPs should use this opportunity to also reduce trade-related red tape and other cross-border frictions.

Most of the southern Mediterranean countries continue to maintain a range of para-tariff measures.[73] These include formalities for the legalization of certificates of origin and import

[71] Financial Times (29 March 2000).

[72] Financial Times (28 October 1998).

[73] Zarrouk, Jamal. 2000. "Para-Tariff Measures in Arab Countries." In B. Hoekman and H. Kheir-El-Din, eds.,

invoices, or the certification of compliance with product and safety standards. Fees collected from importers in return for such services are considered para-tariffs if they exceed the costs of service provision (e.g. charges collected on an *ad valorem* basis). A second category of para-tariffs are internal charges (collected beyond the border), such as value added or sales tax that discriminate against imported products. Both types of para-tariff measures are prohibited under World Trade Organization (WTO) rules and the latter is also prohibited under the framework of the Greater Arab Free-Trade Area.[74] They also run counter to the provisions of the Euro-Med Association Agreements prohibiting the imposition of customs duties and charges with equivalent effect. As shown in box 1.10, however, they are still wide-spread and should be phased out in coming years.

Box 1.10 Some Examples of Para-Tariff Measures in the Mediterranean Partners (1999)

Jordan

- 'Service' charges affecting importers: (i) Fees for customs overtime wages are levied on all goods at 0.2 percent of the cost, insurance, and freight (CIF) value of imports and 0.1 percent of the value of exports. (ii) Legalization charges of JD2 for certifying import invoices and certificates of origin and their attachments are levied on free on board (FOB) value of imports ranging between JD 1,000 and JD 10,000. The certification fee is JD 20 for FOB imports value exceeding JD 10,000. (iii) Additional specific duties are expressed as a fixed monetary amount per physical unit of the product imported.
- Internal taxes or charges violating the national treatment of imports: Sales taxes of 10 and 20 percent of the CIF import value plus customs tariff and customs duties are charged. Sales tax is levied on both locally manufactured and imported goods, except for staples (wheat, corn, sugar, gas, agricultural machines and equipment, and medications).

Morocco

- 'Service' charges affecting importers: A para-fiscal tax (*taxe para-fiscale*) is collected at the rate of 0.25 percent of the CIF import value and levied on all imported goods, except those exempted from or subject to minimum customs tariffs. This tax is collected to assist standards and quality inspections of export-oriented goods, the Moroccan crafts industry, the Moroccan Center for Export Promotion, and the Industrial Development Council.
- 'Special' import taxes complementing tariffs: (i) Fiscal withholding on imports (*prélèvement fiscale à l'importation*) is levied at 15 percent of the CIF import value plus the customs tariffs, and (ii) specific import duties on timber (except wooden manufactured articles) are levied at the rate of 6 percent on the CIF import value, plus tariffs and other customs duties as well as the fiscal withholding import tax.
- Internal taxes or charges violating the national treatment of imports: (i) Value-Added Tax (VAT) is levied on both imported and locally manufactured goods. This tax comprises five rates: 0 percent granted to certain foodstuffs; 7 percent levied on the consumption of electricity, water, medications, petroleum products, table oils, medical services, legal services, and bank and other financial services; 10 percent levied on imports of sugar and other derivatives; 14 percent levied on transport; and 20 percent levied on some other goods. The VAT levied on imports is calculated on the basis of the CIF value plus tariffs and the fiscal withholding, as well as other customs duties and charges. (ii) Consumption tax is levied as a specific duty as a surcharge on imported alcoholic beverages, sugar, artificial sweetener, rubber sheets, pneumatic tubes, and wheel tires.

Source: Zarrouk.(2000).

Trade Policy Developments in the Middle East and North Africa. MDF and World Bank Institute.

[74] According to Article II (2c) and Article VIII (1-a) of the GATT, a "state desiring to levy charges on imports or exports in addition to customs duties shall collect such charges or taxes [only] in return for specific services rendered and [...] these shall be computed on the basis of actual cost of services rendered in the conduct of a commercial transaction (be it an importation or exportation transaction). The GATT prohibits party-states from imposing additional charges or taxes on imports in any other form for the purpose of protecting national products or collecting additional revenues for the State treasury in an indirect manner."

The delays and frictions resulting from cumbersome border-procedures are often more distorting than the actual costs of tariffs and para-tariffs. Most of the measures listed in box 1.10 involve their own formalities and can be a breeding ground for bureaucracy and corruption. "Export checks and import clearance procedures may impose a considerable burden on producers, traders, and investors, in addition to consumers. Imposition of costly procedural requirements to assure that imports satisfy formal specifications and national product standards can be especially burdensome for importers."[75] A 1995 World Bank study on Egypt found that trade was being regulated by the Customs Authority, the Ministry of Health, the Ministry of Supply, the General Organization of Veterinarian Services, the General Organization for Quarantine, the Atomic Energy Association, the Industrial Control Authority, and the General Authority for Export and Import Control.[76] Details about documentation requirements and procedures for imports/exports in Egypt and other MPs can be found on the Arab Chambers web-site.[77]

In Egypt, 1,550 tariff lines are subject to product standards and depending on the product category, different forms must be submitted to several agencies. "Each agency samples and tests the consignment independently [and all involved] agencies must approve the shipment before release is granted. [...] For some products the fees involved are significant. [...] Delays of two to four days to inspect the product are not uncommon. Duplicative testing is the rule. All consignments are sampled, regardless of compliance history. [...] Inspection is carried out by a technical committee of three individuals and leads to an excessive use of manpower."[78] Another example of the disproportionate administrative and compliance costs that product standards can impose is Jordan. Of the 51,000 import transactions processed by the national standards institute in 1997, only 65 failed to meet Jordanian standards (i.e. 0.1 percent).[79] While this is an extreme example, it is symptomatic of the red tape that disrupts transport flows at southern Mediterranean borders. In many of the MPs, border formalities continue to be governed by outdated rules and cumbersome procedures. Duplicative inspections and a lack of inter-agency coordination are another common problem. Several countries in the region have successfully started to reduce red tape at borders, but much work remains to be done.

Customs clearance, in particular, remains one of the most important cross-border transport bottlenecks. Lebanon's customs reform program exemplifies the reform needs in the southern Mediterranean countries and is discussed in section 4.4. Supported by the World Bank, the program was launched in 1995 with a streamlining of tariff structures (simplification, alignment with international nomenclature). A single administrative document replaced a plethora of 26 different forms. Combined with a streamlining of administrative procedures, this made the clearance process computerizable and starting in late 1997, a computer system modeled on international and EU standards was installed. All trade-related regulations of different agencies were summarized in a user-friendly matrix and the simultaneous performance of all border-related controls is being planned. Due to the efficient use of a customer data-base and selective testing, the percentage of inspected shipments was reduced from 90 to 60 percent, while average tariff revenues remained constant. Between October 1997 and March 1999, average clearing times were reduced from six to four days. An EDI system was rolled out and a new customs law adopted. Two other useful

---

[75] Kheir-El-Din, Hanaa. 2000. "Enforcement of Product Standards as Barriers to Trade: The Case of Egypt." In *Trade Policy Developments in the Middle East and North Africa*. MDF and World Bank Institute.

[76] A study by Bernard Hoekman cited in: World Bank. 1995. *Claiming the Future*.

[77] Under (*www.arabchamber.com*) see the respective country section, heading "Business and Economy," subheading "Trade Regulation and Standards."

[78] Kheir-El-Din, Hanaa. 2000. "Enforcement of Product Standards as Barriers to Trade: The Case of Egypt."

[79] Al Khouri, Riad. 2000. "Trade Policies in Jordan, Lebanon, and Saudi Arabia." In B. Hoekman and H. Kheir-El-Din, eds., *Trade Policy Developments in the Middle East and North Africa*. MDF and World Bank Institute.

instruments to reduce customs-induced frictions are pre-shipment clearance and the physical transfer of customs controls from (air)ports to the warehouses and factories of key importers (*in situ* clearance).[80] Tunisia, Jordan, and Lebanon already operate such a system. Morocco, where recent reforms under a World Bank-sponsored project have also dramatically improved customs performance, plans to do the same.

Box 1.11 The Central American Logistics Corridor

One region that might offer some lessons for trade and transport integration between the southern Mediterranean countries is Central America. It consists of a culturally homogenous group of small economies in close geographic proximity to a large trading block (NAFTA). The Central American Integration System (SICA) was launched in the early 1990s and has seven members: Guatemala, Belize, El Salvador, Honduras, Nicaragua, Costa Rica, and Panama. A partly completed single market and a dozen specialized agencies exist, but progress towards regional integration has been hampered by political instability in some member states as well as insufficient follow-up to agreed initiatives. The SICA countries are situated along the isthmus connecting North and South America. Exploiting a natural transit role and gaining better access to the NAFTA market have long been high on the agenda. Since the mid-1990s, regional policy makers were discussing plans to build a four-lane highway all the way from Guatemala to Panama. The renown Central American business school INCAE – affiliated with Harvard and founded with the help of USAID in the 1960s – presented a study on a Central American Logistics Corridor. It showed that the main bottlenecks were not due to a lack of physical infrastructure, but to cumbersome border procedures as well as regulations that restrained competition in road haulage and the development of a logistics industry. Technical regulations for trucks differed widely between countries. INCAE compared cross-country routes of equal length and found that freight rates in Central America tended to be twice as high as those in Europe – despite much lower labor costs. It argued that policy problems made the isthmus a 'broken bridge' and that a logistics corridor was needed, instead of an expensive new highway. To prove their case, the authors of the study used an unconventional research method. They "put two guys with a camera on a truck" from Guatemala to Costa Rica to film the causes of delays. Of 75 hours spent on the journey, 22 hours (i.e. 30 percent) were spent in customs. Translating the diagnosis into actual reforms, however has proven difficult as vested interest groups in customs and road haulage prevented policy reforms, while many policy makers remained preoccupied with grandiose infrastructure projects. There is now hope that this might change, as the plans for a logistics corridor developed by INCAE recently "became the basis for the Plan Puebla-Panama, the attempt by President Vincente Fox of Mexico to extend southwards the benefits of NAFTA."

Source: Quote from Financial Times (1 April 2002); other information from INCAE Business School.

1.9 Cross-Border Logistics: Bilateral and Multilateral Initiatives

While the majority of transport reforms have to take place at the national level, some policy issues need to be addressed bilaterally or multilaterally. Both the Maghreb and the Mashrek form natural sub-regions within the Euro-Mediterranean FTA and some multilateral transport issues could also be addressed within such smaller groupings. Air transport is arguably the mode where bilateral and multilateral policy coordination is most critical for cross-border traffic. An important issue on the bilateral reform agenda is the liberalization of cross-border traffic rights, which requires the revision of bilateral air service agreements that regulate market access to international routes. An important multilateral European policy initiative that could in principle be extended to the southern Mediterranean is the European Civil Aviation Area (ECAA), discussed in section 2.6. Other European agreements and institutions that might be of interest for the MPs are Eurocontrol and the Single European Sky Initiative (see box 2.14).

[80] In this case, goods are transported in-bond from the port to the warehouse. Bonded warehouses, where goods are subject to clearance only when they leave the warehouse, and free-trade zones are other examples, where customs authorities treat goods as if they were not entering the country, in order to facilitate trade.

Another important item on the cross-border reform agenda are the bilateral free-trade agreements, which the MPs are concluding between each other, in complementarily to their Association Agreements with the EU.[81] While the provisions for cumulative rules of origin in the AAs are an intermediary step to move from the bilateral North-South agreements to a multilateral FTA, South-South agreements that liberalize trade between the MPs will eventually be needed.[82] About 20 such bilateral agreements have already been signed, but the main challenge will be to ensure their effective and rapid implementation.[83] Sub-regional initiatives could also be a useful vehicle, but their track record is not very good. Of the 35 multilateral agreements by the Arab Maghreb Union (AMU), for example, only 5 have so far been implemented. In 1998, the 18 members of the Arab League initiated the creation of the Greater Arab Free-Trade Area by 2008 and tariff dismantling has started.[84] One of the most promising recent developments is a four-country initiative between Morocco, Tunisia, Egypt, and Jordan, launched in May 2001. Referred to as the 'Agadir Process', this agreement is open to other MPs and could substitute many bilateral agreements.[85]

While such free-trade agreements are necessary to reduce tariffs and quotas, parallel efforts are needed to remove non-tariff barriers at land borders between the MPs. Some borders are still closed for political reasons (e.g. Morocco-Algeria or Israel-Lebanon). They need to be reopened if traffic is to flow freely. Other policy issues that arise at land borders are being discussed in sections 4.1 (general land-based transport), 4.2 (roads and trucking), and 4.3 (railways). These issues include joint border crossings and juxtaposed controls (especially customs); the streamlining and coordination of trade-related procedures; cross-border railroad concessions and network access; as well as a harmonization of standards (e.g. for rolling-stock, vehicles, or personnel).

Any import is also an export, and as goods move across borders from one jurisdiction to another they are often subjected to duplicative checks. To minimize such frictions, the participants of the Euro-Mediterranean Partnership should strive for a convergence of controls throughout the region. The harmonization or mutual recognition of norms and standards, as well as a systematic exchange of information between national customs authorities could considerably reduce cross-border red tape. The MPs should bring their national standards in line with those of multilateral bodies, such as the International Organization for Standardization (ISO) and the Centre Européen de Normalisation (CEN), to facilitate trade and market integration. A harmonization of intermodal technology (e.g. technical specifications for unitized cargo, compatibility between EDI systems) is another area, where regional and multilateral cooperation is called for.

Customs reform is a challenge that each of the MPs has to address domestically, but there are also some issues that countries in the region should tackle jointly. Cross-border cooperation between customs authorities or the connection of ports to regional IT networks, for instance, could help avoid duplicate submission of data and minimize clearance times. The North American Free-Trade

[81] It should be taken into account that if the MPs sign bilateral AAs with the EU without effectively liberalizing trade between themselves, they would reduce their chances to increase exports and FDI. A hub-and-spoke pattern of trade and investments could emerge, with investors having an incentive to locate trade-related production in the hub (the EU), from where they would have free access to all MP markets.

[82] As intermediate goods move through international supply chains, *rules of origin* are needed to identify in which country which part of the added value was produced. Tariffs and taxes can then be collected accordingly. A pan-European (EU plus EFTA) system already exists and in May 2001 EMP trade ministers created a working group to explore how this could be extended to the MPs to replace the bilateral systems that currently exist. A detailed discussion of the issue can be found in: Handoussa, H. and J.-L. Reiffers. 2001. *The Evolution and Structure of Trade and Investment Between the EU and its Mediterranean Partners*. FEMISE Research Network.)

[83] The agreements vary considerably with regard to content and status of implementation.

[84] The Economist (10 October 1998).

[85] Reuters Business Briefing (30 December 2001).

Area, for example, has a tri-national group, the International Border Clearance Planning and Deployment Committee, "to streamline processes and coordinate the incorporation of technology for transportation and customs purposes at North American border crossings. This committee provides recommendations to governments at all levels in Canada, the United States, and Mexico regarding the use of new technologies and processes."[86] Another example of multilateral trade facilitation is the Asia-Pacific Economic Cooperation Forum. "As part of facilitating electronic commerce, the group's goal is to eliminate the requirement for paper documents, both regulatory and institutional, for key messages relevant to international transportation and trade for the next 10 years."[87] The initiative receives substantial assistance from the express carriers UPS and FedEx. Customs cooperation between the EU and the accession countries in Eastern and Central Europe could also provide lessons for similar initiatives in the Euro-Mediterranean.[88]

At the regional level, the Euro-Mediterranean partners should also identify priority transport corridors and systematically remove bottlenecks along them. In the case of land-based transport, this would imply a regional backbone network of roads and railways. In the case of air and maritime transport, it would be a network of key ports and airports. Bottlenecks along these transport corridors and at key nodes of the multimodal system can be either policy-induced or physical. A common regional approach to such priority corridors could look as follows: The Transport Forum could, with support from the regional MEDA transport projects and other donors, identify corridors and nodes with high traffic volumes. This should be a relatively straightforward exercise. Studies would then identify the most important bottlenecks and propose measures for their removal. On that basis, funds could be mobilized to finance policy reforms (TA grants) and infrastructure investments (loans) in return for clear reform commitments from countries participating in a corridor. An interesting example for the combination of physical investments and policy reforms at a key node is Beirut airport, where the EIB partly funded expansion under the condition that the airport be privatized. International trade corridor committees with multi-jurisdictional boards are another instrument to oversee the implementation of corridor strategies.[89] Finally, multilateral agreements on policy reforms between Euro-Mediterranean governments could be considered. The Interbus Agreement (section 4.2) and the negotiations of the European Civil Aviation Area (box 2.7) between the EU and the CEECs could provide useful models.

The various national, bilateral, and multilateral transport sector reforms discussed in this and the following chapters can all be regarded as building blocks for the creation of a common Euro-Mediterranean transport space. Such a common transport space would facilitate trade, tourism, and investment throughout the FTA. MP governments should tackle this agenda with speed and determination, if they want to increase exports, foreign direct investment, the competitiveness of their economies, and the living standards of their citizens. The World Bank, the European Commission, and other donors should stand ready to facilitate this important adjustment process through technical assistance, policy advice, and financial support.

---

[86] K. Burr in OECD Trilog. 1998. *Conference Proceedings: Public Policy Issues in Global Freight Logistics*.

[87] K. Sample in OECD Trilog. 1998. *Conference Proceedings: Public Policy Issues in Global Freight Logistics*.

[88] Tunisia was to receive EU assistance to introduce a single administrative document (*liasse unique*). This € 600,000 project, the only customs reform initiative under MEDA I, was subsequently cancelled. This compares to multi-million Euro customs programs for the Eastern European accession candidates.

[89] Another instrument to reduce trade-related barriers are *free zones*. Such areas, usually located near ports or airports, have a legal status that grants customs exemptions, preferential tax regimes, or simplified administrative procedures. An interesting case are the US-sponsored qualified industrial zones (QIZs) in Jordan. Companies located in these QIZs and meeting certain conditions (e.g. joint inputs from Israeli and Jordanian partners) are granted duty-free access to the US-market. The advantages of free zones are that they help to attract FDI and encourage the emergence of industry clusters by bundling resources. The granting of such privileges to small legal enclaves, however, cannot be a substitute for policy reform and improvements of the business environment for a country at large.

Box 1.12 Multilateral Transport Agreements and the Euro-Mediterranean Partnership

Several dozen international agreements for the facilitation of cross-border trade and transport exist. The Euro-Mediterranean partnership in the transport sector should take full account of these. Perhaps most relevant are the EU institutions and the acquis communautaire for the transport sector, which are discussed in detail throughout this publication. Other important initiatives that should be factored into the Euro-Mediterranean transport partnership are those of the European Conference of Ministers of Transport (ECMT). Founded in 1953, the ECMT has 40 member countries (Turkey is a member and Morocco has observer status). It seeks to harmonize transport policies in an enlarged Europe through sector analysis, policy dialogue, and multilateral agreements. Resolutions and agreements cover subjects such as the removal of obstacles at border crossings, the allocation of infrastructure costs, dimensions of loading units, combined transport, rules for international road freight, technical standards for equipment, and the streamlining of customs procedures.[90] This overlaps with the work of the transport division of the UN Economic Commission for Europe, whose main focus is on the implementation of the UN transport facilitation conventions. European countries have ratified most of these conventions, but the MPs are still lagging considerably. Of 16 key UN transport conventions, for instance, Italy ratified all 16, France 15, and Portugal 13 – while Algeria has only signed 4, Tunisia 5, and Morocco 6.[91]

Besides these European initiatives, several international organizations are also involved in trade facilitation. The implementation of simplified customs procedures codified by the World Customs Organization's (WCO) Kyoto Convention is one example. The International Civil Aviation Organization's (ICAO) International Convention for the Unification of Certain Rules for International Carriage by Air or the Agreement on Pre-shipment Inspection by the World Trade Organization (WTO) are others. The model laws developed by the United Nations Commission on International Trade Law (UNCITRAL) can provide guidance in the reform and harmonization of the legal framework. The Convention on Facilitation of Maritime Traffic by the International Maritime Organization (IMO) has been ratified by most IMO members and the Commission actually plans to use it as a basis for an EU directive on the harmonization of documents used in ports. The United Nations Conference on Trade and Development (UNCTAD) offers discussion fora and technical assistance, including its Trade Efficiency Program. The World Bank launched a Global Facilitation Partnership in 2000. One of its first initiatives was the establishment of a standardized Facilitation Audit Framework.[92] The International Chamber of Commerce (ICC) has developed standard documentation and contract terms for cross-border trades and payments (e.g. the INCOTERMS).[93]

The WTO could eventually become the most important driver of transport sector liberalization, but to date its role is rather limited. With regard to aviation, the transport annex of the General Agreement on Trade in Services (GATS) thus far only includes marginal services such as aircraft repair, computer reservation systems, and the selling and marketing of air transport services. Traffic rights, however, are excluded and the system of bilateral ASAs actually runs counter to two main pillars of GATS: the Most Favored Nation (MFN) and National Treatment Principles. Important services, such as airport management and groundhandling, are also excluded. A number of organizations, including the Organization for Economic Cooperation and Development (OECD) and the ICC, have launched initiatives to liberalize air cargo in the next round of multilateral WTO negotiations. With regard to maritime transport, shipping is largely liberalized already, but port services could become an issue in future WTO discussions. The situation in land-based transport and the potential importance of the WTO varies, with parts of the market more liberalized than others.[94]

---

[90] A full list of publications and policy documents of the ECMT can be found under (*www.oecd.org/cem/*).

[91] Magold, Martin. May 2001. *Transport Facilitation in Europe*. UN Economic Commission for Europe.

[92] Raven, John. 2000. *Trade and Transport Facilitation – An Audit Methodology*. World Bank and International Express Carrier's Conference (IECC).

[93] More information on the transport-related work carried out by the International Chambers of Commerce can be found under (*www.iccwbo.org/home/menue_transport.asp*).

[94] *Air Transport Services* (November 1998), *Maritime Transport Services* (November 1998) and *Land Transport Services* (October 1998) all by the World Trade Organizations (not published).

Chapter 2

Air Transport

Chapter 2

Air Transport

2.1 Introduction

The main competitive advantage of air transport, as compared to other modes, is in passenger traffic as well as in the transportation of high-value and perishable goods. Air transport is both a key driver of globalization and one of the sectors which benefits from it most. Between 1981 and 2000, global passenger traffic grew by an annual average of 6 percent, almost twice that of underlying world GDP growth (3.5 percent).[1] During the past five years, the growth rates were even higher (see diagram 2.1).[2] In the southern Mediterranean, air traffic has also grown considerably, albeit at a lower rate. The terrorists attacks of September 2001 led to a dip in traffic volumes, but the long-term growth trend was expected to resume faster than during the downturn that resulted from the Gulf war in the early 1990s.

Across the world, air transport reform is advancing fast. The two largest markets, the United States and the European Union, have been fully liberalized. In Latin America, the process of privatization and deregulation has virtually been completed and an increasing number of other developing countries have started to move in the same direction. According to the International Air Transport Association (IATA), the "regulatory scene is evolving rapidly" but there "are increasing signs that the industry is becoming a 'two-tier system' in which the industrialized nations are moving ahead [with liberalization, while] leaving the developing nations behind."[3]

Diagram 2.1 Growth in Global Air Transport

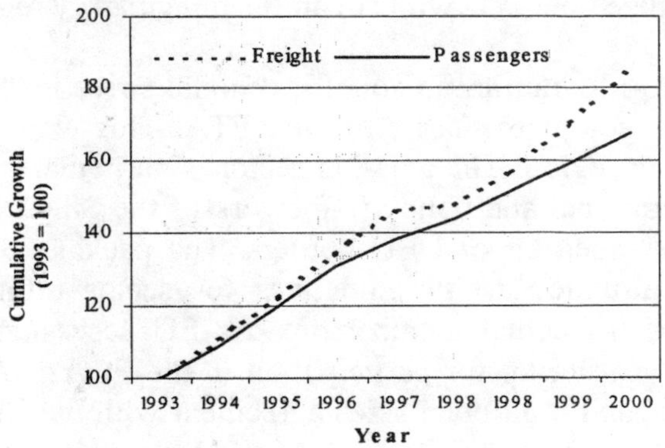

Source: IATA.

Air transport reform in the Mediterranean Partners (MPs) is at an early stage. Throughout the region, aviation services are still largely provided by state-owned airlines and airports. Competition is restrained by restrictive licensing regimes and international air service agreements (ASAs), as well as rent-seeking public monopolies and the cartellized markets they are prone to create. Government interference, outdated institutional structures, and red tape further reduce efficiency. If the air transport industry in the southern Mediterranean is to fulfill its essential role in tourism, export-driven economic development, and regional integration, comprehensive reforms will be needed. In several of the MPs, sector reforms are underway. In most countries with a strong tourism

---

[1] IATA. 2002. *Passenger Forecast 2001-2005 – Special Interim Edition.*

[2] IATA. 2001. *World Air Transport Statistics 2001.* Between 1993 and 2000 cumulated growth in total passenger-kilometers performed was 67 percent and in total freight-kilometers flown was 86 percent.

[3] IATA. 1999. *Annual Report 1999.*

industry, the market for charter flights is largely competitive. Jordan and Morocco recently signed open skies agreements with the United States, while Lebanon adopted a general open skies policy. The majority of the MPs have announced or started to implement plans to privatize their flag carriers, including Turkey, Lebanon, Jordan, and Algeria. Egypt has mobilized private investments for several new regional airports and Algeria is considering to do the same in its capital, Algiers. The Inter-Arab Freedom of the Air Program and the pan-African Yamoussoukro Agreement set promising targets for cross-border liberalization, but are yet to be implemented.

On the northern shore of the Mediterranean, EU countries have spent more than a decade liberalizing, privatizing, and integrating their aviation markets. The Single Market framework for air transport includes legislation to deregulate licensing regimes, route access, and tariffs; strict competition and state aid rules; a directive to liberalize groundhandling; regulations on slot allocation; as well as multilateral cooperation on safety and air traffic control. With EU-internal reforms largely completed, the European Commission is now focusing its liberalization efforts on traffic with non-EU countries and particularly on the extension of the Single Market for air transport to neighboring countries. Agreements to that effect have been reached with Norway, Iceland, and Switzerland. Negotiations with the accession candidates of Central and Eastern Europe for the creation of the European Civil Aviation Area (ECAA) were concluded in mid-2001. The ECAA will extend the Single Market for air transport to the Central and Eastern European Countries (CEECs) prior to their full accession to the EU. By the time the Euro-Mediterranean free-trade area (FTA) is completed, the ECAA will include up to 30 countries. State ownership of airlines and key airports will largely be a phenomenon of the past, and European carriers, operating in liberalized markets with streamlined regulatory regimes, will be highly competitive.

The Euro-Mediterranean countries should strive for the gradual creation of a common air transport space, in complementarity to their FTA. This would facilitate trade, tourism, and business travel within the region. The aviation sector is particularly well-suited for such deeper integration, since the institutional and policy framework of the Single Market for air transport is explicitly designed to be extended beyond EU borders. The package of policy measures that lie at the heart of the ECAA provides useful guidelines for sector reform that the MPs should consider adopting, regardless of actual membership. As EU accession candidates, Cyprus, Turkey, and Malta are already gearing up for participation in the ECAA. As the first Arab MP, Morocco has requested negotiations for an open skies agreement with the EU. Intermediate steps towards a common civil aviation area between the EU and the MPs could be the multilateral liberalization of air transport among the MPs, combined with more liberal provisions of the ASAs between the EU and the MPs.

The air transport sector comprises several interdependent market segments. These include passenger and cargo, scheduled and charter flights, airport infrastructure and services, as well as air traffic control. A comprehensive reform strategy and correct sequencing of individual measures are required to modernize the legal, regulatory, and institutional framework of the sector. Licensing regimes and domestic traffic rights should be overhauled to foster competition, increase transparency, and cut red tape. Bilateral air service agreements between countries need to be amended to allow for cross-border liberalization and integration of aviation markets. State-owned airlines and airports should be restructured and privatized to improve performance and attract much needed investment. Groundhandling and airport charges should be regulated in a fair and transparent manner; and airport slots allocated in a way that facilitates market entry of new airlines to stimulate competition. Institutional reforms should include the separation of operational and regulatory functions, the transfer of commercial activities to corporatized entities, capacity building in sector ministries, and the strengthening of regulatory agencies.

Box 2.1 Air Transport Liberalization and Cross-Border Integration in the Americas

The comprehensive liberalization and privatization of air transport markets across Latin America and their integration with the North American market during the past decade, might provide a precedent for reform in the MPs and for the gradual integration of their aviation markets with that of the EU. According to the trade journal Avmark Aviation Economist, the "first half of the 1990s was a period of intense industry restructuring in Latin America [...] The privatization process was completed in record time. At the turn of the decade, two thirds of the Latin American flag carriers were government owned, but by the end of 1995 all were in private hands [...]. Privatization put in place more commercially-oriented managements and raised funds for fleet modernization and other badly-needed investments [...]. They also accelerated the airline consolidation process in the region. [...] Numerous start-up carriers have been the real driving force behind the changes that have taken place [...] with modern fleets, entrepreneurial management and aggressive marketing and pricing strategies. [...]" After the dual shock-therapy of quick privatization and radical liberalization, the region's carriers have "staged an impressive return to profitability. [...] The recent privatizations proved instrumental in turning around chronically loss-making carriers."[4]

In addition to reforms at the country-level, cross-border traffic between Latin American countries and vis-à-vis the United States has been de-regulated. Since the creation of a free-trade zone between its members in 1992, "the Andean Pact has liberalized air services. At the end of 1996, the Mercosur customs union agreed to liberalize sub-regional air services." In 1997, Caribbean states concluded a multilateral agreement to liberalize 3rd and 4th freedom services.[5] As one of the first countries in Latin America, Mexico de-regulated bilateral air traffic with the United States. The countries modified their air traffic agreement "to include open routes, no capacity restrictions, freedom to transfer cargo for 'onward flights', and operational flexibility."[6] In May 1998, six Central American countries signed Open Skies agreements with the US (see table 2.4). In December 1998, representatives from 33 American states attended the third *Western Hemisphere Transportation Meeting* in New Orleans, with the objective of developing an integrated multi-modal transport system throughout the Americas. The biennial Air Cargo Americas International Congress has evolved into an important forum for discussions on sector policy and regional integration.[7]

Despite overall progress, however, a series of macroeconomic shocks has struck the region. Combined with strong competition, this led to the bankruptcy or takeover of several inefficient airlines and rapid market consolidation. As in other markets, however such 'creative destruction' is an integral part of competitive dynamics. While individual airlines have suffered, the overall market, customers, and well-managed companies have benefited. Lan Chile, for instance, was a small private airline in the early 1990s. Between 1994 and 1999, it doubled its turnover to $ 1 billion, took over the ailing Chilean flag carrier, rescued the Peruvian flag carrier, was invited to become a member of the OneWorld alliance, and was recently ranked among the best 15 international airlines in terms of service, safety, and efficiency.[8] Latin America has been one of the most rapidly growing aviation markets in the world and this trend is likely to continue. According to Boeing's 2000 global market outlook, it is expected to feature the highest growth rates of any world region – 7.7 percent per year compared to a global average of 4.8 percent.[9]

2.2 The Structure of Air Transport Flows in the Southern Mediterranean

A number of structural characteristics of the region's air transport market and associated policy implications can be identified:[10]

[4] The Avmark Aviation Economist (January 1998).
[5] IATA. 1997. *Regulatory Developments in 1997.*
[6] Lakshmanan, T. and William Anderson. 2001. "Transport and Trade in the North American Free Trade Agreement." In *Integration of Transport and Trade Facilitation*. World Bank.
[7] World Trade (October 2001).
[8] Financial Times (1 March 2000).
[9] Financial Times (25 July 2000).
[10] Unless otherwise stated, all data in section 2.2 have been taken from the MED-Trans database of Eurostat.

- Despite some cyclical fluctuations and the severe downturn during the Gulf conflict, the sector is characterized by long-term growth, particularly in tourism-related passenger transport. Growth rates in the Arab MPs, however, tend to be lower than international averages, as illustrated by diagram 2.2. The underlying factors for this growth differential are many, but more liberal transport policies certainly would have helped. Growth has been particularly pronounced in Egypt, thanks to economic growth and an important tourism sector. In general, figures are worse for cargo than for passengers. This reflects high growth rates in tourism on the one hand, but relatively low economic growth and the inability to diversify exports into higher value-added products on the other hand.

Diagram 2.2 Country Growth Compared to World Average (cumulative 1994-2000)

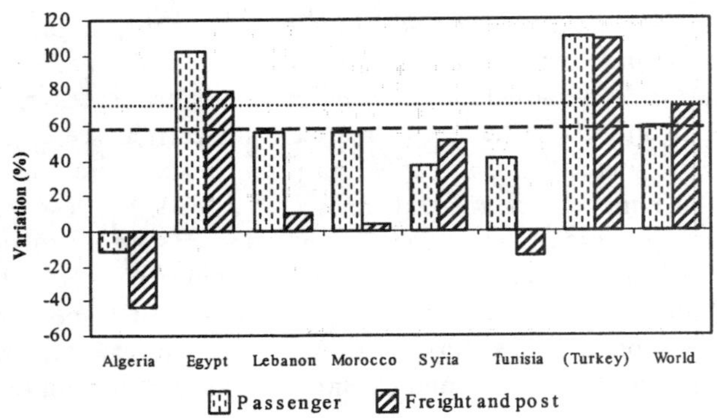

Source: Eurostat /IATA.

- The competitive advantage of aviation vis-à-vis maritime and land-based modes lies in the transport of passengers as well as perishable and high-value goods (e.g. fruit, cut-flowers, electronics, textiles). The strong bias toward freight with a high value-to-weight/volume ratio is demonstrated by trade statistics between the EU and the MPs. In terms of volume, only 0.2 percent of trade between the two regions was carried by air, while the figure in terms of value was 16 percent (i.e. 80 times as high). In Tunisia, for example, 30,000 tons of trade is carried by air, compared to around 3.5 million by sea. Perishables and high-value added products are those cargo items for which speed, reliability, and service quality matter most. Hence, a policy framework that encourages competition and high performance in the air transport sector would help attract more foreign direct investment and diversify the export base of the southern Mediterranean countries towards products with higher value added.

Table 2.1 Air Traffic by Country (1999-2000)

Country	Domestic Passengers	International Passengers	Total Passengers	Freight (tons)	Share of Main Airport in Total Passengers (%)	Transit Passengers (%)
Algeria	3,888,189	1,956,403	5,844,592	21,788	46	1
Egypt	7,955,646	11,517,568	19,473,214	188,782	45	3
Jordan	73,795	2,436,292	2,510,087	85,620	92	1
Lebanon	0	1,997,103	2,222,344	59,243	100	4
Morocco	1,772,063	4,375,132	6,147,195	51,522	50	2
Syria	163,296	1,713,965	1,903,493	31,077	83	6
Tunisia	590,334	8,947,761	9,646,360	27,835	41	n.a.
WB&G	0	88,009	88,009	245	100	0
Total/Av.	**14,443,323**	**33,032,233**	**47,835,294**	**466,112**	**70**	**2**
Israel	1,128,734	8,734,100	9,862,834	342,799	85	n.a.
Turkey	12,931,771	17,079,887	30,011,658	276,166	45	5

Source: Eurostat (MED-Trans Database).

- The other market segment in which aviation has an edge over competing modes, and thus a high market share, is international passenger transport. The Maghreb and Mashrek countries recorded a total of about 40 million passengers by air, compared with about 5 million by sea. Passengers expect high standards in terms of service, flexibility, interconnections, and safety. This requires well-managed airlines with competitive services, new fleets (comfort and safety), and integrated networks (flexible routing and good interconnection). Passengers also expect airports that can offer state-of-the-art facilities and services.

- Air transport is particularly important for cross-border tourism. Even though ferry traffic plays a significant role for general passenger traffic in the Maghreb and road traffic in the Mashrek, most tourists arrive by air. In Egypt, the share of air transport in foreign arrivals is 74 percent, in Lebanon 70 percent, in Morocco 66 percent (23 percent by sea), and in Turkey 69 percent (19 percent by road).[11] About 85 percent of international passengers to and from Tunisia are tourists. Tourism also accounts for the high market share of charter traffic in many MPs (see also section 2.8). Another consequence is that it increases the seasonal fluctuation of air traffic. For most MPs, tourism is an essential and growing source of revenues. In 1999, tourism receipts amounted to $ 3.9 billion in Egypt, $ 1.6 billion in Tunisia, and $ 2 billion in Morocco. This was equivalent to shares of total exports of 29, 18, and 18 percent respectively. As a job-intensive service industry, tourism also makes an important contribution to employment (see box 2.10). Between 1990 and 1999, tourist revenues increased by 255 percent in Egypt, by 55 percent in Morocco, and by 65 percent in Tunisia. Starting from a low base, they more than quadrupled in Syria.[12] Given the increasingly global nature of the tourism industry, the MPs will need competitive air transport if they are to maintain their market share in this important sector.

Table 2.2 Tourist Statistics (1999-2000)

Country	Inbound Tourists ('000)	Tourism Receipts ($ million)	As Share of Exports (%)	EU Share of Nights Spent by Non-Residents (%)
Algeria	755	24	0	52
Egypt	4,489	3,903	29	61
Jordan	1,358	795	23	37
Lebanon	673	807	67	26
Morocco	3,824	1,960	18	82
Syria	1,386	1,360	25	26
Tunisia	4,832	1,560	18	87
Total/Average	**17,317**	**10,409**	**26**	**53**
Israel	2,275	3,050	9	56
Turkey	6,893	5,203	11	60

Source: World Bank (columns 1 to 3), Eurostat (column 4).

- In most countries of the region, domestic air traffic is considerably less important than international traffic, especially for cargo. Lebanon and Jordan, for instance, have virtually no domestic flights, while less than 10 percent of passenger traffic in Tunisia and Syria takes place within national borders. Exceptions are larger countries and/or those in which tourism plays a lesser role. In Algeria, 67 percent of total passenger traffic is domestic, in Egypt it is 41 percent, and in Turkey 43 percent. As far as international traffic is concerned, for most MPs the majority of passengers and cargo traffic is bound to and from the EU. In 1999, the share of the EU in air

[11] Eurostat. 2001. *Tourism Trends in the Mediterranean Countries.*

[12] World Bank. 2001. *World Development Indicators 2001*. More tourism statistics and related information can be obtained from the World Tourism Organization (*www.world-tourism.org*).

passenger traffic, for instance, was 78 percent for Tunisia, 47 percent for Morocco, and 43 percent for Egypt. This traffic creates important economic and social links between the two sides of the Mediterranean. To foster these links, regional liberalization, regulatory harmonization, and commercial integration (e.g. through airline alliances) with the EU should be a priority of sector reform. Moreover, the liberalization of international traffic rights will be particularly important on the key North-South routes in the region.

- In most of the MPs air transport is heavily concentrated at one or two airports. This pattern is less pronounced in countries with a strong tourism industry (e.g. Morocco or Tunisia). These tend to have important charter airports close to key resorts. In Tunisia, 72 percent of scheduled passenger traffic and 90 percent of cargo traffic is concentrated in Tunis, whereas 89 percent of charter traffic is processed through Monastir and Djerba. In Syria, Damascus airport accounts for 85 percent of total passenger traffic. In Egypt, about 99 percent of international airfreight is processed through Cairo. This high concentration of traffic implies that efficient ground transport and domestic connecting flights are needed to bring cargo and passengers from these points of entry to their final destination. Another policy implication is that airport reforms – such as privatization, competition in groundhandling, or the streamlining of customs – are most needed at key airports. Fortunately, high traffic levels make such reforms easier at large airports since they are more attractive for investors and since they have the critical mass needed for effective competition in groundhandling.
- A peculiar feature of air traffic flows in the southern Mediterranean is the relative lack of international hub airports. In most of the region's key airports, less than five percent of all passengers are in transit.[13] Even though the potential for regional hub-and-spoke structures might be limited, there seems to be potential for long-haul transit traffic. Since regional hubs can potentially be located in different places (e.g. European passengers flying to the Far East are indifferent if their transfer takes place in Dubai, Beirut, Amman, or Cairo), the countries in the region are competing for the internationally mobile investments and jobs associated with them. More transit traffic could also enhance competition between national airlines (see diagram 1.1). The most promising strategy to attract transit traffic is through a liberalization of traffic rights, for example by allowing foreign carriers to take on board passengers during stop-overs or to operate domestic feeder services. Other measures include state-of-the-art infrastructure services and the privatization of flag carriers to facilitate the participation in international alliances and the integration of route networks. Dubai, for example, has been highly successful in turning itself into a hub and has about one million transit passengers per year (see box 2.9).

[13] Unfortunately, the only transit figures available are for direct transit (i.e. stop-overs where the passenger continues with the same plane and flight number). Figures for transfer or connecting transit (i.e. where passengers transfer between two flights) are better indicators for hub structures, but are difficult to obtain.

Airlines

2.3 Restructuring and Privatizing State-Owned Airlines

The privatization of state-owned airlines can yield important benefits to the carrier, to the transport sector, and to the economy at large. It reduces government interference and permits the introduction of modern management techniques. It improves incentives to cut costs, innovate, and upgrade services. It facilitates the introduction of competition in the sector and strengthens the airline's international competitiveness. It enhances access to financial markets, while permitting cross-ownership with international strategic partners. Finally, it increases transparency and reduces public subsidies, which distort markets and drain government budgets. For these benefits to fully materialize, however, privatization should be embedded in broader sector reform, particularly liberalization (discussed in the following sections). Given these advantages, it is not surprising that there has been a wave of airline disposals in recent years. According to International Civil Aviation Organization (ICAO), "97 of the top 194 world airlines [were private] and a further 18 [had] less than 50 percent governmental shareholding" in 1996.[14] This trend has continued since.

A common problem of public ownership, especially when combined with a lack of competition, is poor management and low efficiency. A variety of performance indicators can be used to measure and benchmark the performance of an airline. One of these indicators is capacity utilization, which comprises aircraft utilization time (the hours per day that planes are in the air) and load factors (the percentage of capacity used during flights). Since aircraft represent high fixed costs, unutilized capacity has a negative impact on profitability. On aircraft utilization time, most MP carriers under-perform relative to global benchmarks (see table 2.3). While utilization times of 10 hours per day and more are the norm for efficient companies, the averages were 5 hours for Air Algérie, 6 hours for Syrian Arab Airlines, and 7 hours for Royal

Table 2.3 Weight and Passenger Load Factors Benchmarked Against World Average (2000)

Country	Passengers (%)	Deviation from World Average (%)	Weight (%)	Deviation from World Average (%)
World Average	73		66	
Air Algérie	59	-19	n.a.	n.a.
Egypt Air	61	-16	50	-24
El Al (Israel)	75	3	59	-11
MEA-Airliban	54	-26	40	-39
Royal Air Moroc	71	-3	51	-23
Royal Jordanian	68	-7	62	-6
Syrian Airlines	43	-41	37	-44
Tunis Airlines	62	-15	60	-9
Turkish Airlines	67	-8	56	-15
Region Average	**62**	**-15**	**52**	**-21**
Emirates	74	1	70	6

Source: IATA (2001).

[14] IATA. 1996. *Regulatory Developments 1996.*

Jordanian in 2000.[15] On passenger and weight load factors, MP carriers also tend to under-perform international standards, often by double-digit percentage figures. Since marginal costs for additional passengers and cargo are low and since capacity is 'perishable' (i.e. once a plane has flown it can no longer be used), load factors also have a strong impact on a carrier's bottom line.

Box 2.2 Airline Privatization and Restructuring in the EU

The liberalization of aviation markets across the EU (see box 2.5 and 2.7) has significantly increased the market share of private carriers. Although the Commission has no explicit policy on airline restructuring and privatization, it has a mandate to scrutinize subsidies by EU governments that could distort cross-border competition.[16] Throughout the 1990s, the majority of EU flag carriers received significant subsidies to cover their losses. In return for the approval of a total of $ 10 billion of state aid by EU member states, however, the Commission imposed strict conditions with regard to restructuring and privatization (see also section 4.6). In fact, this pressure has been credited for accelerating wide-spread restructuring, privatization, and the successful turn-around of most EU airlines during the past decade. In the five years from 1990 to 1994, the members of the Association of European Airlines incurred collective losses of about $ 8 billion. In the five following years, their total profits amounted to $ 6 billion.[17] Other factors contributing to this reversal have been a general trend towards privatization and the efforts of governments to prepare their domestic carriers for international competition.

In early 2002, the privatization of airlines in the EU was far advanced. British Airways (BA), Lufthansa, and Dutch KLM are each 100 percent privately owned. In 1999, Spain sold 46 percent of Iberia to a group of strategic shareholders and floated the remaining shares in April 2001. State-ownership has been reduced to 57 percent in Air France, 47 percent in Alitalia, 40 percent in Austrian Airlines, and 59 percent in Finnair. In early 2001, plans of the Swissair group to take over 34 percent of TAP-Air Portugal as well as the Belgium government's residual stake in Sabena were cancelled due to the financial difficulties of the Swissair group. In December 2000, the Greek government launched a tender for the privatization of a majority stake in the loss-making flag carrier Olympic Airways, but insufficient restructuring and strained labor relations dampened investor interest. Due to the small size of the Nordic countries, Scandinavian Airlines Systems (SAS) is the flag carrier with the most unusual ownership structure in the EU. Half of SAS is jointly owned by the governments of Sweden, Denmark, and Norway while the other half has been floated on the stock exchanges of the three countries. The accession candidates of Central and Eastern Europe are also privatizing their airlines. The Danish carrier Maersk bought two-thirds of Estonian Air in 1996, while SAS purchased one-third of Latvia's Air Baltic. In November 1999, the Polish government sold 38 percent of its flag carrier LOT to Swissair as a strategic investor and after failed privatization attempts in the mid-1990s, Hungary and the Czech Republic are also re-launching efforts to sell their flag carriers.

A range of other statistics can be employed to assess airline performance and restructuring needs. Average fleet age is a good indicator for investment needs. Some of the region's airlines, like Tunis Air, have recently implemented ambitious fleet renewal programs. Many of them, however, are left with outdated aircraft after years of under-investment under public ownership. Operating profits (or losses) can be a useful performance indicator in competitive markets. In protected markets (the case for most MP flag carriers), however, the earnings of incumbents are often inflated by monopoly

[15] IATA. 2001. *World Air Transport Statistics 2001*. These figures are averages across different aircraft types and do not take account of differences in fleet-composition. It should be noted that the route network of most MP carriers is biased towards short and medium-haul flights and thus average aircraft utilization times are bound to be relatively low. On the other hand, the chosen benchmarks are relatively low: they are not best practice but international averages, which also include poor performers.

[16] According to the EU's founding Treaty, the Commission has the obligation to enforce EU competition laws and to prevent state aids by individual countries, if they distort cross-border competition. The Treaty also explicitly stipulates that the EC has no mandate on privatization issues. Nonetheless, many of the Commission's liberalization initiatives have encouraged privatization by Member States.

[17] Association of European Airlines. 2001. *Yearbook 2000*. Air transport is a notoriously cyclical business. These figures, however, largely reflect the results of restructuring.

rents. This hides the negative effects of inefficiency and renders this indicator less useful. The usefulness of operating profits is also reduced by a lack of transparency. "Few non-quoted airlines [in the region] provide any financial information [...]. Regional airlines which do issue financial statements frequently fail to meet international accounting standards, making international comparisons and valuations difficult."[18] For most southern Mediterranean countries, reliable performance indicators for the air transport sector are difficult to find and further analysis will be needed (see also box 3.2).

Despite such measurement problems, there is strong evidence that poor performance under public ownership imposes high economic costs. While Tunis Air and, after recent restructuring, Royal Air Moroc (RAM) are profitable and operating efficiently by most standards, some national carriers in the region have been making heavy losses. Royal Jordanian (RJ), for instance, had accumulated losses of $ 848 million by 1998 – about $ 150 for each Jordanian citizen or about 10 percent of GDP.[19] Middle Eastern Airlines (MEA), a formerly private carrier that went bankrupt during the civil war, is owned by Lebanon's Central Bank, which has sunk almost $ 450 million into the loss-making airline during the past five years.[20] Until the recent wave of restructuring and privatization, EU flag carriers were also notoriously unprofitable. Between 1991 and 1997, seven EU governments transferred a total of $ 10 billion to their national airlines.[21] Before Commission-imposed restructuring, Portugal's TAP made losses for 22 years, while Belgium's Sabena recorded profits for only 2 of the past 40 years before its bankruptcy in November 2001. Greece's Olympic Airways had only one profitable year in two decades.[22] An example from a developing country is Kenya Airways. Under public ownership, it made losses in each year between 1977 and 1993. Following restructuring and privatization, it was consistently profitable between 1994 and 1998.[23]

Privatization is virtually complete throughout North and Latin America and well advanced in the European Union. Diagram 2.3 illustrates how the continued prevalence of state-ownership in the southern Mediterranean compares with the situation in South America.[24] In Latin America, virtually all airlines are privately owned. This contrasts with the southern Mediterranean, where all flag carriers are still fully or largely publicly owned. Recently, however, several MPs have launched restructuring and privatization strategies. A minority share of Tunis Air was sold several years ago, although 80 percent of the airline remains in public hands. In 1999, the Moroccan government hired privatization consultants to find a strategic investor and sell 40 percent of RAM. Following the reduction in global traffic after the terrorist attacks in the United States, however, these plans were postponed. A restructuring and fleet renewal program prepared Turkish Airlines for privatization and in December 2000, the tender documents for a 51 percent stake of the carrier were published. The government wanted to attract a foreign strategic investor who can integrate the carrier into a global alliance.[25] As discussed in more detail below, the sale of up to 49 percent of RJ has been under preparation. Lebanon's government has wanted to sell MEA for a number of years and in

[18] Oxford Analytica (25 February 2000).

[19] Total debt figure from MEED (5 June 1998).

[20] While the airline's problems are not only a result of public-sector control, state-ownership has politicized and thus significantly delayed the process of restructuring and re-privatization. Although 4,000 employees have been operating a mere 8 planes, for example, the payroll remained constant for years.

[21] UK Civil Aviation Authority. 1998. *The Single European Aviation Market – The First Five Years.*

[22] Financial Times (4 February 2000, 30 October 2000, 11 December 2000).

[23] Avmark Aviation Economist (November 1996).

[24] The method used to compile the data for diagram 2.3 was the following. The percentage of public ownership for each country's flag carrier was multiplied with the carrier's revenue-passenger-kilometers for scheduled traffic (to account for different size). These figures were added to calculate weighted averages per region. In two cases, where privatized airlines had gone bankrupt, the largest carrier of those countries was used instead.

[25] Financial Times (18 September, 17 October, and 14 December 2000).

mid-2000 presented a three-stage strategy for restructuring and privatization.[26] In early 2001, MEA launched a redundancy program for 1,500 staff and started to restructure its debt. In December 2000, the Algerian authorities announced their intention to sell 49 percent of Air Algérie and hired privatization advisors in mid-2001.[27] The Israeli government would also like to sell shares in El Al, but has encountered political obstacles. Although a privatization of EgyptAir is not yet in the cards, a study for the airline's restructuring was commissioned in mid-2000. Around the same time, Saudi Arabia appointed privatization advisors for its flag carrier. These privatizations could enhance efficiency and facilitate the integration of MP carriers into international alliances by permitting cross-shareholding. However, the current market environment will make disposals difficult.

Diagram 2.3 State-Ownership in Airlines: South America and the Arab MPs Compared

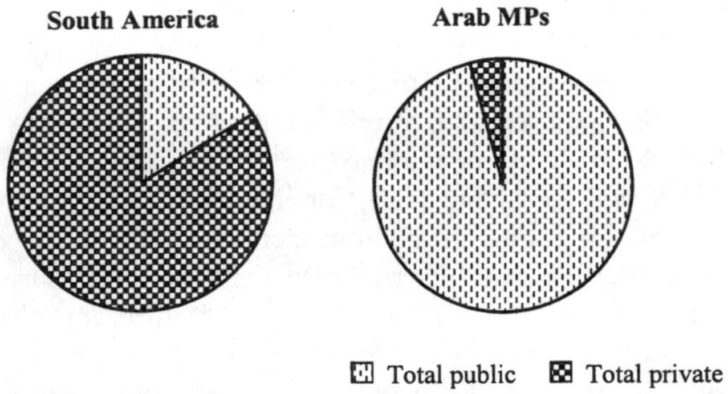

Source: Author's calculations.

When choosing a privatization strategy, governments should take into account the importance of corporate governance. Minority privatizations can infuse much needed management expertise if they involve a strong strategic investor, normally a foreign carrier. In general, however, minority and particularly 'pseudo' privatizations (i.e. cross-shareholding between state-owned companies) have only a limited impact on airline and sector performance. The economic benefits of privatization mainly arise from the effective transfer of company control to private investors. Without the prospect of full privatization, strategic investors also tend to be reluctant to acquire a stake, or will expect a price discount to compensate for the risk of continued government interference. In 1999, for instance, BA took partial ownership of Iberia but insisted on the option to reverse the transaction if the Spanish government did not dispose of its remaining share by a certain deadline. In mid-2000, Dutch carrier KLM terminated its alliance with Alitalia, citing privatization delays as a key reason.[28]

In most cases, privatization requires prior restructuring. The restructuring needs of RJ, described in box 2.3, are typical for many of the state-owned airlines in the region. The challenges that the carrier had to deal with included an over-extended route network, government interference in operational decisions, high levels of debt, overstaffing, excessive vertical integration, and unfunded public service obligations such as the maintenance of loss-making routes.[29] According to RJ's president, a state-owned airline "is run by rigid government rules which limit management from doing real commercial business. When you work under the public sector it is a political liability,

[26] MEED (31 March 2000 and 18 May 2001).

[27] MEED (22 June 2001).

[28] Financial Times (1 May 2000).

[29] *Traditionally, most airlines were vertically integrated and produced a range of ancillary services in-house*, such as groundhandling, maintenance, training, catering, or duty free shops. More recently, however, many have started to focus on their core business (i.e. airline operations) and outsourced other activities. The main reason is that many of these activities are subject to economies of scale and it is more inefficient for one supplier to provide such services to a number of airlines than for each carrier to produce them in-house. In principle, market dynamics should determine the degree of vertical integration, but in some cases regulatory restrictions are needed. This is particularly the case for groundhandling services, where vertical integration can permit an incumbent airline to extend its dominant position further up or down the value chain, or to use it to gain an unfair advantage over a competitor.

Box 2.3 The Restructuring and Privatization of Royal Jordanian

The example of RJ illustrates the complex web of interrelated reforms, needed to successfully restructure and privatize a loss-making airline. The disposal of Jordan's flag carrier had been under discussion since 1993. After a number of false starts, initial restructuring included staff reductions and a streamlining of the extensive route network. An agreement with employees on the shedding of surplus staff was reached and by mid-2001 the payroll had been reduced from 5,000 to 3,600. Six non-core businesses, including duty free shops and engine repair facilities were split off from airline operations and were sold as separate companies through international tenders. By June 2001, the duty free shops had been privatized for $ 60 million, the training facilities for $ 18 million, and catering services for $ 20 million. Other measures included:

Financial Restructuring: A precondition for the financial viability and eventual sale of RJ was the reduction of its crippling debt ($ 848 million in 1998). The cornerstone of the balance-sheet restructuring, which should restore the debt/equity ratio to sustainable levels, is the transfer of liabilities to the government. Following successful restructuring efforts, RJ recently recorded a net profit of $ 36 million.

Legal Restructuring: The airline used to be a government corporation established by a special decree (10/1969), which gave it full monopoly rights for air transport from and within Jordan, as well as for groundhandling at all three national airports. It also obliged the government to cover its losses and guarantee all commitments (loans or leases). Over the years, the decree resulted in government interference with the day-to-day operation of the airline. The absence of market pressures as a consequence of legal monopolies and guarantees, created perverse incentives for management and a complex web of opaque interdependencies between commercial and political interests. To overcome these problems, the decree was revoked and RJ was transformed into a private corporation under company law, initially fully owned by the government. This also involves the end of all explicit and implicit subsidies and the clarification of the relationship between the airline and the civil aviation authority (CAA).

Operational Restructuring: Further operational restructuring is expected to be carried out after the partial sale to a strategic foreign investor. The advantages of this approach are that the private partner has a financial interest in a quick turn-around of the airline and brings in managerial expertise (under public ownership, RJ did not even have a functioning management information system), fresh capital, and synergies through international network integration. Latter would help to further streamline RJ's overstretched international network. The carrier serves about 40 destinations world-wide, many of which at sub-optimally low frequencies. Given Jordan's favorable geographical location and a small domestic market, Amman could try to position itself as an East-West hub. This, however, will require RJ to integrate its network with that of a strategic partner, while providing the high service standards that most transit passengers expect. An expensive overhead, which could be reduced through a strategic partnership, is RJ's over-sized network of about 50 international offices. Many of these service less than two flights per week while acting as tourist offices for the country. They account for about a quarter of all operating expenses. Once the operational restructuring has been completed and a strategic investor found, the privatization strategy foresees that the government sells its remaining stake through an initial public offering on the stock exchange.

Complementary Reform of the Regulatory Framework: An integral part of the privatization process will be a redefinition of the relationship between the airline and the CAA in order to fully separate operational and regulatory functions. RJ used to receive implicit subsidies through artificially low airport fees and the operation of commercial airport activities (monopolies for groundhandling and duty free), without corresponding payment of concession fees. This starved the CAA of revenues and undermined its ability to make necessary investments in airport and air navigation infrastructure. RJ's monopoly rights will be maintained for a few years but should eventually be phased out. As is the practice elsewhere, the airline would instead be granted traffic rights for a limited period of time and against the payment of an adequate fee to the CAA. Moreover, Jordan's airports should be transferred to the private sector in order to reduce the involvement of the CAA in operational activities. To further strengthen its regulatory function, the government would ideally grant CAA financial and operational autonomy. Other costly legacies of the era of state-ownership also need to be addressed, including the servicing of certain loss-making international routes for political reasons as well as tariff discounts for public officials (25 percent) and members of the armed forces (35 percent).

Sources: World Bank, Middle East Economic Digest (MEED).

privatization gets rid of all that and gives management a free hand."[30] The restructuring of the Jordanian flag carrier also illustrates the complementarities between sector reform and airline privatization. These include a separation of regulatory and operational functions, gradual market liberalization, and a clear distinction between commercial activities and public service obligations.[31] The overhaul of the regulatory framework and the clarification of sector policies should precede privatization. On the one hand, this helps to avoid policy lock-in resulting from the creation of private property rights. On the other hand, it reduces the political and regulatory risk for private investors and thus increases privatization receipts.

2.4 Modernizing the Regulatory and Institutional Framework

A web of economic and technical regulations – both at the national and the international level – influences the market structure and economic behavior of participants in the air transport industry. Although safety and environmental regulation are also an integral part of the regulatory framework, this analysis will focus on economic regulation. Critical economic and business variables such as market entry and exit, pricing, route network design, and capacity adjustments, are a function of the legal and regulatory framework. In fact, there are few industries where government interference has removed so many critical business parameters from the control of managers. For the sake of economic efficiency and growth the MPs need to streamline the legal and institutional framework of their aviation markets, reduce bureaucracy, and cut red tape. At the national level, licensing regimes, tariff regulation, infrastructure access, and competition are the main policy issues to be addressed. At the international level, bilateral ASAs that regulate cross-border traffic rights should be the main target of reforms.

The central objective of regulatory reform should be to foster transparency and competition. A liberalized environment gives operators the incentive to improve efficiency while passing cost reductions on to consumers through lower prices and better services. In the United States, for instance, studies found that fares on routes with two competitors were on average 8 percent lower than those with only one airline. Prices on routes with three airlines were another 8 percent cheaper.[32] An example for the benefits of cross-border liberalization is Ireland. Two years after deregulation of traffic between Britain and Ireland, economy fares between London and Dublin (with three operators) were reduced by half, while those between Dublin and other European capitals (with duopolies) had actually increased.[33] Diagram 2.4 illustrates the effect of competition on airfares in Germany. On most domestic routes where Lufthansa encountered competition (light bars), fares declined by 10 to 20 percent over the five year period from 1992 to 1997. On monopolistic routes, they rose by 20 to 50 percent.

---

[30] MEED (5 June 1998).

[31] *Several southern Mediterranean countries have domestic routes on which traffic is too thin* to permit commercially viable services. Many governments have used their control over state-owned airlines or have granted exclusivity rights to permit cross-subsidization between profitable and loss-making routes. Such non-transparent subsidies, however, hamper competition and tend to be disproportionately expensive instruments to achieve these objectives. A more efficient alternative is free competition and private participation, complemented by targeted subsidies for the provision of well-defined public services. Where possible, subsidies should be tendered to the company offering to provide services at the lowest cost. Examples of subsidies in liberalized markets are the national regimes permitted under the EU's Public Service Obligations rules and the US Essential Air Service Program. The latter minimizes fiscal costs by using competitive bidding between private operators to allocate subsidies.

[32] OECD. 1997. *The Future of International Air Transport Policy.*

[33] The only exception was Madrid. The two examples in this paragraph are from studies quoted in: OECD. 1997. *The Future of International Air Transport Policy.*

For private participation and competitive dynamics to unfold, the institutional framework of the sector needs to be overhauled. Responsibility for sector policy ought to remain with the sector ministry. The CAA should be in charge of safety and economic regulation (e.g. licensing and the allocation of traffic rights). Like any regulatory agency, it should be given political and institutional independence. Air traffic control could either be handled by a separate entity or, in the case of small countries, a department of the CAA. All commercial functions (airline operations, airport management, groundhandling) should be fully separated from both the ministry and the regulatory agency and transferred to independent entities. To improve their performance and to reduce the scope for government interference, these would then be corporatized, commercialized, and – to the extent possible – privatized. Institutional reforms in many southern Mediterranean countries are still at an early stage. In Jordan, the CAA is still an integrated government department, has no financial and operational autonomy, and retains important commercial functions with respect to airports. However, the government plans to separate regulatory from operational functions and to eventually privatize airports. In Lebanon, the Ministry of Transport has virtually no policy capacity following institutional erosions during years of civil strife. In mid-2001, a draft law was presented to Parliament, which should pave the way for the establishment of an independent CAA. Running counter to international best practice, Tunisia merged its CAA with the airport authority into an Office de l'Aviation Civile et des Aéroports. The Egyptian government, in contrast, has announced plans to "turn the Cairo Airport Authority and the Egyptian CAA into two entirely independent bodies" and recently created a separate ministry for air transport.[34]

Diagram 2.4 The Impact of Competition on Fares

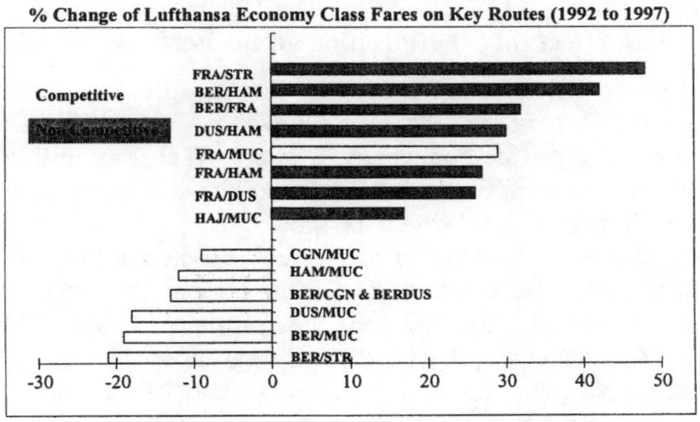

Source: United Kingdom Civil Aviation Authority (1998).

The regulatory framework of the European Civil Aviation Area could provide useful guidance for sector reform in the MPs. The rules and regulations governing the Single Market for air transport and the ECAA are outlined throughout the following sections. In principle, multilateral liberalization of air traffic between the Euro-Mediterranean countries in accordance with ECAA principles would be easier than cumbersome re-negotiations of all bilateral ASAs. Alternatively, the EU and the MPs could agree on a standard set of liberal provisions, to be included in all ASAs between them. ECAA rules also provide a framework for the regulation of groundhandling, airport charges, and slot allocation; the harmonization of safety standards; and a coordination of air traffic control. The adoption of such common rules by the MPs would provide industry participants with a transparent and harmonized regulatory environment across the entire region. This would facilitate their efforts to optimize route-networks, develop cross-border alliances, and mobilize investments.

Despite these advantages, the creation of a civil aviation area across the Euro-Mediterranean region can only be a gradual process. As EU accession candidates, Cyprus, Turkey, and Malta are already gearing up for ECAA membership. As of 2002, Cyprus is adopting an open skies policy vis-à-vis the 15 EU countries as well as the 12 other accession candidates. Morocco has also requested

[34] MEED (28 January 2000).

negotiations for an open skies agreement with the EU. Whether current ECAA members would accept the formal accession of the Maghreb and Mashrek countries remains to be seen. Even if their *de jure* membership is unlikely in the near future, their *de facto* participation through the adoption of the ECAA policy framework is feasible. To prepare their aviation industry for such a move and to demonstrate their reform credentials, the MPs should adopt the comprehensive reform agenda outlined in the following sections. Whatever the mechanism chosen, the ultimate objective should be the creation of a common civil aviation area across the Euro-Mediterranean region.

Box 2.4 The Effects of Liberalization on the Performance of Emirates Airline

While privatization and liberalization are two mutually reinforcing policy instruments, the example of the Dubai-based Emirates shows that radical liberalization can induce even fully state-owned carriers to act like private companies. It is crucial that an airline is run along commercial lines and that a competitive environment forces it to make continuous improvements in its operations. Located in the highly competitive Dubai market, which is served by more than 90 international airlines, Emirates has been doubling in size every three-and-a-half-years since its creation. In 1999 it overtook Saudi Arabian Airlines as the largest international freight carrier in the region. Created in 1985, Emirates has been profitable in each single year, except for one, and generates profits of about $ 100 million per year. They are paid to the government as dividends. The airline has won more than 150 international quality awards and is widely recognized for its high service standards. As part of its international expansion program, it bought a 40 percent stake in Sri Lanka's national carrier Air Lanka in March 1998 and immediately launched a radical restructuring program. Even after the traffic dip caused by the terrorist attacks of September 2001, Emirates ordered further aircraft and plans to triple the size of its fleet from 36 planes in 2001 to 100 in 2010. According to Shaikh Ahmed, the chairman of the Emirates Group, "operating in the open-skies environment of Dubai, without subsidies or protection, we have managed to beat the competition by operating a high-quality airline, and profitably so. This is how it should be all over the world, for it is beneficial to the customer, which must always be our ultimate goal. [...] Governments in some countries [...] protect their national carriers [...]. They believe this is good for their economy but, in fact, it weakens the carriers they are trying to protect which eventually need subsidies from them."

Source: MEED (4 September 1998 and 16 November 2001), Financial Times (11 April 2000).

2.5 An Agenda for Domestic Liberalization

Licenses ought to be awarded on a non-discriminatory, transparent, and non-bureaucratic basis by a public entity without any links to the state-owned carrier. While the technical and financial fitness of operators needs to be scrutinized, such regulation should not impose disproportionate costs and delays. Neither should it act as a barrier to entry or protect the incumbent operator. Technical and safety regulations should be pro-competitive and comply with international standards to allow for mutual recognition between countries.[35] The selection of routes, capacity, and flight frequency should not be constrained by licenses, but determined by market conditions and management decisions. National ownership and control rules, which are also part of the licensing regime, ought to be kept to a minimum. This will encourage foreign investment and allow domestic operators to participate in international alliances through cross-shareholding. Inter-modal links and the creation of multimodal transport companies should not be unnecessarily constrained by stringent license conditions or red tape. Neither should the regulatory environment (including accounting and tax laws) discourage leasing – an important instrument for capacity adjustments and the spread of investment costs over time.

[35] EU safety and environmental standards generally exceed ICAO minimums and all aircraft entering EU airspace need to comply with them. EU countries have agreed to create a European Aviation Safety Agency (see box 2.14).

Box 2.5 Air Transport Liberalization in the EU

The deregulation of EU aviation markets was carried out in three stages. The Commission's first and second 'package of measures' relaxed rules on fares and the allocation of seat capacity, while generally granting 3rd and 4th freedoms. It was the 'third package of measures' however, that brought full liberalization. Gradually implemented between 1993 and 1997, it consisted of four pieces of legislation:

- The common rules on the licensing of air carriers (Council Regulation (EEC) 2407/92) permit free market access for all carriers, as long as they meet clearly defined technical and financial standards.
- The rules for the freedom of access to the market (Council Regulation (EEC) 2408/92) grant free access to all routes within the EU for any carrier holding a Community license, starting with cross-border routes in 1993 and including cabotage as of April 1997. This effectively terminated the exchange of traffic rights through bilateral air service agreements (ASAs) between EU countries.
- The rules on fares and rates (Council Regulation (EEC) 2409/92) generally liberalized tariffs and forbid member states to subject airfares to the requirement of prior authorization.
- The rules on the full application of competition rules to the air transport market (Council Regulations (EEC) 3975/87 and 3976/87) gave the Commission important powers to counter anticompetitive behavior and government subsidies (see also box 2.2 and section 4.6).[36]

Since April 1997, when the last measure of the third package entered into force, both freight and passenger air transport within the EU have been completely liberalized. The regulatory distinctions between scheduled and non-scheduled services as well as those between cargo and passenger services were abolished, as were national ownership and control requirements. Besides lower fares and better services, the main effects of liberalization have been the following:

- As a response to liberalization and privatization, most EU flag carriers have undergone radical restructuring and significantly increased their profitability and efficiency. Between 1992 and 1996, the revenue-passenger-kilometer (RPK) per employee of EU airlines rose by 48 percent.[37]
- Privatization, restructuring, and liberalization have forced incumbent airlines to significantly cut costs and shed surplus staff. The sector as a whole, however, has benefited. According to the Commission, total employment of the EU's civil aviation industry increased from 435,000 to 490,000 between 1988 and 1996 (the main period of reforms).[38]
- As new competitors have entered the market, the aggregate share in output of flag carriers fell from 80 percent in 1992 to 70 percent in 1997.[39] One of the main effects of liberalization has been the rapid growth of the low-cost travel market, which doubled between 1996 and 1997 and continued to grow at 25 percent in 2000.[40] Ryanair, which was the pioneer in this market segment a decade ago, is now one of the world's most profitable airlines and has a higher market capitalization than British Airways.[41]
- Like in Latin America and the United States, market exit of airlines through mergers or bankruptcies has been part of the sector metamorphosis. In the five years after 1993, 131 carriers entered the sector, half of which have since ceased operations.[42] Such 'creative destruction' is an integral part of the renewal process. While inefficient airlines have lost out from reforms, well-managed ones have gained.

In most MPs, flag carriers have long been artificially protected by rigid licensing regimes. Across the region, however, liberalization is now underway. In Jordan, RJ has a monopoly on scheduled flights. Jordan Aviation, the country's first private carrier, recently launched charter flights to

[36] One of the few remaining block exemptions is *IATA fare coordination for interlining* (see section 4.6).

[37] UK Civil Aviation Authority. 1998. *The Single European Aviation Market – The First Five Years*. Not all of this increase is due to increased productivity. Some is the result of outsourcing and economic growth.

[38] European Commission. 1999. *Communication on the European Airline Industry: From Single Market to World-Wide Challenges*.

[39] UK Civil Aviation Authority. 1998. *The Single European Aviation Market – The First Five Years*.

[40] World Air Transport (July 1998) and The Economist (26 May 2001). Growth is expected to continue as 'no-frills' flights constitute 3 percent of the EU market, compared to 24 percent in the US. (Financial Times, 23 September 1999).

[41] Financial Times (8 November 2000) and The Economist (2 March 2002).

[42] Association of European Airlines. 1999. *Yearbook 1999*.

Scandinavia, but it only flies routes not served by RJ. In Lebanon, MEA and Trans-Mediterranean Airlines have the only international licenses for passenger and cargo flights, respectively. Of Tunisia's two licensed scheduled carriers, the flag carrier is 80 percent state-owned (Tunis Air) and holds 40 percent in the second one (Tuninter).[43] In Algeria, licenses for eight private airlines have been issued since 1998. The largest one, Khalifa Airways, not only operates domestic services but also flies to Spain and France. In April 2001, it ordered 18 large aircraft as part of an aggressive expansion strategy for international traffic.[44] By mid-2001, Air Algérie's share of domestic traffic had fallen to 54 percent as a result of competition.[45] Morocco licensed the first private competitor to RAM in 1997. Regional Air Lines operates domestic charter flights as well as services to Spain and Portugal.[46] In Egypt, the government announced plans to permit private companies to serve domestic routes in January 2000.[47] The entry of private airlines into MP markets is an important development, but few of them can effectively compete against entrenched incumbents. Most of them remain niche players, with a small market share. State-owned airlines retain a strong influence over sector policies due to political and other linkages, and often obstruct reform at the expense of consumers and taxpayers. According to ICAO, for instance, Egypt's "extension of domestic liberalization to international operations is being vigorously opposed by Egypt Air."[48]

2.6 An Agenda for Cross-Border Liberalization

Air transport has two layers of regulation, a national and an international one. While licensing regulates market access at the national level, bilateral air service agreements (ASAs) between governments regulate cross-border traffic rights. ASAs are based on the notion of national sovereignty over airspace and on other principles defined by the 1944 Chicago Convention. These agreements stipulate which routes may be served. They regulate capacity and tariffs, specify the number of airlines each country can designate, and contain provisions on issues such as taxation and airport charges. The traffic rights granted by ASAs are also referred to as freedoms of the air (see box 2.6). While no two agreements are the same, they can be categorized according to how much leeway they give to market forces. Under the traditional 'predetermined ASAs', each country designates a carrier to operate on each bilateral route. This tends to create legal monopolies or duopolies on individual routes. Moreover, predetermined ASAs limit the number of routes that may be served; fix capacity and frequency ex ante; grant few 5th freedoms; and require double approval of tariffs by both governments. 'Bermuda-type agreements' are slightly more liberal. They allow for the designation of more than one airline, grant more 5th freedoms, and leave capacity to be negotiated between airlines.

Open skies agreements are ASAs with a minimum of regulatory constraints on capacity, frequency, tariffs, and equipment. It should be noted, however, that 'some skies are more open than others' and not all of these agreements fully live up to their name.[49] The United States pioneered open skies

[43] There are two other private companies: Nouvelair (formerly Air Liberté Tunisie), which has a charter license and Tunisavia, a small player, providing mainly air-taxi services.
[44] MEED (6 April 2001).
[45] MEED (15 June 2001).
[46] Economist Intelligence Unit. 2001. *Morocco Country Profile 2001.*
[47] Air Cairo, one of the few airlines that have managed to enter the market, is 80 percent owned by EgyptAir.
[48] IATA. 1997. *Regulatory Developments in 1997.*
[49] One *difference between open skies agreements* is the number of routes affected (point-to-point liberalizing individual routes vs. multiple-point liberalizing several or all routes). Another important distinction is with respect to air traffic rights. US open skies agreements, for instance, usually only grant 5th freedom rights but do not allow 7th freedom rights or cabotage. 5th freedom rights, in turn, can be sub-divided between 'intermediate' and 'beyond', with latter being much more rare and contentious. In fact, the US has been criticized for using a set of

agreements in the early 1990s, by developing a set of provisions which can be inserted into bilateral ASAs when they come up for periodical re-negotiation. By early 2001, the United States had reached agreement on about 40 such bilaterals, covering more than 50 percent of international US traffic.[50] The benefits of open skies policies are illustrated by the US-Canada agreement, which entered into force in 1992. It led to an average tariff decrease of 20 percent, the opening of 102 new scheduled cross-border routes in 1995, and an increase of traffic by 11 percent in the three subsequent years – compared to growth rates of only 4.3 percent in each of the three years prior to liberalization.[51] Rigid bilateral agreements do not only reduce competition and traffic but they also prevent optimal network design and route scheduling, which are important determinants of efficiency both at the company and at the sector level.

Box 2.6 Freedoms of the Air in Bilateral Air Service Agreements

FIRST FREEDOM
To overfly one country en-route to another

SECOND FREEDOM
To make a technical stop in another country

THIRD FREEDOM
To carry freight and passengers from the home country to another country

FOURTH FREEDOM
To carry freight and passengers to the home country from another country

FIFTH FREEDOM
To carry freight and passengers between two countries by an airline of a third country on route with origin / destination in its home country

SIXTH FREEDOM
To carry freight and passengers between two countries by an airline of a third country on two routes connecting in its home country

SEVENTH FREEDOM
To carry freight and passengers between two country on a route with no connection with its home country

EIGHTH FREEDOM OR CABOTAGE
To carry freight and passengers within a country by an airline of another country on a route with origin / destination in its home country

TRUE DOMESTIC
To carry freight and passengers within a foreign country with no connection with the home country

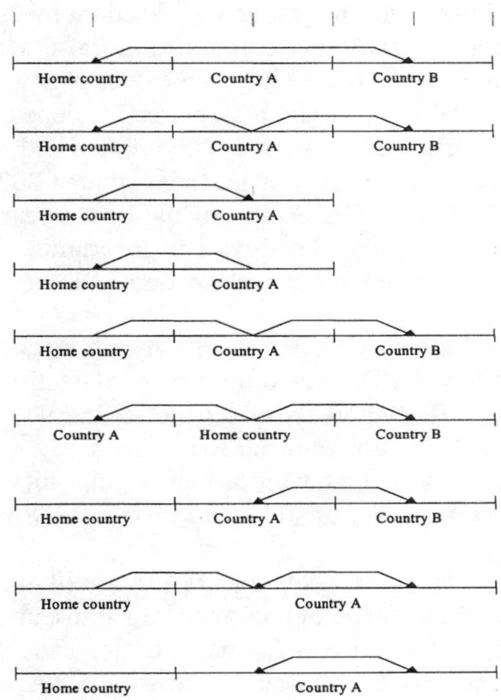

Source: OECD (1999b).

Despite these adverse effects, multilateral efforts to reform the anachronistic system of international air transport regulation, based on the 1944 Chicago Convention, have thus far failed. Air transport was largely excluded from the General Agreement on Trade in Services (GATS) but is likely to be eventually incorporated into the World Trade Organization (WTO) framework. The GATS comprises a chapter on air transport but does not yet liberalize the core of the sector: air traffic rights. Future WTO negotiations on the liberalization of trade in services could become an effective vehicle for multilateral liberalization. In the meantime, bilateral open skies and regional agreements

bilateral open skies agreements without 5th freedom and cabotage rights to create a hub-and-spoke structure, which gives US airlines an advantage over their foreign competitors. A key provision of open skies are free market access for designated carriers (free choice of routes, capacity, and frequency) as well as pricing freedom.

[50] IATA. 1999. *Regulatory Developments in 1999*. and The Economist (10 March 2001).

[51] (1) IATA. 1996. *Regulatory Developments in 1996*. (2) IATA. 1997. *Regulatory Developments in 1997*.

like the EU's Single Market for air transport described above, or the ones between the Mercosur, the Andean Pact, or the Caribbean countries are driving cross-border liberalization.

Given the relatively small size of the domestic aviation markets in most MPs, international liberalization ought to be the main focus of air transport reform. Most southern Mediterranean countries are still concluding traditional pre-determined or Bermuda-type ASAs. They should start to revise their bilateral agreements, either when they come up for re-negotiation or through memoranda of understanding that amend existing ASAs. The priority should be point-to-point liberalization on key routes. Several of the MPs have started to liberalize cross-border traffic. In 1996, Jordan was the first country in the region to enter into open skies with the United States. It also negotiated complementary 5th freedom agreements with Ireland and the Netherlands to allow RJ to pick up passengers on routes to and from New York and Chicago. In October 2000, Morocco concluded negotiations for an open skies agreement with the United States, which foresees a gradual liberalization up to the 7th freedom by 2005. As part of its strategy to turn Casablanca into an international hub, the authorities are also seeking more liberal bilaterals with other countries. Morocco recently reached agreement on a new ASA with Italy and is currently negotiating with Jordan and Egypt. Lebanon's approach to open skies is currently the most liberal in the southern Mediterranean. A trial-period with unrestricted 3rd and 4th freedom rights during the 1998 summer season was deemed successful. In November 2000, the government introduced a general open skies regime, including 5th freedom rights. Half a year later, this had already led to a noticeable increase in traffic.[52] In 2000, the Egyptian government liberalized scheduled flights to key resorts, in an effort to stimulate tourism (see section 2.8).

The liberalization vis-à-vis the EU should be a priority, since this market is the most important one for most of the MPs. About 80 percent of Tunisia's international traffic, for instance, is with the EU countries.[53] Sixty percent of scheduled and 90 percent of non-scheduled international flights from and to Morocco are with the EU.[54] Currently, competition on scheduled flights between Morocco and France as well as Morocco and Spain, for instance, is very limited – due to a combination of restrictive ASAs and an alliance between RAM with Air France and Iberia.

The most comprehensive strategy for cross-border liberalization in the Euro-Mediterranean region would be the creation of a common air transport space through the gradual accession of the MPs to the ECAA. The three MPs that are also candidates for EU enlargement – Cyprus, Turkey, and Malta – are expected to accede to the ECAA in the foreseeable future. According to Morocco's Transport Minister, the reason why his country was the first Arab MP to apply for an open skies agreement with the EU was to "integrate Moroccan airspace in the European space to end the current legal restrictions contained in the bilateral accords."[55] An advantage of using the ECAA as a vehicle for cross-border liberalization in the region is that it would require only twelve agreements instead of a few hundred bilateral ASAs (i.e. between 30 members of the ECAA and the countries of the region. Regional liberalization would also overcome the inherent weakness of the bilateral system in accommodating traffic flows in multilateral route networks.

As an intermediate step, or a less ambitious alternative, for the creation of a Euro-Mediterranean common civil aviation area, the EU and the MPs could agree on a standard set of liberal provisions to be used for bilateral ASAs between them. This could be somewhat similar to the open skies provisions

[52] MEED (18 May 2001).
[53] World Bank. 1997. *Tunisie: Etude sur la stratégie des Transports*.
[54] Loir, Michel and Pierre Guislain. 1997. *Royaume de Maroc: Participation du Secteur Privé dans les Infrastructures*. World Bank.
[55] Reuter (9 October 1997).

used by the United States. An interesting precedent for air transport liberalization between the EU and the MPs are in fact the open skies agreements between the United States and several Latin American countries. These agreements, most of which were concluded in 1997, had important repercussions as seen in table 2.4. Within one year, countries that adopted open skies experienced an average growth of traffic to and from the United States of 20.5 percent. During the same period, countries that maintained restrictive policies, saw virtually no traffic growth at all (1.6 percent on average). Moreover, flag carriers in countries that liberalized air traffic registered higher growth in turnover than those in countries without open skies, even though they were exposed to greater competition.

Box 2.7 Cross-Border Liberalization in the EU

In international air transport, still dominated by the Chicago Convention and the concept of national sovereignty, the EU's Single Market rules for air transport are a radical innovation. All regulatory distinctions between international and domestic services have been abolished. Bilateral air traffic agreements between member countries no longer exist. And with national ownership restrictions practically abolished, airlines no longer have a 'nationality'. Non-EU ownership is still limited to 50 percent but within the EU no cross-border ownership restrictions apply. Moreover, a common regulatory framework (regulation of groundhandling, competition policy etc.) provides a harmonized business environment and a level playing field for competition.

With internal reforms largely completed, the Commission's efforts to liberalize air transport are now transcending the EU's external boundaries. The Single Market framework for air transport has already been extended to several non-EU countries in Western Europe (Norway, Iceland, Switzerland). In late 1996, the Commission received a mandate to negotiate the ECAA with the ten EU accession candidates of Central and Eastern Europe. By mid-2001, multilateral negotiations with these countries (except for Hungary) had been concluded and preparations for the implementation of the agreement were being made.[56] Cyprus will be the first MP to join the ECAA. Turkey and Malta are expected to follow soon. An important side-benefit of multilateral negotiations, cited by Commission officials, has been that sector officials from the CEE countries got to know each other and were able to learn from the reform experience of their peers.

In addition, 11 of the 15 EU member states have signed far-reaching open skies agreements with the United States, whose internal aviation market (the world's largest) was liberalized in the late 1970s.[57] Going one step further, the Commission has asked EU member states for a mandate to negotiate a Trans-Atlantic Common Aviation Area (TCAA) between the EU and the United States. The TCAA would cover two-thirds of global air traffic.[58] At the company level, the international integration of markets is reflected by the business strategies of European airlines. Some of them have invested in foreign carriers and almost all of them have joined global airline alliances.

In addition to the liberalization of cross-border traffic to the EU, the southern Mediterranean countries should consider multilateral liberalization between themselves. Two interesting developments in that context are the Yamoussoukro Agreement and the liberalization efforts of the Arab League. In November 1999, 49 African countries (including Morocco, Algeria, Tunisia, and Egypt) adopted a continent-wide policy framework for gradual liberalization of African air transport markets at a conference in Yamoussoukro. A group of donors, including the World Bank and the European Commission, supports the process through policy advice and technical assistance. The two-phase strategy foresees open skies within the region to be introduced immediately, followed by liberalization of all flights to and from Africa two years later.[59]

[56] Agence Europe (14 July 2001).

[57] Financial Times (4 February 2002).

[58] The Economist (10 March 2001). The Commission does not yet have a general mandate to negotiate ASAs with third countries, but a 2002 court ruling should strengthen its role. (Financial Times, 4 February 2002).

[59] This would mean that all designated African carriers will be free to negotiate bilateral agreements for freight and passenger services on any combination of routes within and between the participating countries. The World Bank and the African Development Bank are expected to finance technical assistance for measures such as training and

The Inter-Arab Freedom of the Air Program is supposed to liberalize intra-Arab air services over a period of five years. It was also approved by the transport ministers of the Arab League countries in 1999.[60] The phased liberalization foresees the removal of restrictions on cargo and non-scheduled flights (starting in 1999); the granting of 3rd and 4th freedoms subject to capacity and frequency restrictions (starting in 2001); the abolition of all remaining 3rd and 4th freedom restrictions (by 2003); and the removal of 5th freedom restrictions (by 2005). These measures are to be implemented through the revision of bilateral ASAs. In 2005, ACAC should also receive a mandate to negotiate traffic rights with third parties on behalf of its member states. This could be particularly useful if the Arab countries and the EU should decide to negotiate a common air transport space. However, many previous efforts of regional cooperation between Arab countries have fizzled out and it is not yet clear to what extent this initiatives will be implemented. With only five MPs members in the Yamoussoukro Agreement and with intra-Arab liberalization proceeding slowly, the MPs should consider additional measures to liberalize and integrate their aviation markets. Moreover, they could eventually create a multilateral negotiating body to act as a counterpart to the Commission. Whatever they decide, however, well-defined implementation mechanisms, a clear timetable, and political commitment will be needed.

Table 2.4 South America: Open Skies and Traffic Growth with the USA (1997/98)

Country	Total Traffic Growth (%)	Growth for National Carrier (%)
Traditional ASAs with US		
Argentina	4.5	0.5
Brazil	-0.2	-14.1
Colombia	3.4	6.3
Total	**1.6**	**-7.1**
1997 Open Skies with US		
Chile	11.8	1
Costa Rica	24.3	5.6
El Salvador	42.8	43.4
Guatemala	17.7	-2.9
Panama	15.5	-3.6
Peru	11.2	-0.6
Total	**20.5**	**8.4**

Source: Avmark Aviation Economist.

Policy reforms can also facilitate cross-border integration at the company level. Airline alliances are becoming increasingly prominent features in international aviation. In 2000, 580 cooperation agreements between airlines existed. Many of these were code-sharing agreements, but more than 50 of them involved equity stakes.[61] In recent years, more limited and largely bilateral forms of cooperation are being eclipsed by a handful of global alliances. In 1999, the four largest of these already accounted for 70 percent of scheduled cross-border traffic (Star Alliance, Oneworld,

regulatory reforms. The World Bank will also incorporate the implications of the accord in terms of national reforms and corresponding TA needs into its respective Country Assistance Strategies (CASs) for the participating countries. In parallel, the Commission plans to provide assistance for public security-related investments. Other donor support includes the Initiative for Safe Skies in Africa by the US government and assistance from the French Cooperation. It should be noted that a number of sub-regional liberalization initiatives already exist in Africa. Most advanced is the Common Market for Eastern and Southern Africa (COMESA).

[60] Fifteen Arab states and the Palestinian Authority are party to the agreement, including Egypt, Jordan, Lebanon, Syria, Morocco, and Tunisia – but not Algeria. These measures were adopted by the Arab Civil Aviation Council (ACAC) in 1998, supported by the Arab Air Carrier Association (AACA), and finally approved by the transport ministers of the Arab League countries in 1999.

[61] Annual survey on airline alliances in: Airline Business (July 2000).

SkyTeam, and Wings).[62] By international standards, most southern Mediterranean airlines are small. If they want to benefit from network externalities and other scale economies (e.g. joint marketing, ticketing, or groundhandling), they need to develop stronger international partnerships.[63] To date, however, none of the MP flag carriers has become a member in one of the large global alliances, even though some cooperate with individual airlines (e.g. MEA and RAM with Air France, or RAM with Iberia).

The longer the region's carriers are excluded from global alliances, the more their competitive advantages will be eroded and the more difficult it will become to catch up. Liberalization would give airlines the commercial incentives and freedom to team up with foreign partners. Privatization would allow them to implement such a strategy by exchanging equity with partner airlines. The privatization strategies for RJ and RAM, for instance, foresee the sale to strategic investors. Despite the advantages of cross-border alliances, governments must ensure that they do not become vehicles for anticompetitive behavior and the creation of cartels. In the EU, the Commission already routinely scrutinizes airline alliances as part of its competition policy for the sector. The risk of collusion is particularly high, where the networks of partner airlines overlap and/or on routes where their combined market share is high.[64] On the routes between Morocco and France, for instance, RAM and Air France dominate the market. At about 10 cents/km, ticket prices were about 25 percent more expensive than those on similar routes between France and Greece.

A final benefit of cross-border liberalization is the development of hubs. As discussed in section 1.4, hubs increase customer choice, competition, and capacity utilization. Countries can attract international hub functions through the liberalization of traffic rights, state-of-the-art infrastructure services, and competitive groundhandling. In most MPs, the percentage of transit passengers (a key hub indicator) is less than 5 percent (see table 2.2). To a large extent, this is the result of regulatory rigidities. Given its high turnover and central geographic position, Cairo for example, would be well placed to become a transit airport and is already a relatively important node in the route network of some airlines. The lack of 5th freedom rights, however, is an obstacle for the development of true hub-structures, as planes that stop over are forced to continue half-empty. Morocco, Jordan, Lebanon, and Dubai are all countries that are trying to use the liberalization of international traffic rights to turn their main airports into regional hubs. Dubai is already an important regional hub, with around one million transit passengers (see box 2.9). The largest international freight carrier Lufthansa Cargo, relocated its regional hub to Sharja in the Emirates to benefit from a low cost and light regulatory environment. With 300 weekly flights, the airport is now the carrier's second biggest hub after Frankfurt.[65] Casablanca could also become an important transit point for US-Africa traffic once the open skies agreement between the two countries is fully implemented.[66] Similarly, Lebanon's general open skies regime might help Beirut regain some of the hub functions it lost during the civil war.

---

[62] Financial Times (24 November 2000).

[63] The 18 members of the Arab Air Carriers Organization agreed on joint aircraft handling at London airports (MEED, 5 June 1998).

[64] A comprehensive analysis of the competition policy issues raised by airline alliances can be found in: OECD. 1999. *The Nature of Competition in the Airline Industry and Airline Alliances and Mergers*.

[65] MEED (5 February 1999).

[66] The government would like to develop Casablanca into a hub for US traffic with Africa and the Middle East (40 percent of RAM's traffic from the US is already in transit to other African destinations) and for EU traffic with Africa. Recently agreed liberal ASAs should bring the network links and traffic volume needed for a successful hub. Small European hubs like Lisbon have eight million passengers/year, while Casablanca has three million.

Box 2.8 ICAO, IATA, and ACI

ICAO (International Civil Aviation Organization) – Headquartered in Montreal, ICAO is a special agency of the United Nations. It was created at the Chicago Convention of 1944 with a mandate to establish international standards for air transport, as well as to recommend practices and procedures on technical, economic, and legal matters of international civil aviation. In recent years, ICAO has become increasingly involved in a wider range of issues, including regulatory, economic, legal and security policies. ICAO has 185 member states, including all Maghreb and Mashrek countries. The regional office for Africa and the Middle East is based in Cairo (*www.icao.org*).

IATA (International Air Transport Association) – The umbrella organization of international airlines, IATA was established as a counterpart to ICAO. A non-governmental organization founded in 1945 and based in Montreal, IATA has more than 230 member airlines. They account for a total of 95 percent of international air traffic. IATA is the prime vehicle for inter-airline cooperation. Its principal aims are to promote safe and efficient air transport and to facilitate cooperation among the companies operating in the sector. Originally a cartel to organize interlining and control international prices, IATA also provides services such as an interline ticket clearing house, data collection, forecasting, and scheduling conferences for airport slots. IATA has a Middle East office in Amman and an office for Africa (including the Maghreb) in Nairobi (*www.iata.org*).

ACI (Airport Council International) – Created in 1991 and headquartered in Geneva, ACI is the international association of airports. It is a non-profit organization with the objective of fostering cooperation among member airports and other partners, including governmental, airline, and aircraft manufacturers. In April 1999, ACI had 531 member airports and airport authorities (9 from North Africa and Middle East), operating a total of 1,400 airports in 165 countries and territories. The regional office for Africa is located in Cairo and the office for Asia (including the Middle East) is in New Delhi (*www.airports.org*).

Source: ICAO, IATA, ACI, World Bank.

2.7 Policy Issues for Air Cargo

Cargo is one of the fastest growing segments of the air transport market. Forty percent of global manufactured exports (by value) are carried by air.[67] The members of IATA, which handle 95 percent of all international freight tons, registered an average growth rate of about 10 percent annually in the five-year period to 1997. Boeing expects an average growth rate of 6.4 percent over the next two decades.[68] World-wide, about 75 percent of cargo is carried by combined passenger/cargo planes, although the share of all-cargo traffic is growing.[69] As can be seen from diagram 2.2 at the beginning of this chapter, growth rates within the southern Mediterranean have been below the global average. Another common structural feature of freight traffic in the MPs is the pronounced imbalances between out-bound and in-coming volumes. In 1997, for instance, Jordan imported 25,600 tons by air while exports were a mere 16,600 tons. Between 1993 and 1996, 28,400 tons were unloaded at Beirut airport, but only 18,100 were loaded. Even in Morocco, where the traffic was less lop-sided, the gap is around 10 percent.[70] This pattern also reflects trade imbalances and the difficulties of MPs to diversify their export base into higher value-added products.

In particular, goods with a high value/weight ratio, as well as products that are perishable or fragile, are transported by air. As discussed in section 1.3, dramatic changes in business practices (e.g. global sourcing, supply-chain management, just-in-time production) are making cheap, fast, and reliable air transport services for goods increasingly important. "About two-thirds of production and sales in OECD countries are processed directly to order, with 'just-in-time' delivery of

[67] The Economist (10 March 2001).
[68] MEED (4 June 1999).
[69] OECD. 1999. *Regulatory Reform in International Air Cargo Transportation.* Besides the global all-cargo carriers that also serve the region, there are a few cargo-only airlines in the southern Mediterranean. In 1998, Tunisia licensed the partly state-owned Mediterranean Air Service (MAS), which provides cargo services between Tunisia and France. Lebanon's Trans Mediterranean Airways (TMA), the oldest private freight carrier in the region, is trying to regain its former importance, which it lost together with Beirut's hub function during the civil war. In mid-1999, Ogden Aviation of the United States took a stake in TMA to gain a foothold in the region. (MEED, 4 June 1999).
[70] Eurostat. 1999. *Transport Trends in the Mediterranean Countries.*

products becoming the norm in many sectors. Significantly, 60 percent of all exports from developing countries go to OECD markets [mainly the EU in the case of the MPs] and must meet OECD standards. As service, delivery, and quality become increasingly critical factors, transportation will replace labor costs in establishing an international competitive cost advantage."[71]

Air cargo should be an integral part of the multimodal logistics chain, but regulatory barriers continue to obstruct seamless integration. In many of the MPs, restrictive ASAs prevent free route development and network optimization. Rigid licensing regimes make a diversification into ground transportation services, as well as self-handling at airports, difficult. Additional frictions are being caused by customs delays; constraints to wet leasing (aircraft leased with staff); or the prohibition to carry freight in the belly-holds of tourist charters (e.g. the case in Tunisia).[72] Arbitrary regulatory distinctions between providers segment the market (e.g. different licenses for all cargo carriers, combined carriers, or express carriers). Morocco provides two recent examples of the impact of regulation on the efficiency of air transport. The express carrier DHL had won a contract to deliver modern telephone equipment for the construction of the country's second mobile phone network. However, DHL was unable to obtain permission to use a larger aircraft (a 26-ton Boeing 727 instead of the 5-ton Convair 580) and thus lost this important contract. In a positive development, the open skies agreement between the United States and Morocco will help to extend the existing RAM/Delta Airlines code-sharing agreement to Delta's European partners, Lufthansa and Alitalia. This is expected to facilitate the export of perishable merchandise such as cut-flowers and fruit.

In both the United States and the EU, the liberalization of the air cargo preceded full liberalization of air transport. In the United States, the Air Cargo Deregulation Act of 1977 became effective before the Airline Deregulation Act of 1978. It liberalized licensing, permitted licensed carriers to operate on all routes, and fully de-regulated domestic rates. By 1984, the number of cargo carriers had almost tripled from 36 to 124, a large number of new routes had been opened, and the new breed of express carriers emerged from this liberalized environment (see also section 1.6). In the EU, liberalization in the freight segment also preceded reform of the overall air transport market. A 1991 directive for cargo deregulation removed national ownership and control rules; granted 3rd, 4th, and 5th freedom rights on all routes without restrictions to all Community carriers (other freedoms followed later); removed regulation on frequency, capacity, and types of aircraft; liberalized tariffs; introduced equal treatment of scheduled and non-scheduled services; and applied EU competition rules to cargo services. [73] In both the United States and the EU, however, the air cargo liberalization was promptly followed by the liberalization of the entire sector.

A number of measures could be considered to liberalize air cargo markets in the Euro-Mediterranean region. ASAs can have different provisions for cargo and passenger services. Australia, for instance, has an open skies policy for cargo, while Mexico and India treat freight services much more liberally than passenger transport. The OECD launched an initiative for the international liberalization of air cargo in 1999 and drafted a protocol that can be used to amend existing service agreements (including reforms to groundhandling and customs).[74] Compliance with

[71] World Bank. 1995. *Airport Infrastructure*.

[72] Customs delays are particularly problematic for air transport, since the time ratio between customs clearance and transportation can be far greater than for other modes.

[73] The effects of EU liberalization on prices were more limited than in the US. A much smaller percentage of EU transport is airborne and well-developed overnight rail and road services had already fostered intermodal competition prior to liberalization of air transport.

[74] Financial Times (29 September 2000). A complementary effort at the company level was made by the European Shippers' Council (ESC), which developed a best practice code for airfreight and a registry of companies adhering to its guidelines. More details can be found on the ESC web-site (*www.europeanshippers.com*).

the World Customs Organization Immediate Release Guidelines, "devised to meet express delivery needs for rapid customs treatment," could be another item on the reform agenda.[75] The MPs should also consider ratifying ICAO's International Convention for the Unification of Certain Rules for International Carriage by Air. This convention, which entered into force in 1999, reforms the 70-year old Warsaw Convention governing air cargo documentation and should considerably streamline procedures. It authorizes "the replacement of the paper air waybill by an electronic information record; simplify the air waybill contents; and introduce more contractual freedom between shippers and carriers."[76] In 2000, it had been ratified by all EU countries and by most EU accession candidates (including Turkey and Malta), but by none of the Arab MPs. Other specific policy reforms to liberalize air cargo include the abolition of restrictions to carry freight in the belly-holds of charter planes; open competition in cargo-related groundhandling services; the removal of regulatory barriers between different categories of cargo service providers; and the development of underutilized secondary airports into cargo hubs.[77] Especially express carriers "need to develop their own airport infrastructures, to guarantee access at will, swiftness, reliability, and cost efficiency."[78] As much as policy initiatives geared at liberalizing air cargo are needed, the majority of airfreight is carried by combination aircraft. This means MPs must eventually liberalize the entire aviation sector, if they want full competition in airfreight.

Box 2.9 The Emergence of Dubai as an Air Cargo Hub

Open skies policies and the highly competitive national carrier Emirates (see box 2.4) have helped Dubai establish itself as an air transport hub for cargo and passengers. It serves transit traffic both within the region and between Europe and Asia. After a capacity expansion in the 1990s, the Dubai Cargo Village (DCV) was approaching its maximum throughput of 675,000 tons/year in 2001. To accommodate future growth, an increase in capacity to one million t/y by 2005 and a further expansion to three million t/y by 2018 are planned. The total cost of these expansions is estimated at $ 500 million. For passengers, a third terminal for about $ 400 million is to be constructed by 2006. Passenger traffic is expected to increase from 12 million in 2000 to 30 million in 2010. Besides double-digit annual growth rates, at least two other aspects of the Dubai example are noteworthy. Thanks to complementary policies and hub structures in maritime transport, the air/sea segment accounted for about 20 percent of total air cargo in 1998 and grew more than twice as fast as the overall market (by 10 percent compared to 4 percent for all air cargo). Besides these intermodal synergies, the developments in Dubai also highlight the importance of modern IT for logistics services. Emirates SkyCargo, which is DCV's largest tenant, launched Emirates SkyChain, an automated system for the management of cargo logistics. Integrated over its entire network, the system allows customers to track shipments, check availability, and make online bookings. SkyChain is seen as an invaluable addition in the airline's efforts to expand its cargo business. A senior manager of Emirates SkyCargo contends "that future growth in air freight will be increasingly tied to IT." Encouraged by the example of Dubai, Yemen announced plans to develop the Cargo Village Aden by 2004. Created as a joint venture between Yemen Airlines, the Port of Aden, and the Yemen Free Zone Public Authority, it is supposed to capitalize on the hub function of the port to offer sea-air transshipment.

Source: MEED (8 June and 16 November 2001).

[75] Raven, John. 2001. *Trade and Transport Facilitation – A Toolkit for Audit, Analysis, and Remedial Action.* World Bank Discussion Paper Series 427. One of the most important facilitation mechanism targeted by these guidelines is the provision of selected declaration data prior to the arrival of the cargo.

[76] OECD. 1999. *Regulatory Reform in International Air Cargo Transportation.*

[77] This is a common trend also in the EU. In 1998, for instance, logistics company TNT moved its European hub from the crowded airport of Cologne/Germany to Liège/Belgium. During the 1990s, the former military air base Hahn, close to Frankfurt, grew into the fourth largest cargo airport in Germany.

[78] OECD. 1999. *Regulatory Reform in International Air Cargo Transportation.*

2.8 Policy Issues for Charter Flights

Non-scheduled (i.e. charter) flights are generally less regulated than scheduled flights. They are not covered by bilateral ASAs, but subject only to unilateral policy decisions. In fact, charter flights are the most competitive segment of the aviation market in most southern Mediterranean countries and can be regarded as a successful pilot case for liberalization. International competition has induced countries with large tourism industries, such as Tunisia, Morocco, and Egypt, to adopt liberal policies in this sub-sector. In Tunisia, for instance, 64 percent of international passengers were non-scheduled in 2000 (5.6 million out of 8.9 million). In Egypt, charter passengers accounted for 45 percent of the total (8.8 million out of 19.5 million).[79] About 20 companies offer scheduled flights to Morocco, compared to 50 charter airlines.[80] In Syria, where the tourism industry plays a lesser role, the market share of charter in passenger transport is below 10 percent. Some MP airports close to important tourist destinations are handling mainly charter traffic, such as Monastir and Djerba in Tunisia or Hurghada and Sharm El Sheik in Egypt. Because charter planes can be easily deployed to service demand peaks, it permits the industry to accommodate the high seasonal fluctuation of tourism traffic.

To prevent the competition from the charter segment of the market from 'spilling over' to protected scheduled services, many MPs maintain regulatory barriers between the two. It is common practice to outlaw split-charters (where capacity is re-sold), the carriage of cargo in the belly holds of charter flights, as well as quasi-scheduled (which fly at regular times) charter flights. It is not clear, however, why only package tourists should benefit from competition while other passengers and cargo customers have to put up with high prices and restricted choice. It is time for southern Mediterranean countries to overcome their asymmetric approach to sector policy by liberalizing scheduled traffic. Cheaper and more frequent scheduled flights would also allow the MPs to more effectively tap the high-end tourist market (where package deals with charter flights are less common) as well as the fast growing market for short holidays. Northern Europeans in particular are showing a strong tendency to go on shorter but more frequent vacations.

An example of the blurring lines between scheduled and non-scheduled traffic is Egypt. In 2000, the Egyptian government decided to liberalize scheduled flights to key resorts in response to strong pressure from the tourism industry and private operators of the new BOT airports (see section 2.12). Previously, foreign tourists going to Hurghada, Sharm el-Shaik, or Luxor only had the choice between direct charter flight or the inconvenience of scheduled flights to Cairo, with connecting domestic flights by EgyptAir on the following morning. This was "a source of great frustration for tourist executives. 'We have two monopolies, one for EgyptAir, which can't do the job properly and the other for the charter companies which are catering to the cheap end of the market' [...] With the proliferation of hotels opening in the Sinai and Red Sea resorts in particular, it is vital that international airlines should be free to operate scheduled flights to resorts to bring in the higher-paying customers."[81] Another reason why the liberalization of scheduled flights to key resorts encourages high-end tourism is airline loyalty schemes. Frequent flier miles cannot be used on charter flights and according to an Egyptian tourist operator, "you have business travelers around the world with 40 million air miles which they could redeem at hotels in Sinai or on the Red Sea, but they can't get on the flights."[82]

---

[79] Eurostat (MED-Trans database).

[80] Loir, Michel and Pierre Guislain. 1997. *Royaume de Maroc: Participation du Secteur Privé dans les Infrastructures*. World Bank.

[81] MEED (2 June 2000).

[82] MEED (4 February 2000).

Bringing charter capacity back into the sector mainstream would allow carriers in the region to reap economies of scale through extended networks, higher flight frequencies and shared overheads. This will require the removal of regulatory barriers between non-scheduled and scheduled services and a liberalization of scheduled traffic. The artificial barriers that persist are fragmenting the market. By thinning out traffic and reducing the frequency on many scheduled routes, they reduce the efficiency of the sector. In this respect, the MPs should learn from the experience of their neighbors on the northern shore of the Mediterranean. According to the OECD, "the European Union has been a precursor in banning all scheduled vs. non-scheduled differentiation [...] In a truly open market, there is no longer any need to make the distinction. The market determines the type of operations."[83]

Box 2.10 Tourists and Migrants

Two groups play an important role for the process of regional integration as well as for cross-border passenger flows in the Euro-Mediterranean area: migrants and tourists. The southern Mediterranean countries are an important tourist destination, especially for Europeans. According to Eurostat, international arrivals to the twelve MPs "are estimated to total 28.9 million in 1998 [...] On average about 50 percent of international tourists to the Mediterranean countries come from the EU. For some countries this figure is much higher (e.g. 85 percent for Malta, 72 percent for Cyprus)."[84] According to the World Tourism Organization, total tourist receipts in the twelve MPs are around € 20 billion per year (see table 2.2). The industry is also an important source of jobs. In Morocco, for instance, 600,000 people are directly or indirectly employed in the sector.[85] In Tunisia, tourism accounts for 7 percent of gross domestic product. It is "the principal source of foreign currency and the second largest employer, providing 80,000 jobs directly and 300,000 indirectly."[86]

At the same time, up to ten million migrants from the MPs live in the EU. France alone has three million inhabitants of southern Mediterranean descent – including 1.5 million from Algeria; 1 million from Morocco; 350,000 from Tunisia; 315,000 from Turkey; and 100,000 from Lebanon.[87] Germany has two million immigrants from Turkey and several other EU member states also have sizable expatriate communities from the southern Mediterranean.[88] While the economic importance of the migrant community goes far beyond the transport sector (remittances of nationals working abroad amounts to about $ 1 billion per year in Algeria, Egypt, Jordan, and Morocco), these migration patterns are reflected in traffic flows.[89] In Algeria, 85 percent of the 680,000 annual visitors from abroad are Algerian nationals. The percentage figures for Morocco (38 percent) and Tunisia (10 percent) are lower, but in absolute terms about half a million nationals residing abroad arrive to Tunisia each year and more than one million to Morocco.[90] Other than in the Maghreb countries, the emigrants from Egypt and Jordan are less concentrated in the EU than in the Gulf states. The Lebanese that left their country are widely dispersed and supposedly more Lebanese now live abroad than in Lebanon proper. While most expatriates visit their country of origin by air, hundreds of thousands arrive by car via RoRo ferries each year, especially in the Maghreb countries.

[83] OECD. 1999. *Regulatory Reform in International Air Cargo Transportation.*
[84] Eurostat. 1999. *Tourism in the Mediterranean Partner Countries 4/1999.*
[85] Eurostat. 2001. *Tourism in the Mediterranean Countries.*
[86] MEED (28 December 2001).
[87] The Economist (28 July 2001).
[88] Website of the German statistics authority, Statistisches Bundesamt (*www.destatis.de*).
[89] World Bank. 1999. *World Bank Debt Tables 1999.*
[90] Eurostat. 2001. *Tourism in the Mediterranean Countries.*

Airports and Air Traffic Control

Transport services are the ultimate output of the aviation industry, but airport infrastructure and services are essential intermediate inputs. Airports have an important impact both on the cost structure of airlines and on the competition between them. In Europe, costs in and around airports account for 24 percent of total airline costs. Roughly half of these are airport charges and the other half groundhandling charges.[91] At the same time, the availability and allocation of airport slots can have important implications for market access and the degree of competition between airlines. For these reasons, the way in which airport services are managed and regulated has significant implications for the entire industry. Airports generally constitute local natural monopolies, except for hub functions or in cases where airports have overlapping hinterlands. Moreover, airports provide an interrelated cluster of services that involve different sets of policy issues, including the regulation of groundhandling, airport charges, and slot allocation.

2.9 Regulating Groundhandling Services

Groundhandling services (or land-side services) include baggage and ramp-handling, surface transportation, storage for cargo, as well as fuel and repair services. They do not constitute natural monopolies, but can efficiently be provided by two or more companies. Exceptions are small airports with low traffic volumes or space limitations. Despite the potential for competition in groundhandling, airport operators often extend their infrastructure monopoly to these services by prohibiting self-handling by airlines or the use of facilities by third-party service providers. Equally problematic and common in the southern Mediterranean are groundhandling monopolies controlled by the flag carrier. In such cases of vertical integration, incumbents has an incentive to abuse this monopoly not only to extract excessive fees, but also to discriminate against competing airlines by providing them with lower quality services.

Diagram 2.5 The Impact of Competition on Ground-Handling Charges

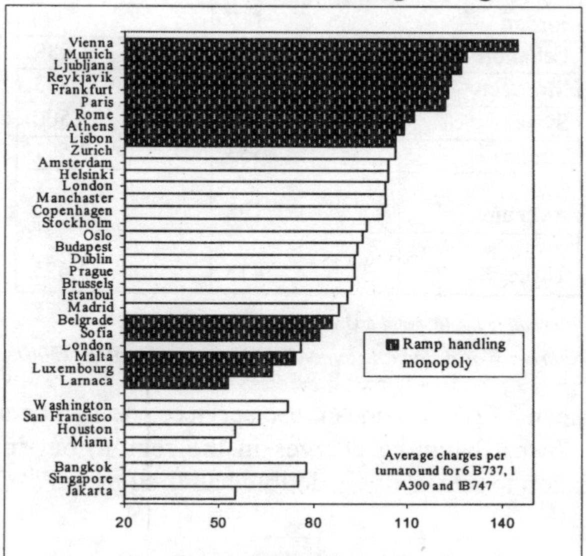

Source: Association of European Airlines (1998).

The results of groundhandling monopolies are higher costs and reduced choice for airlines. A 1998 study of European airports by Cranfield University found that "monopolistic tariffs are 40 to 75 percent above competitive rates," depending on the type of aircraft serviced.[92] The findings are

[91] Figure for members of Association of European Airlines from the *AEA Yearbook 1998*. The IATA Annual Report 1999 notes that "In 1998, IATA Member airlines paid $ 7.4 billion in airport landing and related charges [including air navigation charges] for their scheduled international operations. Together, they represented 10 percent of the airlines' international operating costs."

[92] OECD. 1999. *Regulatory Reform in International Air Cargo Transportation*. Cranfield University carried out this study on behalf of the Association of European Airlines.

illustrated by diagram 2.5, which ranks airports according to cost, with the most expensive at the top of the diagram. All high ramphandling charges are levied by airports with ramphandling monopolies (dark bars), while those with service competition (light bars) have notably lower prices. To achieve competition in groundhandling, regulation needs to unbundle groundhandling both from airport and airline operations. Third-party handlers and self-handling operators need to be able to obtain licenses and to physically access facilities. In return, they ought to pay adequate fees for their use of airport infrastructure. The EC directive on groundhandling (see box 2.11) codifies these and other principles for the regulation of such activities. MP governments should consider applying these principles, but with lower traffic thresholds.[93] In particular, restrictions to self-handling by airlines should be removed, and in cases where monopolies are maintained, they should be awarded by competitive tender.

European carriers frequently identify groundhandling as a key problem in the region. Especially restrictions to third-party handling are wide-spread. Some countries apply the principle of reciprocity (or barter) to groundhandling charges by requiring a foreign carrier to pay the same price that the domestic airline pays for groundhandling at the foreign carrier's home airport. Given the large difference in costs between a Moroccan and a Dutch airport, for instance, this results in excessive profit margins. It also runs counter to ICAO guidelines, which stipulate that handling charges should be cost-related. In Morocco, Tunisia, and Jordan, where the national carriers operate groundhandling monopolies, charges tend to be high and service quality low. One MP where some degree of competition in groundhandling exists is Lebanon (Beirut). The Jordanian CAA has prepared regulations for cargo handling by private operators after the abolition of RJ's monopoly. In Cairo, the semi-private company EAS provides these services. As can be seen from table 2.5, Egypt has long had some of the lowest handling charges in the region, but in mid-2000 EAS made the highly controversial decision to retroactively double handling prices at Cairo airport.[94]

Table 2.5 Handling Charges by Country

Country	MD-80 ($)	B 747 ($)
Algeria	118	1,317
Egypt	87	822
Jordan	117	900
Lebanon	167	1,039
Morocco*	358	2,953
Syria	206	1,500
Tunisia	333	3,581
Average	**198**	**1,730**
Turkey*	473	2,625

** Including landing and approach fees.*

Source: World Bank. Lebanon Civil Aviation Strategy (2001).

[93] The *size thresholds of the EC directive* are 1 million passengers or 25,000 tons of freight per year for the introduction of competition in self-handling and 3 million passengers or 75,000 tons in the case of third-party handling. In January 2001, the latter was lowered to 2 million passengers or 50,000 tons. With these minima, only Algiers, Cairo, Casablanca, Monastir, and Tunis-Catharge would have to introduce third-party handling. The number of airports above the self-handling threshold would be larger, comprising at least one airport from each of the MPs. Traffic growth, however, would soon take other airports above the thresholds. Given the lower price of labor and less wide-spread use of modern equipment in the region, the minimum efficient scale for most groundhandling services should be lower in the MPs than in Europe. This justifies the application of lower thresholds.

[94] Egyptian Aviation Services (EAS) was created in 1989 as a joint venture by six foreign airlines, Egypt Air, the CAA, and two local banks. The advantage of this unusual structure is that it involves key stakeholders. The drawback is that it effectively precludes competition in Egypt's main airport. The shareholders are contractually obliged to use EAS, while the company is expected to maintain competitive charges that guarantee it a 20 percent annual return on paid-up capital. Even before the doubling of charges, however, the return was in fact 200 percent. According to the Financial Times, the "threat by the powerful former air force generals who control Egypt's civil aviation services [the chairmen of EgyptAir and EAS, as well as the head of the CAA are all former generals] to

Box 2.11 The EC Directive on Groundhandling

EU directive 96/67/EC, which became effective at the beginning of 1998, defines general principles for the regulation of groundhandling services.[95] It is part of the package of legislation that all ECAA members have to adopt. The directive covers groundhandling services such as ground administration and the supervision of airlines; passenger and baggage handling; ramphandling (e.g. maneuvering and loading of planes); aircraft maintenance; catering; and crew administration. All ECAA countries are obliged to ensure legal and physical market access for both self-handling and third-party handling in the airports of their jurisdiction. For most categories of services, at least two competing providers have to be licensed per airport. At least one of the third-party handlers should be fully independent from the body in charge of airport administration as well as the dominant airline (i.e. unbundling of groundhandling from airports and airlines). In those cases where these incumbents continue to provide groundhandling services, they have to fully separate their accounts. EU member states have to enforce this separation. Restrictions to competition are only permitted "on the basis of relevant, objective, transparent and non-discriminatory criteria" (e.g. space constraints). They ought to be temporary and they should "not extend further than necessary" (the principle of proportionality). Governments have to submit a request to the Commission for any exemptions they grant. This request has to include a detailed explanation and a clear strategy to remove the constraints justifying the exemption. For the sake of transparency, the Commission is to publish its decisions on these requests. In each airport, an Airport Users' Committee, open to all users, has to be created. Even though this directive has been an important step towards competition in groundhandling, airlines have voiced concerns that many airports have failed to go beyond the minimum requirements of the directive.[96]

2.10 Regulating Airport Charges

Groundhandling services can be made competitive by unbundling them from the airport infrastructure. The core services provided by airports, however, constitute a natural monopoly. These are the aeronautical or airside services such as the use of runways, aprons, or terminals. To prevent an abuse of monopoly power, airport charges need to be regulated. A Commission draft directive on airport charges, modeled on ICAO principles, provides some useful guidelines whose adoption the southern Mediterranean countries should consider.[97] First, charges are supposed to be cost-related to permit the airport to recover costs and earn a fair return, while preventing it from extracting monopoly rents from its clients. One of the few exceptions should be scarcity pricing in the case of capacity constraints as a means to allocate capacity efficiently and fairly. Second, airport charges should be non-discriminatory to prevent the distortion of competition between airlines. Third, charges ought to be transparent to reduce the scope for monopolistic pricing and price discrimination (e.g. a detailed breakdown of bills, specification of charging principles, institutionalization of user consultations through user councils). Following airport lobbying and political resistance by some member states, the adoption of this EC directive has been blocked for years. In the meantime, however, the Commission as the EU's competition authority, has applied EU competition rules to some precedent cases in order to roll back the practice of discriminatory charges. It has thus indirectly enforced the main principles with regard to airport charges as laid out

---

withdraw groundhandling services erupted as foreign investors are becoming concerned that a decade of economic reforms has not improved transparency and accountability in Egypt." (Financial Times, 3 and 13 July 2000).

[95] European Commission. 1996. *Council Directive 96/67/EC on Access to the Groundhandling Market at Community Airports*.

[96] European Voice (23 November 2000).

[97] ICAO endorsed these principles in Article 15 of the 1944 Chicago Convention on International Civil Aviation, in the Statement by the Council on Charges for Airports and Air Navigation Services (ICAO Doc. 9082), and elaborated on these principles in the Airport Economics Manual (ICAO Doc. 9562). (See also: *www.icao.org*) The EC directive explicitly refers to these documents.

in the draft directive.[98] In fact, this is an illustrative example of the complementarity and substitutability between sector-specific regulation and cross-sectoral competition policy (see section 4.6).

Another regulatory approach to the natural monopoly problem is price regulation for airport charges, such as the price-cap regulation used in the United Kingdom.[99] At London Heathrow, annual increases in charges are limited to less than inflation and as a consequence real costs for the operation of a B747-400, for instance, fell by three-quarters between 1979 and 1989.[100] There has been a surprising but powerful side effect of this regulatory squeeze on charges. It has not only induced the operator BAA (formerly: British Airport Authority) to continuously reduce costs, but also to aggressively develop airport retailing, as money earned from this commercial activity is not subject to regulation. The company had neglected that part of its business when it was an unregulated public monopoly, but it is now widely credited with having revolutionized airport retailing and "taught the world that airports could be turned into shopping malls."[101]

Competition between airports can also create incentives for better management and lower charges. An interesting example, where such competition would be feasible, if political obstacles could be removed, is between Damascus, Beirut, Tel Aviv, and Amman. Geographically, these four cities constitute the corners of a rectangle. Each of them is in a 200-kilometer radius from two of the others, and in a 100 km radius of at least one of them.[102] Damascus-Beirut or Amman-Tel Aviv could in theory compete for overlapping hinterlands. In practice, however, political conflicts, inadequate land transport, and delays at borders prevent such competition.

2.11 Allocating Airport Slots

The regulation of groundhandling and airport charges creates the necessary incentives for airports to increase efficiency and lower prices. The allocation of take-off and landing slots has to be regulated in order to create a level playing field between competing airlines. Airport slots are a critical determinant of market access and thus competition between carriers. The liberalization of international traffic rights is of little use to airlines if their access to airport infrastructure is

[98] Until a few years ago, the structure of airport charges in most EU countries discriminated between domestic and foreign carriers, to the disadvantage of the latter. For example, charges for a plane landing in Strasbourg/France were much higher if it came from Frankfurt/Germany than if it came from Bordeaux/France, even though the domestic flight had to cover a greater distance and the costs for the airport in both cases were the same.

[99] Under a *price-cap* regime, airport charges are fixed by the regulator and periodically adjusted either according to a general formula (e.g. annual reduction by a fixed percentage) and/or more comprehensively revised at the end of a multi-year period. The objective is to adjust profit margins to normal levels. In contrast to *profit or rate-of-return regulation*, regulated companies have an incentive to cut costs (the higher the gap between costs and fixed prices, the higher the profit) and thus reveal their true cost structure (asymmetric information about costs is one of the biggest problems in the regulation of natural monopolies). The regulator can then use this information for the next periodic review of the price cap.

[100] The Avmark Aviation Economist (May 1998). Charges were reduced from £ 40 to £ 10 in 1998 real terms.

[101] Financial Times (1 May 1998). In fact, airport charges in many developed countries have been falling in recent years as concessions for landside services contribute increasingly to airport revenues. At Heathrow, regulation actually obliges the airport to reduce landing charges as retail profits rise. (The Economist, 6 December 2000).

[102] *Competition between airports* is more difficult to achieve than that between ports (discussed in section 3.6). The main traffic categories in airports, passengers and high-value cargo, are sensitive to time-consuming modal transfers and long land-legs. In contrast, the key business of ports is cargo, where indirect routing, modal transfers, and longer land-legs are less of a problem. In some cases, however, airports can compete effectively in the freight segment of the market, as well as for hub functions. Another important segment where competition between airports is possible is tourism. Tourists tend to be relatively flexible with regard to their choice of holiday destination, and the price and service quality of air transport is an important criterion for their decision.

constrained. The issue of slot allocation is particularly important if they are scarce, as at congested airports and during peak times. Carriers that hold a disproportionate share of slots at a specific airport can use this dominance to extract monopoly rents. British Airways, for instance, holds about 40 percent of all slots at Heathrow airport, Europe's largest airport and main trans-Atlantic hub. Competitors accuse the company of abusing its entrenched position. According to British Midland, a business class ticket from London to New York costs $ 3,033 more than an equivalent one from Frankfurt to New York.[103] American Express has calculated that business class travelers pay € 1.43 per mile between Britain and the United States, compared to € 1.01 per mile between other European airports and the United States.[104]

Box 2.12 Slot Allocation Rules in the EU

In the EU, both sector-specific regulation and general competition rules are being used to address the issue of slot allocation. Competition policy is a useful tool to deal with abuses on a case-by-case basis (see section 4.6). A 1993 regulation defines general principles for slot allocation across the ECAA:[105]

- All member states have to designate congested airports to which the regulation applies. Twice a year, a capacity analysis at each of these airports has to be carried out.
- A designated coordinator monitors the use of slots and allocates them in accordance with the regulation. A coordinating committee, consisting of airlines and other concerned parties, considers complaints and proposes improvements. The coordinator should be sufficiently independent. Its accountability should be ensured by transparent decision making and effective complaints procedures.
- Grandfather rights (i.e. airlines can keep slots once they have them) are complemented by a use-it-or-lose-it rule, whereby they have to return those slots that they did not use sufficiently in the previous season (i.e. 70-80 percent of the time).
- New and returned slots go into a slot pool. To stimulate competition, 50 percent of these slots are given to new entrants.

Current rules have two main drawbacks. First, the independence of the coordinator is not always ensured. While the UK coordinator is an independent company owned by 13 airlines and the coordinator in Spain is the airport authority, the flag carriers fulfill this function in France and Germany.[106] Second, grandfather rights have largely secured the dominance of national carriers in many European hubs and flag carriers have repeatedly lobbied EU governments to prevent reforms.[107] The Commission has reviewed these rules and a number of options for amendments have been discussed. One proposal is to limit the periods for which slots are allocated to ten years, with airlines returning 5 to 10 percent of their slots to the pool each year. Moreover, a secondary market for the trading of slots between airlines could be introduced and the decisions of coordinators and coordinating committees could become subject to judicial review.

To ensure both economic efficiency and equity, slots need to be allocated on a fair and competitive basis. The same holds for corresponding facilities such as aprons and parking space. In many cases, the key question is not only whether an airline is able to obtain a slot at all but also at what time. Business travelers in particular, by far the most profitable category of passengers, are very sensitive with regard to timing. The ability to obtain certain slots is also a prerequisite for the development of an efficient route network. The allocation procedure should be designed carefully and the entity in charge of slot distribution ought to be independent and impartial. In many countries, however, the allocation process is ill-defined, non-transparent, or biased towards incumbents. Often, national airlines or state-owned airports allocate slots, giving rise to conflicts of interest or discriminatory

103 Financial Times (15 February 2000).

104 Financial Times Deutschland (1 February 2002).

105 European Commission. 1993. *Council Regulation (EEC) 95/93 on Common Rules for the Allocation of Slots at Community Airports*.

106 Aviation Economics. 2001. *Slot Allocation – A Review of the European Situation.* (not published).

107 European Voice (20 December 2001).

treatment of foreign carriers and new competitors. Airport congestion, and thus slot scarcity, might be less of a problem in the southern Mediterranean than in the EU. However, it seems to be relevant to some of the main airports, especially during high season and at peak times.

2.12 Introducing Private Participation in Airports

The function of airports is to provide sufficient infrastructure capacity and to supply airlines with high-quality services at minimum cost. Commercialization, corporatization, and private participation help to increase the efficiency with which these functions are fulfilled. In terms of operations, commercial management helps to reduce costs, exploit new business opportunities, and use existing infrastructure more effectively. In terms of physical infrastructure, private capital can mobilize funding for the maintenance and construction of facilities. The profit motive induces private investors to strive for investment efficiency, that is to choose technical parameters and investment instruments which minimize costs and risks while maximizing returns. Better services and modern facilities (e.g. airport lounges, duty free shops) also help attract transit traffic and tourists. Especially for tourists, the airport is the first and last impression they get from a country and can therefore have an impact on a country's reputation as a tourist destination. The largest German newspaper Bild, for instance, published a four-page survey of tourist airports at the beginning of the 2001 holiday season. It contained a detailed assessment of facilities, baggage handling, connecting transport infrastructure, and cleanliness. The only two airports that received the top rating were the private airports in Antalya (Turkey) and Athens (Greece).[108]

Under public ownership such incentives are weakened or distorted. A survey comparing the passenger-friendliness of 201 airports in 67 countries found that privately managed airports were significantly more responsive to passenger needs than those that are government-owned.[109] Several examples of poor investment planning under public ownership can also be found in the southern Mediterranean. In 1993, for instance, the Moroccan government initiated a large-scale airport expansion program that created capacities in Agadir three times in excess of 1996 traffic turnover. A private operator would probably have opted for a more economical, phased approach.[110] In Tunisia, the Tabarka airport was in low demand for years after completion. In Cairo, plans for a third terminal have been under study since 1989. Contractors submitted pre-qualification bids for the $ 300-400 million project in 1996. After they were left in limbo for three years because of budget constraints, the government notified them in 1999 that it had decided to re-tender the terminal as a concession. At the end of 2001, the government hired consultants to prepare the terms of reference.[111] A particular problem is the fact that the existing terminal was designed in a non-modular fashion. The result of this short-sighted decision is that the terminal cannot be expanded, but that a much more expensive new terminal will have to be constructed.[112] The Algerian government launched a project to modernize and expand Algiers airport in 1986. Partially completed and starved of funding, however, this project has been lingering until a decision in 2000 to concession it to a private investor.

Governments have a range of policy instruments at their disposal to increase private participation in airports. They differ in the degree to which risk, ownership, investment, and management functions are being transferred to the private sector. Vehicles for private participation include concessions to

[108] Bild am Sonntag (24 June 2001). This tabloid is estimated to reach 20 percent of the German population.
[109] Advani, A. 1999. *Passenger-Friendly Airports: Another Reason for Airport Privatization*. Reason Foundation.
[110] World Bank. 1997. *Morocco: Private Participation in Infrastructure – Synthesis.*
[111] MEED (4 June 1999, 2 June 2000, 6 April 2001, 2 November 2001).
[112] MEED (24 August 2001).

build and operate airports, leases, and management contracts (see section 3.5). Even in cases where airports remain publicly owned, there is plenty of scope to improve performance through corporatization and commercialization. A recent World Bank study found that between 1990 and 1998, private sponsors "participated in projects involving 89 airports in 23 developing countries, with investments totaling $ 5.4 billion."[113] As can be seen from diagram 2.6, there has been an acceleration in private airport investments over recent years.[114] With a share of a mere 3.6 percent of total investments, the Middle East and North Africa region is lagging behind other regions. Again, Latin America (45 percent) punches far above its weight and has attracted almost as many investments as the other developing regions together. "As of mid-1999, some 60 [Latin American] airports had been privatized or commercialized [...] and a further 58 are in the process."[115]

Diagram 2.6 Investments in Airport Projects with Private Participation in Developing Countries (cumulative)

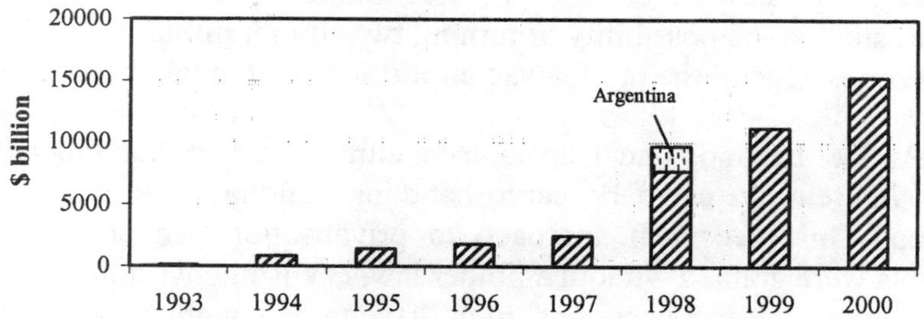

Source: World Bank (PPI Database).

The most widely used mechanisms for airport privatization are concession-type contracts. According to a World Bank study, all "airport projects involving terminals have granted private sponsors the right to raise revenue by selling concessions for commercial activities (such as restaurants, parking facilities, and duty-free shops). On average these projects derive about half their revenue from non-aeronautical services." As two unusual examples from Colombia and Northern Ireland demonstrate, the contractual details of private participation offer great flexibility and can be tailored to meet specific needs and circumstances. For Bogotá airport, the CAA awarded a build-operate-transfer concession (BOT) for the construction and maintenance of a new runway, with landing fee revenues going to the private operator. At Belfast Airport, where issues of national security were a major concern for the government, full privatization was supplemented by a golden share that permits the authorities to intervene in cases where national security is at stake.

Several southern Mediterranean countries have initiated airport privatization. In 1998, the Egyptian government awarded 40- to 50-year concessions for three BOT airports, in return for around 10 percent of the respective airport revenues. Private consortia are to construct and operate the airports in Marsa Alam, El Alamein, and Ras Sudr as part of large-scale tourism developments and a free zone. Total investment commitments exceed half a billion dollars. In September 1999, the Swiss-Swedish company ABB initialed a 50-year BOT-concession for two other airports in the oases of Farafra and Bahariya. Investments of about $ 110 million per airport, as well as $ 280 million to develop integrated facilities, have been pledged. In the popular Sinai resort of Sharm el-Shaikh, investments of around $ 100 million will be needed for an expansion of the airport, which currently

---

[113] Silva, Gisele. 1999. "Private Participation in the Airport Sector – Recent Trends." World Bank Viewpoint Note Series 202. All Viewpoint notes contain case studies on public policies for the private sector and can be downloaded from the World Bank website (*www.worldbank.org/html/fpd/notes/*).

[114] The year 1998 was an outlier, as Argentina's airport privatization attracted investment commitments of $ 2 billion, as shown in diagram 2.6.

[115] IATA. 1999. *Regulatory Developments in 1999.*

handles around two million passengers a year. A BOT tender was launched in 2001.[116] The recent decision to liberalize scheduled flights to key resorts will make Egypt's airports more attractive to investors. As part of its ambitious privatization program, Turkey will sell some larger airports. In 1999, the rapidly expanding Antalya airport was sold to a consortium led by Frankfurt airport. In 2001, the privatizations of Bodrum, Dalaman, and Izmir were being prepared. In late 2001, consultants finalized the design for a third large international airport in Tunisia. The tender for the country's first BOT airport in Enfida was to be launched in 2002.[117] It is expected to cost $ 400 million and will have a capacity of five million passengers per year.[118] In 1998, Lebanese authorities studied the possibility of turning two former military airfields into private cargo airports with free zones. One of them, Moawad airport in Qleiat, might eventually be offered to investors.

Some MPs, like Lebanon and Tunisia, have attracted private funding and management for ancillary facilities. In Beirut, a car park, cargo handling buildings, and duty-free shops were tendered for concession. This piecemeal approach to privatization had at least two drawbacks. First, the concessions were granted without a proper law, exposing investors to a high degree of political risk. Second, some of these concessions might have to be bought back should the government proceeds with plans to fully privatize Beirut airport. In Tunisia, minor involvement of the private sector in airport related activities include the concessioning of car parks in Tunis and Djerba, the renting of buildings outside the customs area, and the concessioning of duty free shops. A new Code de l'Aviation Civile should permit more substantial private involvement in Tunisian airports.

The construction of new secondary airports through BOT schemes and the privatization of ancillary services is an encouraging start. The main challenge in the southern Mediterranean, however will be to privatize the core of the sector: the large existing airports. None of the key airports in the region, which constitute critical nodes in the multimodal transport system of the region, have yet been privatized. Algeria could become one of the first MPs to sell a major airport. Plans for a capacity expansion of Algiers airport to six million passengers per annum were launched over a decade ago, but subsequently abandoned for lack of funds. In May 2001, the government selected a privatization advisor, who will develop a concession strategy and draft the concession documents for the $ 300 million project.[119] In late 2001, the government of Cyprus prepared a shortlist from more than ten international consortia, that have expressed interest in the $ 300 million privatization of the country's two airports in Paphos and Larnaca.[120] Malta has also offered 40 percent of Malta International Airport to strategic investors and would like to place the remaining shares on the stock exchange.[121] After the completion of a $ 600 million renovation and expansion project, the Lebanese government has submitted a law for the full privatization of Beirut airport to parliament. In fact, the European Investment Bank (EIB) made the disposal a condition for a loan that helped fund the rehabilitation.[122] In Morocco a new airport at Marrakech, the need for a new passenger terminal at Casablanca, or the potential for a cargo hub in Casablanca all provide opportunities to increase private participation. Another interesting project for private investors might eventually be the joint Jordanian-Israeli airport at Aqaba, which transport officials from both sides started discussing in late 1999. The European experience with airport privatization (see box 2.13) could be of interest not only because it provides examples of successful privatizations, but also because the new private operators in the EU are potential investors and strategic partners for MP airports.

[116] MEED (5 June and 28 August 1998, 2 June and 13 October 2000) and Reuters (24 November 2000).
[117] MEED (15 February 2002).
[118] Reuters Business Briefing (30 May 2001).
[119] MEED (6 April and 4 May 2001).
[120] Reuters Business Briefing (11 September 2001).
[121] Financial Times (19 November 2001) and The Times of Malta (17 December 2001).
[122] MEED (9 November 2001).

Box 2.13 Airport Privatization and Competition in the EU

There are no specific EU rules concerning the ownership structure of airports. However, member states are increasingly turning to privatization in order to mobilize private investments for airport expansion and to attract regional hub functions to their countries.

- As the first European airport operator, the British Airport Authority (BAA) was floated on the stock exchange in 1987. To prevent an abuse of its monopolistic position in London, Europe's largest air transport hub, the company is being monitored by an independent regulator (see section 2.11). Managing seven airports in Britain and eight abroad, BAA handles a total of 116 million passengers per year and has become the largest airport operator in the world.[123]
- In June 2000, the Italian government sold its remaining 51 percent stake in Aeroporti di Roma for € 1.3 billion.[124] The company operates Rome's two airports, which had a combined turnover of 27 million passengers in 2000. Its predominance in international traffic to and from Italy is being challenged by Milan's new Malpensa airport. SEA, which operates Malpensa, intends to float 30 percent of its shares on the stock market.[125]
- In November 2000, the regional authority of Zurich raised around $ 300 million in a secondary offering of 28 percent in Switzerland's largest airport. Passenger numbers at Zurich airport have almost doubled in the 1990s to 21 million in 2000. The company plans an aggressive expansion to 34 million passengers by targeting international transfer traffic in competition to other European airports.[126]
- In late 2000, the Dutch government announced its intention to float its 76 percent in Amsterdam-Schiphol airport in several tranches. The move should value the company at € 2.5 billion, provide funds for further investments in Europe's fourth busiest airport, and pave the way for international expansion. In November 2000, Schiphol and Frankfurt airport announced their Pantares alliance, to position themselves as bidders in international airport privatizations.[127]
- Frankfurt, the second largest airport in Europe, has strategic stakes in several foreign airports, including facilities in Turkey and the Philippines. In April 2001, it became the fifth European airport to be partly privatized through a stock-market floatation of 31 percent, raising around $ 800 million.[128]
- Athens' new € 2.1 billion airport, constructed and operated by the international consortium Athens International Airport (AIA), opened in March 2001. A 26 kilometer, € 1.5 billion private toll road links the terminal to the Greek capital. With an expected 16 million passengers initially, the airport has the ambition to establish itself as hub for southeastern Europe and the eastern Mediterranean region..[129]
- Other cases of European airport privatizations abound. In October 2000, the Austrian government further reduced its stake in the publicly quoted Vienna airport, which had been floated in 1992.[130] In early 2002, arrangements for the multi-billion Euro BOT contract for Berlin's new airport were still pending, following a non-transparent and poorly managed tender process. In late 2000, the Belgian government announced plans to privatize Brussels airport, another important European hub. Two Danish airports, including the one in Copenhagen, were listed at the stock-exchange in 1994.
- Most European hubs are still dominated by one airline (e.g. Heathrow by BA, Frankfurt by Lufthansa, Schiphol by KLM) and airport performance is closely associated with the international competitiveness of the incumbent airline. Paris Charles de Gaulle (CDG) airport illustrates these interdependencies. Air France doubled the weekly connections it offers from CDG from 5,000 to 14,000 in only four years – overtaking its two main competitors, BA (5,000 connections at Heathrow) and Lufthansa (9,000 connections at Frankfurt).[131] This was achieved through Air France's partial privatization and comprehensive restructuring; its alliance with Delta Airlines (permitting it to service a large number of

[123] Website of the British Airport Authority (*www.baa.co.uk*).
[124] Financial Times (16 June 2000).
[125] Dow Jones International News Service (3 May 2001).
[126] Financial Times (14 February 2000).
[127] Financial Times (20 November 2000).
[128] Financial Times (28 May 2001) and Financial Times Deutschland (11 June 2001).
[129] Financial Times (17 October 2000).
[130] Financial Times (23 October 2000).
[131] The Economist (25 November 2000).

US destinations); a synchronization of incoming and outgoing flights in six daily waves (for better connections); heavy investments in facilities (a third runway was opened in 1999 and a fourth in 2001); and more efficient airport management (to handle complex transfer flows).

- An example of how such interdependencies can work the other way is Hungary. After a decade of poorly managed restructuring and privatization attempts, the flag carrier Malev is still weak and not part of an international alliance. Despite significant investments in new terminals, it is questionable if Budapest can make up for lost time and establish itself as a Central European hub, now that Vienna and Munich have filled the void. Warsaw airport might be better positioned, following the privatization of flag carrier LOT and its integration into the Qualiflyer group. The government plans to corporatize the airport and to build a second terminal by 2005, before Berlin's new airport (a potential competitor for central European transit traffic) comes on stream.[132] Other Eastern European countries that have launched airport privatization include Estonia, Bulgaria, and Slovakia.[133]

2.13 Reforming Air Traffic Control

Air traffic control (ATC) provides those services that are needed to ensure the safe and efficient use of airspace. It requires a system of navigation infrastructure (e.g. control towers, area control centers, flight service stations) as well as an institution managing the airspace and providing ATC services. Charges for such services account for about 6 percent of the cost base of European airlines. If the indirect economic costs arising from system inefficiencies and delays are added, this figure doubles according to some estimates. Another indication of the potential for increased efficiency in ATC is a benchmarking study carried out on behalf of the Association of European Airlines. It revealed large discrepancies between the performance of different ATC centers. Compared to Vienna, Athens had only 60 percent of the traffic but 96 times more delays. "London productivity was 19 percent lower than Vienna, and charges 26 percent higher."[134]

To minimize the costs and frictions arising from ATC, a number of policy issues have to be addressed. The main ATC service – to ensure spatial separation of aircraft and thus avoid collisions – is a natural monopoly. However, it is usually bundled with potentially competitive ancillary services, such as communication, navigation, surveillance (transmission of aircraft position to ATC), aeronautical services (e.g. maps), and meteorological information. Several of these services are potentially competitive and others will become so thanks to technological progress. Once the European satellite system Galileo is operational (see box 3.10), for instance, aircraft could use on-board satellite navigation systems instead of ATC ground aids. The main objectives of ATC reform are the separation of operational functions (service provision) from regulatory functions; the opening of potentially competitive services to competition; and the regulation of quality and prices for monopolistic services by an independent entity.

In addition, ATC should be institutionally separated from the provision of other services, especially airport operation. Cross-subsidies between them should be eliminated. Another useful institutional reform for the improvement of efficiency, is the corporatization of air traffic control. Many countries have already taken that step, including the majority of EU member states. As the first country in Europe, Britain is preparing the partial privatization of its National Air Traffic Services (Nats). The government wants to separate service provision from regulation (to remain with the CAA); inject private sector management; and mobilize more than € 2 billion for investments. By

---

132 Reuters Business Briefings (25 June 2001).

133 Reuters Business Briefing (30 October 2000, 11 January 2002, 22 March 2002).

134 Association of European Airlines. 1999. *Yearbook 1999*. To facilitate the assessment of comparative performance, a Eurocontrol Performance Review Commission is developing performance indicators for ATCs.

doing so, it also wants to position Nats for the consolidation of European ATC service providers. The British transport minister expects the number of ATC systems to be reduced from the current 49 to 4 or 5. Canada has pioneered a particularly promising reform model. In 1996, the private corporation Nav Canada took over the country's civilian air traffic control network, one of the world's largest. It purchased the publicly-owned ATC infrastructure for C$ 1.5 billion and hired 6,400 former civil servants. To ensure efficient management and avoid monopolistic behavior, Nav Canada is non-profit (profits are invested or charges lowered) and co-managed by stakeholders (airlines, pilots, employees).

As far as the cross-border rationalization of ATC is concerned, the issues of national sovereignty associated with airspace represents a major political obstacle. Even within the EU, where member states have increasingly ceded national sovereignty to supranational institutions, ATC has long been exempt. This failure to rationalize Europe's fragmented airspace is imposing high costs on airlines and passengers. In 1999, a third of all European flights were delayed by more than 15 minutes, mainly due to ATC problems. The potential cost savings for airlines that could result from ATC reforms have been estimated to be around € 2.5 billion per year, or 5 percent of total operating costs.[135] This figure does not include the costs borne by passengers. There is now a broad consensus that the fragmentation of European airspace is the root cause of these problems and that the technical ATC cooperation between European countries through the European Civil Aviation Conference (ECAC) and through Eurocontrol does is no longer sufficient to deal with rapidly increasing traffic. The Single European Sky initiative was thus initiated in 1999 with the objective of integrating the air space and ATC systems across the continent (see box 2.14).

Table 2.6 Examples of Overflight Charges

Country	A320 ($/100 km)	B747 ($/1000 km)
Algeria	33	753
Egypt	125	480
Jordan	83	511
Morocco	25	582
Syria	27	146
Tunisia	434	434
Average	**121**	**484**
Turkey	55	1,277

Source: World Bank, Lebanon Civil Aviation Strategy (2001).

For most MPs, an overhaul of their national air traffic control might not be the main short-term reform priority for the air transport sector. Their airspace is less crowded than in Europe and other reforms are more pressing. Nonetheless, governments in the region should ensure that ATC is organized as cost-effectively as possible and in line with international best practice. In particular, they should eliminate cross-subsidies between ATC and other parts of the sector (e.g. airports); separate ATC service provision and regulation; and corporatize ATC to create entities with financial and legal independence. With regard to cross-border ATC issues, MPs should consider a number of measures. To the extent possible, political constraints to the optimization of route networks should be removed. The lifting of the air embargo on Libya as well as Israel's decision to permit aircraft from and to Amman to overfly its airspace above Tel Aviv were two encouraging recent developments. Equally important is stronger technical harmonization and cooperation between national ATCs. ICAO and Eurocontrol appear to be suitable institutional vehicles for promoting such cooperation.[136] One possibility would be the eventual accession of the remaining MPs to Eurocontrol. Another option would be to set up sub-regional centers for the control of the upper airspace, such as those operated by Eurocontrol.

---

[135] Study cited in: Association of European Airlines. 1999. *Yearbook 1999*.

[136] The Middle East Office of ICAO, for instance, is working on an Air Navigation Plan for the Middle East region. Another organization is the Arab Civil Aviation Commission, a specialized institution of the Arab League, in Rabat.

Box 2.14 Eurocontrol and the Single European Sky Initiative

Eurocontrol, based in Brussels, has 29 member states, which include the 15 EU countries; the CEEC accession candidates; Switzerland; Norway; and the MPs, Turkey, Cyprus, and Malta. The thrust of Eurocontrol's work is on technical harmonization and the introduction of new technology. It defines mandatory and recommended standards for ATC interoperability. Through the manuals, seminars, and training sessions Eurocontrol promotes harmonization and spreads best practice. It has long maintained regional centers for the management of the upper airspace (relevant for pan-European traffic). In preparation for their EU accession, the CEECs recently agreed to set up such a center in Vienna by 2006. In 1997, Eurocontrol opened its Central Flow Management Unit (CFMU), which has taken over some important functions of national ATCs and provides aircraft with end-to-end routings across Europe. One of the collective planning tools developed by Eurocontrol is the Convergence and Implementation Program (CIP), which defines targets to be met by all national systems. As one of the latest initiatives for further integration of European ATC systems, Eurocontrol launched its ATM 2000+ strategy. In summary, technical harmonization and coordination by Eurocontrol has brought important benefits, but inefficiencies persist. Despite a 1997 revision of the Eurocontrol convention, enforcement mechanisms are still weak, decision making complex. The European airspace remains a patchwork with 49 ATC centers, 31 national systems, 22 operating systems, and 30 computer languages.

As the core group of Eurocontrol members, EU countries have come to the conclusion that they need to fundamentally rethink the process of ATC integration. As in many other sectors, they have decided to transcend multilateral coordination and cede national sovereignty to supranational institutions. In December 1999, the EU Council of Transport Ministers launched the Single European Sky initiative and appointed a High Level Group on Air Traffic Reform, chaired by the Commission. The report and proposed action plan of the High Level Group, presented in December 2000, offer a blueprint for reform:

- Airspace should be treated as a common resource, open to all users and managed as a continuum. The civil and military management of air traffic should gradually be integrated.
- A strong community regulator, independent from ATC service providers, should define and monitor performance targets for ATCs. It should regulate the quality and prices of monopolistic activities and establish a transparent licensing regime to ensure competition for ancillary services. For both safety and economic regulation, decision making should be transparent and involve stakeholders (air service providers, airlines, equipment manufacturers, staff).
- Synergies between the Commission's legislative and regulatory capacity and Eurocontrol's technical expertise should be developed through Commission accession to Eurocontrol, the conversion of Eurocontrol standards into EU legislation, and through the functional distinction between regulation (domain of EU institutions) and service provision (domain of national ATCs and Eurocontrol).
- Systems architecture and technology should be standardized to enhance interoperability and reduce duplication. Human resource policies should be coordinated (e.g. a European license for controllers).

The safety aspects of ATC regulation shall soon be taken over by the to-be-created European Aviation Safety Agency (EASA). Similar to the Federal Aviation Administration (FAA) in the United States, EASA would be an independent safety regulator granting EU-wide licenses for aircraft and technical personnel. It should also provide "technical assistance in contacts and negotiations with aeronautical authorities of third countries and international organizations. [...] The Commission's proposal will permit [it] to associate all countries linked to the Community by agreements under which they adopt and apply Community legislation in the air transport area [i.e. ECAA members]."[137] Just as Eurocontrol and EASA are open to non-EU countries, it seems conceivable that the Single European Sky could eventually be extended to neighboring countries.

Sources: (1) European Commission. 1999a. (2) European Commission. 2000a. Single European Sky – Report of the High Level Group. (3) Eurocontrol (www.eurocontrol.be). (4) The EASA strategy was set out in Communication COM (2000) 598.

[137] Quote from: European Commission website. There are three areas of air safety regulation: (i) airworthiness and maintenance of aircraft, (ii) licensing and registration of cockpit staff and ground personnel, (iii) definition and supervision of air corridors.

Chapter 3

Maritime Transport

Chapter 3

Maritime Transport

3.1 Introduction

The vast majority of trade in the southern Mediterranean is seaborne, especially in the countries of North Africa where this mode accounts for up to 95 percent of the total. The speed, cost-effectiveness, reliability, and diversity of maritime transport services is therefore critical for the promotion of exports, the attraction of foreign direct investment (FDI), the integration of these countries into the global economy, and the ultimate success of the Euro-Mediterranean free-trade area (FTA). Despite recent progress, the efficiency of the maritime transport chains in the southern Mediterranean remains low by international standards. Ports, which are the key intermodal nodes and entry points for trade into most Mediterranean Partners (MPs), are among the weakest links.

Port deficiencies are largely rooted in flawed policies. Most ports in the region are managed by public port authorities, operating within ill-defined incentive frameworks that undermine performance and accountability to users and even governments. Insufficient competition in port services (exclusivity rights, unregulated monopolies, and collusive practices) reduces the quality and increases the costs of cargo handling, warehousing, and bunkering. Government budget constraints, combined with obstacles to private participation, often prevent timely modernization and maintenance of port facilities. Outdated regulations distort market dynamics and create red tape. Cumbersome trade and customs procedures cause significant delays and disruptions in maritime chains, while creating a fertile breeding ground for corruption.

Current sector structures are increasingly at odds with rapidly changing technical and economic requirements. Port hinterlands and ocean transport networks have been reshaped dramatically by new shipping technology, unitization of cargo, specialization of vessels, electronic data interchange, and demand pressures such as just-in-time production. At the same time, global trade and transport liberalization have dramatically increased traffic levels. The changing pattern of demand for services and physical infrastructure requires new forms of service delivery and large investments that the current organizations, dominated by the public sector, cannot provide.

During the past 20 years, a large international pool of experience and best practice regarding port reforms has emerged that the MPs should tap to design much needed reforms of their own.[1] Between 1990 and 2000, 169 port projects with private participation reached financial closure in developing countries, with investment commitments totaling more than $ 16 billion.[2] "Public port agencies have been moving away from the service port model, under which the port authority provides all commercial services as well as regulatory functions, and are increasingly adopting the landlord model. Under this approach public port authorities retain their regulatory functions and continue to own the land and basic infrastructure assets such as berths and breakwater facilities. But they divest themselves of the managerial and financial responsibility for commercial facilities such as terminals and equipment in the port area."[3]

---

[1] A useful technical guide to port reforms is the World Bank *Port Reform Toolkit* (2000). This can be downloaded free of charge from the World Bank website (*www.worldbank.org/html/fpd/transport/ports/toolkit.htm*).

[2] World Bank (PPI Database).

[3] Sommer, Dirk. 1999. "Private Participation in Port Facilities – Recent Trends." World Bank Viewpoint Note Series 193. Viewpoints case studies are available online (*www.worldbank.org/html/fpd/notes/*).

Box 3.1 Maritime Transport and Regional Integration in the Baltic Sea Region

The Baltic Sea region, with a total population of about 80 million people, provides some instructive lessons for maritime policy and regional integration in the Mediterranean. When the Soviet Union disintegrated in the early 1990s, the EU countries on the one side of the Baltic (Finland, Sweden, Denmark, Germany) and the transition countries on the other side (Poland, Lithuania, Latvia, Estonia, and Russia) launched policy reforms and cross-border initiatives with some remarkable results. A decade later more than a third of total port throughput (250 of 700 million tons) is intra-regional. "Both east-west and north-south trade across the Baltic sea is rising at a much faster rate than the 3 to 5 percent growth rates of the region's economies."[4] Sector restructuring and investments have been particularly ambitious in the four countries preparing for EU accession. Strong competition for the important transit traffic with Russia has given additional impetus to reforms in Estonia, Latvia, Lithuania, and Finland.

At the regional level, several conferences of ministers of transport have taken place. A Memorandum of Understanding on information exchange and studies on port matters was signed between the ten countries bordering the Baltic Sea and the European Commission in 1996. An Agreement on Cooperation on Waterborne Transport followed in 1997 and a joint coordinating committee now meets regularly to carry forward this process. As part of these efforts, the Swedish Maritime Administration proposed an action plan for the facilitation of trade and the improvement of maritime transport in 1999. One year later, it presented a comprehensive regional study of the sector, the Baltic Maritime Outlook 2000.[5] Various regional networks have been created, including the Baltic Ports Organization and the Union of 99 Baltic Cities.[6] At the same time, the Commission is helping the three Baltic republics and Poland to adapt their sector framework to EU rules and regulations. The Swedish Institute of Shipping Analysis and the BPO are setting up a port statistic database on the internet (*www.bpo.sai.se*), based on standardized reports submitted by the individual countries on a regular basis. As far as hinterland connections are concerned, a 930-kilometer backbone road from Helsinki to Warsaw is being upgraded and reconstructed. Along this Via Baltica, governments and donors coordinate investments and facilitation measures.[7]

At the national level, the reform momentum is equally impressive. During the 1990s Estonia, Latvia, and Lithuania fully privatized stevedoring services. Estonia's major port Tallinn became a joint stock company in 1996. Most of the superstructure was sold to private operators that now handle more than 75 percent of all cargo. The government also privatized the state-owned shipping company and in late 2000 sold a majority stake in the state railway company to an international consortium in an effort to upgrade the hinterland connections to Russia. Tallinn is also "one of the fastest growing liner and ferry ports of the world."[8] In Lithuania, government policy is to eliminate all subsidies to the maritime sector and to privatize the three public shipping lines. The main port Klaipeda was transformed into a landlord port and most commercial activities were privatized, mobilizing substantial foreign investment. Both intra-port competition (between different terminal operators) and inter-port competition have led to significant improvements in efficiency. Klaipeda has become an important transport hub and a $ 36 million World Bank loan will help fund further expansion.[9] In Poland, the three state shipping companies were corporatized and are earmarked for privatization. A 1997 sector law created the basis for maritime reforms and the transformation of the country's main ports into autonomous landlord ports. Up to 49 percent of their equity may be sold to private investors. Gdansk, Poland's largest port, has attracted significant foreign investment and is implementing an ambitious expansion plan. A free zone and a logistics center were set up. Once the motorway from Gdansk to Vienna (a TEN corridor) is completed, the port should become an important transit hub for traffic to Central Europe. In late 2001, the Baltic Container Terminal, Poland's first full-fledged container terminal, was offered for privatization.

---

[4] Financial Times (19 May 2000). Population figure in first sentence from Financial Times (8 April 2000).
[5] Swedish Maritime Administration. 2000. *Baltic Maritime Outlook 2000*. (*www.sjofartsverket.se*).
[6] Financial Times (8 April and 19 May 2000).
[7] World Bank. 2000. *Transport Sector Restructuring in the Baltic States – Proceedings of a Seminar*.
[8] Journal of Commerce (13 December 2000) and Financial Times (19 May 2000).
[9] World Bank. 2000. *Staff Appraisal Report: Klaipeda Port Project* (not published).

This chapter is organized as follows. Section 3.2 provides an overview of maritime transport flows in the region. With ports as the main bottleneck in maritime chains, most of this chapter is devoted to the issues of port reform (sections 3.3 to 3.8). The remaining sections address policy issues in the shipping industry (3.9) and those related to the competition for transshipment hubs (3.10). Land-based transport and issues related to hinterland connections are discussed in chapter 4. As in air transport, Latin America is the developing region that has progressed furthest with port reforms. Boxes 3.4 and 3.5 thus review the experience of Colombia and Argentina.

3.2 The Structure of Maritime Transport Flows in the Southern Mediterranean

Maritime transport is a heterogeneous sector and it is important to distinguish between different market segments. Dry and liquid bulk; containerized and non-containerized general cargo; roll-on, roll-off (RoRo) truck and car traffic; as well as passenger transport require different vessels and terminals. Traffic patterns, infrastructure needs, and policy issues vary considerably between market segments. As a basis for the discussion of sector policy, this section provides an overview of transport flows in the region.[10]

- Throughout the southern Mediterranean, the majority of cross-border trade is seaborne, especially in the Maghreb. In Morocco, Tunisia, and Algeria, 95 to 98 percent of all trade in terms of volume is processed through ports. The dominance of maritime transport in trade flows is less pronounced if measured by value instead of weight, since many high-value products are being transported by air. In 1997, seaborne trade between the EU and the MPs (including Turkey, Cyprus, Israel, and Malta) accounted for 83 percent of trade in terms of weight, but only 53 percent in terms of value. The predominance of maritime and air transport in trade is due to the fact that several land borders remain closed for political reasons, little trade takes place between neighboring countries, and most MPs are separated from their main trading partners by water. Road haulage and especially rail transport – the alternative modes for the transport of bulky or high-volume goods – play a relatively small role for cross-border flows, particularly in the Maghreb countries and Egypt. Land-based transport is more important in the Mashrek. In Jordan for instance – the only MP without access to the Mediterranean – 65 percent of all imports by weight arrived by truck and only 34 percent by sea.
- The pattern of growth in maritime traffic varies considerably from country to country. In the seven Arab MPs for which data were available, the weighted average growth rate for 1997 to 2000 was 8 percent, or less than 1 percent per year. In this period, growth was negative for Egypt (-15 percent) and Lebanon (-14 percent).[11] Growth was also low for Jordan (2 percent) and Syria (5 percent), but high for Algeria and Morocco (12 and 17 percent respectively). Overall, the relatively poor growth performance was from a low base. Most ports in the region have medium to low throughputs and many of the maritime routes are thin. The economic gap between the Arab MPs on the one hand and the accession candidates (Cyrus, Malta, Turkey) and the high-income country Israel on the other hand is also reflected in maritime traffic. Turkey has the same population as Egypt but thrice the port throughput. Malta has one-tenth of Lebanon's population but a slightly higher traffic volume. Israel's ports (population five million) handle more than double the gross tonnage as those in Tunisia (population nine million). The countries with the largest maritime trades in the region were Turkey (149 million

[10] Unless otherwise stated, all data in section 3.2 have been taken from the MED-Trans database of Eurostat.

[11] The data for Egypt need to be taken with caution because they came from two different sources: the MED-Trans database of Eurostat (2000) and the Egyptian Maritime Databank.

tons), Algeria (100 million), Morocco (53 million), and Egypt (46 million). This largely reflects bulk commodity exports and the size of the population.

- In most MPs, imbalances between imports (mainly processed goods and consumer products) and exports (often commodities) are reflected in the lop-sidedness of maritime transport flows. In countries with strong commodity exports (phosphates in Morocco and Jordan, oil in Algeria and Syria), the weight of exports tends to be significantly higher than that of imports. Jordan, for example, exported seven million tons by sea in 2000, but imported only five million tons. In the same year, Algerian ports loaded 81 million tons but discharged a mere 18 million. Otherwise, however, most countries of the region import considerably more goods by sea than they export. In Lebanon, the ratio is 15 to 1 (5.2 million compared to 0.4 million). In Egypt, the 37.2 million tons unloaded were more than four times the 8.6 million tons loaded in 2000. In 1997, Tunisian ports processed 14.4 million tons of imports but only 7 million tons of exports. Such imbalances lead to considerable unused capacity as well as to differences between out-bound and in-bound fares, depending on vessel type and direction.

Table 3.1 Maritime Transport Flows (2000)

Country	Passengers	Freight				Share of Major Port (%)
		Loaded ('000 tons)	Unloaded ('000 tons)	Loaded as % of Unloaded	Growth ('97-'00 %)	
Algeria	587,247	81,772	18,529	441	12	36
Egypt	2,568,003	37,233	8,608	433	-15	n.a
Jordan	638,542	7,193	5,360	134	2	100
Lebanon	46,001	352	5,195	7	-14	89
Morocco	2,668,392	23,884	29,560	81	17	37
Syria	30,711	20,705	8,959	231	5	57
Tunisia	414,222	7,005	14,432	49	8	25
Total/Av.	**6,953,118**	**178,144**	**90,643**	**197**	**8**	**57**
Cyprus	n.a.	1,805	5,475	33	-3	42
Israel	158,000	13,866	29,196	47	11	43
Malta	210,650	577	5,134	11	67	51
Turkey	1,242,639	45,322	103,707	44	23	21

Notes: (1) Loaded/unloaded 2000 data for Egypt from Egyptian Maritime Databank.
(2) Passengers do not include cruise traffic.

Source: Eurostat (MED-Trans Database).

- In general, it should be noted that all these traffic figures, measured in tonnage, are distorted by dry and liquid bulk cargo. The most demanding traffic in terms of port facilities and labor-intensive handling is general cargo (break bulk), and especially unitized cargo. Bulk traffic is especially pronounced in four commodity exporters among the MPs. In Algeria, 81 percent of 2000 port throughput was in petroleum products (81 of 100 million tons). In Syria, oil and oil derivatives made up to 69 percent of maritime traffic. In Jordan and Morocco, the share of phosphate and other minerals accounted for 54 percent and 19 percent of total maritime trade respectively. In general cargo, the lopsidedness of trade is a cause for the high proportion of empty containers and RoRo trucks. Empty runs of 46 percent in Algeria, 47 percent in Morocco, or 40 percent in Jordan show that most trucks and containers leave these countries empty (see table 3.2). This has an adverse effect on the costs and development of the important trade in unitized cargo.

- In general, maritime traffic is heavily concentrated on a few key ports per country. This is due to economies of scale as well as the geographical concentration of industry and population. In Algeria, about two-thirds of maritime traffic in non-petroleum products flow through the ports of Algiers, Oran, and Annaba, while three specialized ports handle the exports of hydrocarbons (Arzew, Skikda, and Béjaïa). Jordan has a mere 13 kilometers of shoreline along the Red Sea and its only port is Aqaba. In Lebanon, practically all international maritime transport is processed through Beirut. In Syria, the two ports of Lattakia and Tartous are the entry points for almost the totality of seaborne trade. In Egypt, the Arab MP with the largest population and the longest coastline, traffic is more dispersed. Alexandria, Damietta, Port Said, and Suez handle 65 percent of all cargo. But even here, the concentration is considerably higher in individual market segments.[12] Tunisia has eight international ports along a rather short coastline, yet Radès and La Goulette near Tunis account for about 50 percent of general cargo and 97 percent of all unitized cargo.

Table 3.2 Container and Ro-Ro Traffic by Country

Country	Total Units		Growth ('97-'00 %)	Empty Units (% in 2000)
	1997	2000		
Algeria	176,857	301,130	70	46
Egypt	n.a.	n.a.	n.a.	n.a.
Jordan	108,482	151,160	39	40
Lebanon	219,659	206,946	-6	47
Morocco	n.a.	n.a.	n.a.	n.a.
Syria	n.a.	n.a.	n.a.	n.a.
Tunisia	n.a.	231,999	n.a.	n.a.
Total/Av	**168,333**	**219,745**	**31**	**44**
Cyprus	267,070	204,456	-23	29
Israel	870,000	975,000	12	26
Malta	n.a.	n.a.	n.a.	n.a.
Turkey	1,680,448	1,969,757	17	3

Source: Eurostat (MED-Trans Database).

- Maritime passenger transport is largely confined to a few countries. In 2000, the Maghreb and Mashrek countries (including Israel) recorded a total of about seven million passengers by sea, compared to about 42 million by air. For some countries, like Lebanon, Algeria, and Syria, the balance between air and maritime is even more strongly tilted towards air transport. The two countries with the highest maritime passengers traffic are Egypt (particularly short-haul routes around the Sinai peninsula) and Morocco (mainly with southern Europe). Each of them recorded more than 2.5 million passengers in 2000. Particularly in the Maghreb countries, many maritime passengers are emigrant workers from the EU, who often arrive by sea with heavy luggage and/or cars and return by air. In Algeria, for example, passenger arrivals in ports (248,000 in 1997) exceeded departures (144,000) by a significant margin. In one year, 565 car ferries made stopovers in Algerian ports, transporting a total of 14 million tons. In Morocco, 76 percent of 1997 maritime passengers embarked and disembarked in the port of Tangiers – mainly on short and medium haul routes across the straight of Gibraltar and to southern France. The ports of Tunis handle more than 97 percent of Tunisian passenger traffic, 52 percent of which is with the port of Marseilles alone. With the exception of some cruise liner traffic (e.g. 192,000 passengers in Tunisia and 536,000 in Israel), few tourists arrive by sea.

[12] Although Alexandria only handled 48 percent of total traffic in 1997, it had a 63 percent market share for general cargo and almost a monopoly for fertilizers. Two-thirds of transit traffic (mainly container transshipment) is handled by Damietta and the remaining third by Port Said.

- The fastest growing sector of maritime transport is the shipment of containers, both globally and within the region. The total capacity of the world container fleet tripled during the past decade. International container traffic increased from 79 to 147 million twenty-foot equivalent units (TEU) between 1989 and 1996.[13] Total container traffic handled by all Mediterranean ports (including European ports) grew by an annual average of 13 percent between 1990 and 1998, albeit from a lower base than in some other regions. In Tunisia, for instance, container traffic soared from 142,000 TEU in 1997 to 215,000 TEU in 2000 – that is, at an annualized rate of 15 percent. Container transshipment (indirect routing with transfer between connecting vessels) grew even faster, by close to 20 percent per annum.[14] It is becoming an increasingly important segment of maritime transport (see box 3.9). Container traffic tends to be highly concentrated in a few ports and so far the Maghreb and Mashrek countries have managed to capture very little of the regional market (see diagram 3.1). Given the particular importance of this market segment and the specific policy issues involved, container traffic is discussed in section 3.10.

Diagram 3.1 Container Transshipment Market Share in the Mediterranean (1998)

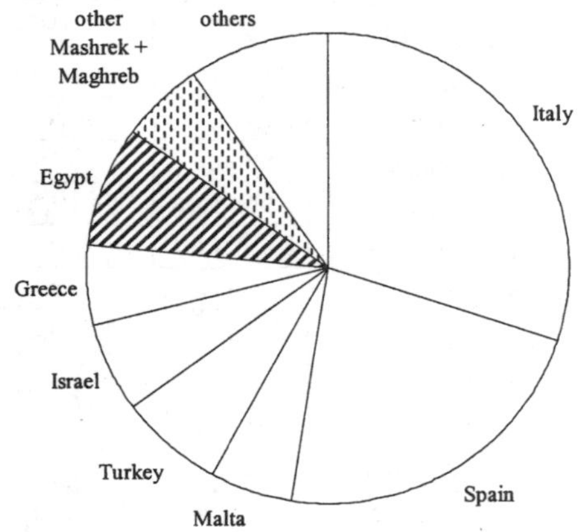

Source: Drewry Shipping Consultants (2000).

- Another form of unitized cargo that plays an important role for maritime traffic in the region, especially in the Maghreb, are trucks carried by RoRo ferries. Moroccan ports, for instance, counted 885,000 RoRo units in 2000 (including passenger cars carried by ferry). For the much smaller island of Cyprus, the figure was 90,000. The advantage of RoRo traffic, as compared to container traffic in cellular vessels (many RoRo trucks carry containers), is that it provides an efficient means for multimodal transport without the need for large and modern port facilities. Especially on journeys where the sea-leg is relatively short compared to the land-legs – such as between southern Europe and the Maghreb – RoRo is widely used. An illustrative example for the importance of RoRo in cross-border supply chains can be found in box 1.6.

- Transport flows to and from the countries of the European Union, as well as those transiting the Mediterranean, dominate maritime traffic in the region. Domestic maritime traffic in most of the MPs is negligible. National coastal traffic accounts for a mere 4 percent of the total in Algeria and for 1 percent in Tunisia. The only MP where domestic maritime traffic is worth mentioning is Turkey (23 percent) with its extremely long coastline. In Jordan, Lebanon, Syria, Morocco, and Tunisia it is practically non-existent. As discussed in chapter 1, South-South trade in the region is also very limited. Trade with other MPs accounts for less than 10 percent of total maritime traffic in countries such as Jordan, Algeria, Cyprus, and Morocco. It is slightly larger in the case of Tunisia (11 percent), Turkey (17 percent), and Lebanon (26 percent) – partly because of the import of oil from neighboring countries. Reflecting trade patterns (see table 1.1), the majority of maritime traffic in many MPs, especially in the Maghreb countries, originates from and is destined to Europe. The share of the EU in maritime traffic flows is 59

[13] OECD. 1999. *Discussion Document on Regulatory Reform in International Maritime Transport.*
[14] Drewry Shipping Consultants. 2000. *Mediterranean Container Ports and Shipping.*

percent for Algeria, 44 percent for Tunisia, and 43 percent for Lebanon. For Jordan, which exports much of its phosphate to Asia, EU traffic made up only 13 percent of the gross tonnage. As a result of the Euro-Mediterranean FTA, the predominance of European countries as trading partners is likely to increase further. Another feature of maritime transport in the region is international transshipment traffic. The Mediterranean is a key transit route for east-west traffic between Asia and Europe via the Suez Canal and for Black Sea traffic via the strait of Bosphorus.

In summary, the structure of maritime transport flows in the southern Mediterranean countries reflects overall economic and trade patterns such as negative trade balances, a non-diversified and often low value-added export base, as well as low levels of intra-regional trade. The structural characteristics outlined above also have implications for maritime sector policies. Due to the importance of maritime transport for trade and investment, any inefficiency in the sector imposes high costs on the entire economy. The dominance of a few large ports and the importance of container transport imply that policy reforms and public sector investments should be geared towards key ports and on the container segment. Rapid growth in the sector, combined with past under-investment, call for increased private involvement to fund new infrastructure and to use scarce capacity more efficiently. Given the predominance of maritime transport in regional freight transport, ports need to efficiently fulfill their role as the primary modal interface in cross-border chains. Due to the footloose nature of container transshipment, including that generated by transit traffic through the Mediterranean, countries with modern and efficient ports are more likely to attract hub functions.

Many performance indicators needed to assess reform needs and policy priorities for the ports in the region are not readily available. Few ports or transport ministries publish indicators such as customs clearance times, ship dwell times, or total cost for cargo handling from ship to gate. Nonetheless, individual case studies and anecdotal evidence illustrate the scope for efficiency improvements. Prior to recent sector reforms in Egypt, a study found that the handling costs for a 20-foot container in Alexandria was \$ 225, compared to \$ 138 in Trieste. Container handling productivity was 20 to 40 percent lower than in comparable ports, while customs and other clearance procedures delayed cargo by 5 to 20 days (1 to 2 days in other countries).[15] In Tunisia, rigid rules for dock labor lead to overstaffing and low labor productivity. The minimum size of a container handling gang, for instance, is eight although four workers would suffice. At the same time, the handling rate of seven to eight boxes per gang-hour is below the twelve boxes of other ports with similar equipment. For RoRo traffic, on the other hand, gang-hour performance is close to international benchmarks (13 units compared to a benchmark of 15).[16] In Morocco's main port of Casablanca, ship handling times could be reduced to about half of today's figure if productivity were increased to international standards.[17] In Algeria, one of the main consignees of the country, EPAL, needs an average of 28 days to process a container through the port of Algiers. The company estimates the excess costs of port inefficiencies to the economy at around \$ 200 million annually – "equivalent to the construction costs of 14,000 units of social housing" every year.[18] Another useful indicator to assess the efficiency of the port sector is the containerization rate of general cargo. As discussed in section 3.10, it is growing but still low for most MPs. In Tunisia – one of the most advanced MPs in this regard – the unitization rate (including RoRo container traffic) rose from 37 percent in 1996 to 50 percent in 2000, but is still far from the 80 percent plus in large ports of industrialized countries. A regional example of the efficiency improvements that reforms can bring is Saudi Arabia, where the "introduction of private sector participation has

[15] World Bank. 1998. *Egypt – Ports Sector Note* (not published).

[16] World Bank. 2000. *Tunisia – Private Sector Assessment Update.*

[17] Paelinck, Honoré. 1999. *Maroc – Facilitation du Transport.* World Bank (not published).

[18] Liberté, Algiers (31 October 2001).

helped to buff up the once tarnished reputation of Saudi ports." According to Saudi Ports Authority, "there has been a 40 percent improvement in average outward clearing times for main-haul container vessels at Jeddah Islamic Port. [...] Four years of private investment has [...] led to a 62 percent increase in tonnage handled per shift."[19]

Box 3.2 Transport Statistics and Sector Reform in the Euro-Mediterranean Partnership

Policy makers, donors, investors, and market participants all need relevant, comprehensive, accurate, and timely transport statistics to make optimal decisions. Efficiency and performance indicators are important to identify bottlenecks and reform priorities, as well as to assess the impact of policy changes through time-series analysis. To compare sector and company performance with that of other countries, harmonized data is needed for cross-border benchmarking ('global markets need global data').

At present, transport statistics for the southern Mediterranean countries, and especially in the Maghreb and Mashrek, are patchy, unreliable, often outdated, and compiled according to different methodologies. Performance and competition indicators are especially hard to come by (e.g. ship turn-around times, ton handled per employee, market share of dominant airline, cost-recovery ratios of ports, amount of direct and indirect subsidies). Official statistics rarely go beyond measuring the flow of goods or physical infrastructure endowments (e.g. tons handled, kilometers of railways and paved roads). Other structural problems include a poor integration of the work of national statistics offices with that of transport sector agencies; insufficient involvement of transport users and the private sector in the generation of statistics (e.g. through user questionnaires); and low levels of transparency. Obtaining statistics about customs clearance times from official sources, for instance, is virtually impossible, even though this information should exist. During the research for this study, it was much easier to obtain sector statistics for the EU, Latin America, and Eastern Europe than for the southern Mediterranean countries.

There has been some donor-sponsored technical assistance (TA) for statistic capacity building, as well as efforts to harmonize statistics across the region. Especially Eurostat's MED-Trans project, supported by the Commission, has made an important contribution to the compilation of better stock and flow statistics. Nonetheless, significant work remains to be done, particularly with regard to policy and performance indicators. Several complementary Euro-Mediterranean Partnership (EMP) instruments can be deployed to build on past efforts.[20] First, a regional MEDA transport project, under preparation at the time of writing, is supposed to help gather and disseminate transport statistics. A MEDSTAT II project, focusing on performance statistics was also being considered. Second, the regional policy dialogue through the Euro-Mediterranean Transport Forum could provide a platform for regional benchmarking exercises. Third, national MEDA projects in the transport sector should include capacity-building measures for transport sector statistics.

[19] MEED (30 November 2001).

[20] It should be noted that modern transport logistics ICT systems, including the computerization of customs, can yield vast amounts of timely data. A source for background information on transport statistics is the web-site of the US Bureau of Transport Statistics (*www.bst.gov*).

Ports

In order to devise adequate policies it is essential to regard ports not merely as pieces of physical infrastructure, but to analyze them in all their functional complexity.

- Ports are critical nodes in intermodal transport chains. They are the location where goods are transferred between vessels and land-based modes. This requires both efficient sea-side connections (e.g. competition between shipping companies, connections to main trade-routes) and land-side connections (e.g. trucking and rail services for effective hinterland connections, high containerization rates of general cargo for smoother modal transfer).
- Ports provide not only physical infrastructure but also a wide range of port services to ships and cargo. These include ship representation; the loading, discharging, and storage of goods; the provision of utilities to ships (bunkering); as well as towage and pilotage. Since transport users are primarily concerned with the availability, cost and quality of these services, so should policy makers. Some of these services are indivisibly linked to the operation of the physical infrastructure (e.g. cargo handling in modern container terminals). Most of them, however, can be unbundled from infrastructure provision and provided competitively.
- Like other transport nodes, ports are naturally destined to serve as platforms for a wide range of value-added logistics services, such as repackaging, the final assembly of goods, stock-management, warehousing, or ship and container repairs. The transformation of ports from intermodal transfer points to major distribution centers (dry ports, distriparks) is a global trend that has reached developing countries. Adequate space and policies are needed to create a favorable environment for the development of industry and distribution clusters.
- As mentioned above, different categories of traffic require specific infrastructure and involve different sets of policy issues. General cargo, and particularly containerized cargo, deserves priority attention from policy makers. These trades tend to involve high-value products and more complex policy issues than, for instance, user-owned terminals for commodity products such as oil or minerals.
- As key entry points into a country, ports are usually the location where transport flows 'hit the administration' – that is, where customs, sanitary, or immigration controls are carried out. To minimize the disruption of transport flows, these border-related procedures need to be streamlined and effectively integrated with overall port operations.

3.3 Institutional and Regulatory Reform: International Best Practice

The following functions should normally be handled by different entities: (i) the management of port infrastructure; (ii) the provision of commercial services; and (iii) the regulation of port activities. While a variety of alternative arrangements are possible, three basic operating structures for ports can be distinguished:

- In the service port, the port authority not only fulfills regulatory functions, but also operates the port assets and provides all commercial services to ships and cargo.
- In the tool port, the port authority retains regulatory functions as well as the ownership of basic infrastructure, superstructure and heavy equipment. However, it rents the equipment to independent operators who provide the commercial services.

- In the landlord port, the role of the port authority is confined to that of the regulator and the owner/developer of basic infrastructure on behalf of the government. It leases the infrastructure to private operators, who invest in superstructure and equipment to provide services to port users. The port authority has no involvement in commercial services, but merely regulates them.

The landlord port, which is becoming the standard operating model worldwide, has several advantages. It allows for the separation of regulatory and commercial functions. It permits to unbundle natural monopoly elements (like provision of basic infrastructure) from potentially competitive functions (like service provision) and thus facilitates the introduction of competition. And it creates a transparent and stable framework for the introduction of private management and investment. It is therefore not surprising that a convergence of institutional arrangements towards the landlord port model has been observed internationally. A survey of the world's 100 largest container ports found that 88 conform to the landlord model.[21] Throughout the EU, the landlord port is also becoming the norm (see box 3.3 and box 3.7).

Countries adopting the landlord port model tend to have a three-tier institutional structure. The government remains responsible for sector policy and planning; autonomous port authorities manage and regulate ports; and private companies provide commercial services. As the first tier, a central government body for sector policy and planning would normally be located at the ministerial level, or preferably an autonomous sector agency would be created to reduce political interference. It would issue key sector regulations to be enforced by the port authorities, but refrain from involvement in the day-to-day management of ports.

Autonomous port authorities should "be granted the right to use state-owned land, administer, maintain and develop port infrastructure assets to the extent required by port activities, manage and enforce navigation safety measures, enforce environmental protection regulations, monitor the concessions and lease contracts governing private sector activities in the port area, and market the port facilities to attract new investors."[22] Port authorities can be established either at the national or the regional level, depending on the size of a country. Port authorities may be public institutions (with a board including central and local government representatives) or public joint stock companies (with a board representing public and/or private shareholders and operating under commercial law). A port council should permit port users and private operators to voice their views and concerns to the port authority.

An important role of the port authority is the promotion of port development, including an assessment of development needs, the maintenance of a master plan, and the mobilization of the private sector for projects fitting that plan. Port authorities should have the right to charge cost-related user fees that allow them to recover operating expenses and capital expenditures.[23] The transfer of government subsidies to port authorities should be transparent and confined to the funding of public service obligations (e.g. the need to maintain a small port essential to the local economy) and cases of market failure (e.g. the need to build indivisible facilities well beyond

---

[21] World Bank. *Transport Subsectoral Issues at a Glance: Ports, Maritime, and Logistics*. World Bank transport website (*www.worldbank.org/transport/*).

[22] Juhel, Marc. 1998. *Globalization, Privatization, and Restructuring of Ports*. World Bank Institute. This document provides a detailed overview over the legal and institutional aspects of port reform.

[23] Normally these are port dues, including berthing fees for vessels and sometimes tonnage fees for cargo and, in the case of landlord ports, concession fees from private operators providing services on port premises. Both berthing fees and tonnage fees are normally paid through one bill by the ship owner to the port authority via the shipping agent. Especially in the tool and service port, port authorities also collect charges for the services they provide, although these are not considered port dues, but service fees.

present market needs). While subsidies should be minimized, port authorities should neither make excessive profits, as this would be equivalent to imposing taxes on imports and exports.

Box 3.3 Maritime Sector Policies in EU Countries: Some Examples

Compared to air transport, the Commission has until recently played a more limited role in the liberalization of ports in the EU. A directive on port services, however, is now being discussed (see box 3.7). To date, reforms have largely taken place at the level of individual countries, and still have some way to go:

- Great Britain: In the 1980s, Britain became the first country to hand over most large ports to the private sector. Privatization went hand-in-hand with radical reforms of dock-labor laws. These changes led to significant private investments and increases in productivity. In the late 1990s, private companies handled 70 percent of all cargo moving through British ports.[24] Despite these achievements, competition for port services tends to be limited since many ports strive to become vertically integrated monopolies.
- Belgium and Holland: The Dutch port of Rotterdam and the Belgian port of Antwerp, two of the world's largest, are in close proximity to each other and compete vigorously. Especially in Antwerp, the role of the public sector is largely confined to the ownership of basic infrastructure and to the regulation of private companies. In Antwerp, 150 shipping agents, 300 forwarders, dozens of cargo handling companies, 40 banks, and a range of other service providers compete for business. The municipal Port Authority ensures administrative control, issues concessions, operates the tug services in the docks, and plans port development. It maintains a comprehensive information processing system connecting the various parties and consults users and private operators through a consultative council.[25]
- Spain: In December 1999, a new Ports Law eliminated the state-holding company for the sector and gave a great degree of autonomy to individual port authorities. Significant investments and increasing competition are now transforming the industry.[26]
- Greece: The country's two major ports of Piraeus and Thessaloniki are being turned into joint stock companies and have launched ambitious investment and modernization programs. In November 1999, the government decided to corporatize five other ports. In the important Aegean ferry industry, private companies are in the process of spending $ 2 billion on fleet modernization in the run up to the liberalization of traffic in 2004.[27]
- Italy: In Italy, policy reforms and private participation have dramatically increased the efficiency of ports, which used to be notorious for their poor performance. Genoa, for instance, has managed to "shake off a history of labor strife, under-investment, low output and political meddling."[28] Italian customers that had re-routed traffic through Northern European ports and shipped them to Italy via land are now returning. A number of private container ports have been concessioned to private operators. The largest of them, Gioia Tauro, received its first ship in 1995 and is now handling around 2.5 million TEU.

Run by commercial managers and hardened by competition, European port operators, stevedores, and shipping lines are now playing an important part in the global consolidation of the maritime transport industry. Together with port users, they are also pushing for further sector reforms in the EU.

As the third institutional layer, private operating companies would then provide commercial services to ships and cargo on a competitive basis. While the policy issues related to this third tier will be discussed in section 3.7, it is important to unbundle infrastructure provision (a monopolistic activity) from the provision of port services (in principle a competitive activity). The draft directive of the Commission, discussed in box 3.7, provides for unbundling by obliging vertically integrated

[24] Trujillo, Lourdes and Gustavo Nombela. 2000. "Seaports." In Estache, Antonio and Ginés de Rus, eds., *Privatization and Regulation of Transport Infrastructure*. World Bank Institute.
[25] Information taken from the website of the Port of Antwerp (*www.portofantwerp.be*).
[26] Financial Times (11 March 1999).
[27] Frankfurter Allgemeine Zeitung (9 July 2001) and Financial Times (30 September 2000).
[28] The Journal of Commerce (4 April 2000).

port authorities to keep separate accounts and by permitting fair and equal access for competing providers of commercial services to port premises.

Another set of institutional and regulatory issues, that policy makers have to address in the context of port reforms are border controls (see also sections 1.8 and 1.9). Administrative procedures such as customs clearance, health checks, or controls for compliance with norms and standards have an important impact on the efficiency with which transport services are delivered. It is thus critical to make them an integral part of efforts to streamline port operations, even though they are strictly speaking not part of it. In most of the southern Mediterranean countries, inefficient trade procedures, including cumbersome customs practices, remain one of the most notorious causes for delays in ports. Reforming them is a vital ingredient of general transport reform, and at the same time a complex challenge (see also section 4.4).

An adequate institutional and regulatory framework can also play a key role in helping ports to become dynamic nodes in international distribution networks, rather than mere interfaces between land and sea transport. As discussed in the case study comparing the Panama and Suez Canals (see section 4.7), ports are increasingly being transformed into logistics platforms where all sorts of transport-related logistics services are being provided. "UNCTAD describes this evolution in defining what it called the 'third generations ports'; after having been at first merely an interface location for cargo between land and sea transport, next a transport, industrial and commercial service center, the 'third generation port' is a dynamic node in the international production/distribution network. [...] As a result, ports are more and more turning into integrated transport centers and logistic platforms for international trade."[29] Policies that induce value-adding activities to settle in port areas can include the establishment of facilities needed for distribution and logistics services within the port, the financing of the first development phases of a dry port, a favorable regulatory regime for logistics services, or the establishment of free zones to permit the provision of logistics services.

3.4 Institutional and Regulatory Reform: Priorities in the Maghreb and Mashrek

If benchmarked against international best practice, the legal and institutional framework in most of the Maghreb and Mashrek countries remains sub-optimal. Most ports continue to be over-regulated by multiple agencies with overlapping responsibilities and cumbersome organizational structures. The service port is still the predominant operating model in the region and landlord ports are practically non-existent. Commercial and regulatory functions are insufficiently separated, while regulatory regimes tend to be opaque. In the absence of competition and private participation, port operators lack the incentives to increase efficiency, innovate, and be more responsive to user needs. Some examples for recent policy reforms and remaining reform needs in the region are outlined below:

- **Lebanon:** Extensive private participation in port services ensures that the ports function reasonably well. The legal and institutional framework, however, is outdated and weak. Key sector laws have not been updated for decades. The main port of Beirut has been run by a transitory public entity with residual commercial functions since a private concession expired in 1991. Private companies in the port operate without adequate contracts and regulation and appear to have been one reason why the privatization of the container terminal failed (see below). By late 2001, the government was drafting a law for private participation in ports. Due

[29] Juhel, Marc. 1998. *Globalization, Privatization, and Restructuring of Ports*. World Bank Institute.

to institutional erosion during years of civil strife and tight budget constraints, the transport ministry's capacity for policy formulation and sector planning is limited.

- **Jordan:** Aqaba on the Red Sea is the country's only port. The state has invested more than $ 500 million in infrastructure, but the facilities operate far below their 20 million-ton/year capacity. In January 2001, the government announced its intention to move towards the landlord port operating model by privatizing commercial functions, while leaving infrastructure ownership and monitoring to the port authority.[30] In early 2001, the 380 m^2 Aqaba Special Economic Zone (SEZ) was established. This ambitious project is to attract tourism, services, and industrial ventures to the area.[31]

- **Israel:** The Israel Ports and Railway Authority controls the three ports of Haifa, Ashdod, and Eilat. The individual ports enjoy only limited autonomy in setting tariffs, planning investments, and managing their commercial operations. Large transfers from the ports to the railway company (a total of over $ 1 billion between 1988-95) have starved the ports of needed investments. Another example of the distortions caused by government intervention has been the use of fee structures to encourage exports. In 1999, wharfage for imports was more than five times that of exports (1.1 percent compared to 0.2 percent).[32] A number of important reforms, however, are now underway. Fees are being brought in line with costs. In 1999, the government decided to run ports as individual profit centers and have them compete for traffic.[33] Private participation is also being introduced (see section 3.5).

- **Syria:** Of all countries in the region, port reforms are least advanced in Syria. According to the trade journal Containerization International, "the state controls everything. The government owns the port authority which in turn supplies all the labor, including the stevedores. There is therefore no competition. Also owned by the state is the Shipping Agencies Company (ShipCo), which handles all the ships which use the port. There are no privately owned shipping agents." The periodical quotes a representative of an international shipping line about his experience with ShipCo: "It operates as per official tariffs, under the supervision of the Ministry of Transport. The staff have their hands tied by regulations, and as government civil servants, they are commercially inefficient and lack all kinds of initiatives, lest they expose themselves to liability."[34] The government is well aware of these problems and wants to modernize the sector. Tariffs are to be reduced and significant investments in the two main ports are foreseen under the ninth investment plan (2001-2005).

- **Egypt:** The Ministry of Transport controls four port authorities as well as the Ports and Lighthouses Authority, which inspects ships and maintains navigational aids. In mid-1997, the autonomy of the port authorities was formally strengthened but is still limited in practice. Through two holding companies, the government owns stevedores, shipping agencies, and shipyards. Through the Ministry of Supply, it retains ownership and control for much of the bulk storage in ports. Cross-ownership between port authorities and these state-owned service companies blurs the boundaries between regulatory and commercial functions. The port authority of Port Said, for example, owns 39 percent in Port Said Container Handling Company. By law, many of the port operating companies were set up as monopolies. Despite the recent licensing of some private operators, important port services remain de facto monopolies. Moreover, the regulatory regime needs to be streamlined and modernized. In 1997, the legal framework of Egypt's maritime sector consisted of a patchwork of several dozen laws

[30] MEED (26 January 2001).
[31] MEED (6 October 2000 and 3 August 2001).
[32] Etzioni, Amir. 1999. *Reforming Israel's Seaports*. Institute for Advanced Strategic and Political Studies.
[33] Journal of Commerce Online (11 May 2000).
[34] Containerization International (April 1999).

and decrees.[35] Some legal restrictions to private ownership of assets or to the right of establishment for foreign companies persist. In an important reform move, Egypt abolished legal restrictions to private participation in maritime services in 1998. More recently, the government has been considering the introduction of the landlord port model.

Box 3.4 Port Reforms in Colombia

A 1991 sector law established the General Port Superintendent as the regulator of port concessions and "defined conditions of operation to ensure free and fair competition among port societies and among port operators. [...] Privatizing the general cargo ports took three years, during which the legal reforms were put in place and [port assets were evaluated]. A separate concession was offered for each port. The concessionaires can set tariffs within guidelines established by the port regulator, and they are obliged to work with the government on future investment plans. The concessions were awarded to the highest lease offer for twenty years, within an ownership structure that encourages a 70/30 split between the private and public sectors, with the government retaining ownership of the port infrastructure. [...] New laws abolished restrictive labor practices and have allowed stevedoring services to compete freely at each port. The liberalization of labor practices along with the privatization of port services has resulted in large and rapid improvements in productivity, lower fees for port users, and very attractive returns for the concessionaires. Productivity levels are higher than in most newly privatized ports in other Latin American countries – where in many cases the ports have been privatized with limited competition. The improvements have been realized with low initial investments, though recently the port societies have gone beyond investing in shoreside equipment and are starting to invest in infrastructure expansion."

Vessel waiting times, averaging ten days in the early 1990s, have practically been eliminated. Working days per year have increased from 280 to 365 and working hours per day from 16 to 24. Tons handled per vessel and day increased from 500 to 2,500 for bulk cargo and from 750 to 1,700 for general cargo between 1993 and 1996. Private investment between 1993 and 2000 is estimated at $ 469 million. "The increases in productivity have prompted many global shipping lines to begin including port calls in Colombia. And the concessionaires' success has ensured a steady flow of lease revenue for the government, amounting to $ 25 million in 1996. [...] As a result of the increase in productivity and the competition among ports [...] and among stevedores at each port, shipping lines and importers and exporters have enjoyed some of the lowest stevedoring and port services rates in South America for the past several years. Between 1994 and 1996 rates fell in real terms by more than 50 percent. And rates per container have dropped from well over $ 600 to less than $ 150." Despite these impressive results, a couple of negative lessons have also emerged from the Colombian experience. Uncertainty about the terms of the concession agreements deterred foreign investors and experienced international operators, thus reducing the government's lease revenue. Second, "ambiguity about the regulator's role has allowed the regulator to become more interventionist over time."

Source: Gaviria, Juan. 1998. "Port Privatization and Competition in Colombia". World Bank Viewpoint Note Series 167.

- **Algeria:** The country's ten service ports used to have the status of autonomous public enterprises, overseen by a state holding company. With these port enterprises as monopolistic providers of all services on their premises, neither private participation nor competition were permitted in Algerian ports. In principle, a new maritime sector law (98/05 of June 1998, modifying the law from 1976) opened commercial activities to private participants, while delegating regulatory functions to the port authorities. Three regional port authorities were created by decree in 1999.[36] The provisions of the new law, however, have not yet been fully implemented through detailed regulations and institutional reforms.

- **Morocco:** Both regulatory and operational functions are essentially carried out by the same public entity, the Office d'Exploitation des Ports (ODEP), even though by law they are formally separated. Private participation in port operations and management is limited. As in Tunisia,

[35] World Bank. 1998. *Egypt Ports Sector Note* (draft, January 1998).
[36] Maghreb Weekly Monitor, 77th issue (4 April 2000).

private stevedores operate on board ships, but depend largely on the equipment of ODEP. On land, ODEP has the monopoly for the main cargo handling operations. Overall, handling prices are high and productivity is low for general cargo, containers, and RoRo. ODEP uses the monopoly rents extracted from larger ports such as Casablanca to cross-subsidize loss-making facilities. The responsible ministry is Le Ministère de l'Equipement. The main opposition against port sector reforms comes from dock workers and ODEP.

- **Tunisia:** The new sector law, Code des Ports Maritimes de Commerce, introduces the concept of port authority, foresees the creation of two consultative bodies for port users, and provides a basis for the award of concessions. This new legal framework permits the creation of landlord ports and the introduction of private participation. The Office de la Marine Marchande et des Ports (OMMP) was created in 1998 through a merger between the Direction General de la Marine Marchande and the Office des Ports Nationaux Tunisien (OPNT) – a move towards a concentration of regulatory functions under a single agency. OMMP owns and develops the country's ports, including Gabès as the latest addition. It has a monopoly for pilotage and towage, and still owns and operates all cranes. The plan to transfer cargo storage and custodial functions to the private sector in secondary ports has been postponed pending resolution of the cargo handling and dock worker issues (see below). Cargo handling is opened to private companies in secondary ports, but a public enterprise has a monopoly in Radès and La Goulette – which account for most of Tunisia's general cargo. In summary, important reforms have been introduced, but more could be done to introduce competition and to upgrade the role of the private sector. As far as border-related red tape is concerned, clearance procedures have long been a major source of delays. However, the government is now addressing this problem. In the port of Tunis, for instance, customs procedures were simplified and opening hours increased.[37]

3.5 Introducing Private Participation in Port Investment and Port Management

An important objective of sector reform is to re-define the respective roles of the public and private sector and create an enabling environment for private participation. This section looks at private participation in port investments and ports operations, while the next section will discuss the reforms required to introduce competition in these activities. The introduction of private participation and competition in port services is discussed in sections 3.7 and 3.8.

Due to technological change and high traffic growth, new port and terminal capacity will be needed throughout the region. Policy reforms can help improve the capacity utilization of existing physical infrastructure and thus reduce the need for investments. Higher vessel turn around times can raise berth throughput. Streamlined customs clearance can release storage space for more productive use. Private management can optimize the flow of vessels and cargo through ports and thus eliminate slack from the current system. Nonetheless, past under-investment and poor maintenance, changing trading patterns (e.g. containerization, increase in vessel size), and growth will still require significant investments in physical infrastructure.

Ports have three layers of assets: (i) land and water, (ii) infrastructure, and (iii) superstructure and equipment. Besides these assets, labor is the other important factor of production in ports (see sections 3.8 and 3.9 on labor issues). "Asset ownership and asset operations are two distinct matters. However, there are combinations of ownership and operations structures which have

[37] North Africa Journal, 109th issue (26 June 2001).

proved over time to be more or less conducive to cost-effective use of assets and to overall efficiency in the delivery of port services."[38]

- Land and water (e.g. port grounds, access areas) should normally remain government property to maintain public control over long-term planning for these strategic assets. Concessions and other instruments permit the transfer of substantial operational rights and quasi-property rights to private operators, without transferring ownership.
- The actual port infrastructure can be sub-divided into basic infrastructure – breakwaters, channels, docks, inland transport connections – and operational infrastructure, such as berths. Most governments continue to fund investments in basic infrastructure. Operational infrastructure is more commonly transferred to private ownership than the former, but the optimal extent and conditions for transfer depend on specific circumstances. To encourage adequate investment in and the maintenance of operational asset located on public land, a lease or concession should be long enough to cover the amortization period of investments.
- With regard to superstructure and equipment – including pavement, warehouses, and cranes – the global trend is unambiguously towards private ownership. It should be noted that investment costs for superstructure and equipment can be higher than those for infrastructure. For modern container terminals they can be up to twice as high.

The preferred policy instrument for the involvement of the private sector in the port investment and operations are build-operate-transfer (BOT) concessions.[39] More than 100 port concessions contracts have been signed world-wide, mostly for container terminals.[40] The majority of these projects are in Latin America and Asia (see diagram 3.2). "A concession [...] is a legal arrangement in which a firm obtains from the government the right to provide a particular service. Concessions can be used to create competition for the market under conditions in which the service provider has significant market power."[41]

Diagram 3.2 Port Projects with Private Participation in Developing Countries by Region (1990–99)

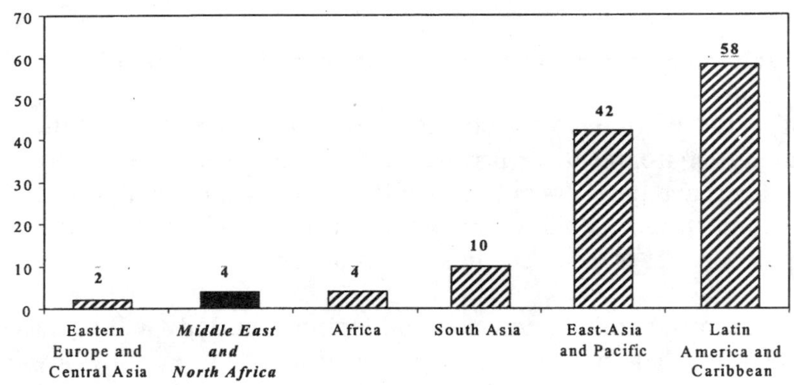

Source: World Bank (PPI Database).

[38] Juhel, Marc. 1998. *Globalization, Privatization, and Restructuring of Ports*. World Bank Institute.
[39] A wide variety of concession arrangements exist, including Build-Own-Operate (BOO), Build-Own-Operate-Transfer (BOOT), Furnish-Own-Operate (FOO).
[40] Juhel, Marc. 1998. *Globalization, Privatization and Restructuring Ports*. World Bank Institute.
[41] Kerf, Michel et al. 1998. *Concessions for Infrastructure – A Guide to their Design and Award*. World Bank. A natural monopoly exists if economies of scale (i.e. high fixed costs for infrastructure and equipment) make it economically more efficient to have only one supplier in a market. In the absence of competition in the market, it is important that a concession (the right to be the one supplier) be tendered competitively' in order to create competition for the market. Like any natural monopoly, a concession needs to be regulated to prevent an abuse of market power. It can be regulated by contract (i.e. through provisions of the concession contract) or by law (i.e. the

Several MPs have started to introduce private participation in port investment and operations. As the following examples show, however, the use of concessions in the southern Mediterranean region is thus far largely confined to stevedoring concessions for new container and bulk terminals.

- **Egypt:** Since a 1998 law legalized private participation in port investment and operation, a number of projects have been launched. For the new container port in East Port Said, Egypt chose the BOT model. Following an international tender, the government signed a 30-year concession with a consortium led by ECT International of the Netherlands and Maersk of Denmark in August 1999.[42] The private venture, Suez Canal Container Handling Company, plans to invest $ 480 million in the port. Annual capacity will one million TEU and might increase to three million TEU in a second phase. The government provides the basic port infrastructure, including dredging, breakwater work, and quay walls for $ 211 million. The port is expected to become operational in late 2003 and will mainly handle transshipment traffic.[43] While this project sets an important precedent, the process that let to it was erratic. The government had started exclusive negotiations with a potential investor, before eventual opting for a competitive tender. It originally wanted the concessionaire to also take over the management of existing facilities in Port Said and Damietta, which would have reduced competition. Finally, it wanted several state-owned companies to participate in the consortium, before accepting full privatization. A second BOT port is under construction as part of the privately developed 2,400 hectare Suez Development Zone at the southern end of the Suez Canal. The government is providing the basic infrastructure, including quay walls ($ 60 million) and dredging ($ 105 million). A private consortium, Sukhna Port Development Company, will operate the port. It includes Stevedoring Services of America (25 percent) and the local partner OCI, which is also one of the main investors in the development zone. A third 30-year concession for the construction of a bulk terminal was to be given to two petroleum companies, who applied to build a $ 50 million oil products pier for their own use in the port of Alexandria.[44] Further BOT projects for tourism and passenger services in this port are under discussion.[45]

- **Lebanon:** After a general concession for the port of Beirut expired in 1991, a transitory public entity (Commission Provisoire) took over the management of common use areas and the provision of storage and certain handling services. Grain silo and handling facilities are managed by the Ministry of the Economy. In early 1999, the Lebanese government awarded a 20-year concession for new container terminal in the Dubai Port Authority (DPA). While other parts of the port will continue to handle general cargo and some bulk traffic, the concessionaire has a monopoly on container handling. The port authority invested $ 150 million in quays and other basic infrastructure, leaving the funding of $ 60 million for gantry cranes and other equipment to the private investor. The terminal was designed to have a capacity of 500,000 TEU with the possibility of a further expansion to one million TEU. With domestic traffic currently limited to about 150,000 TEU, much of this is to be used for transshipment and gateway traffic to the Middle East. Bids were on the basis of income per container, which operators were prepared to receive. At $ 84, the DPA offered less than half of the second bidder ($ 183). In mid-2001, however, DPA withdrew from the contract. Apparent reasons were traffic projections that turned out to be unrealistic, as well as difficulties of the authorities to resolve

---

general regulatory framework). Many countries have cross-sectoral concession laws that define key principles related to the award, design, design, or monitoring of concessions.

[42] MEED (20 August 1999 and 26 January 2001). The two foreign companies own 60 percent of the venture, local investor Kamel 10 percent, National Bank of Egypt 5 percent and other local investors 25 percent. The only other bidder was the Australian P&O Ports. (Financial Times, 20 August 1999).

[43] MEED (8 March 2002).

[44] MEED (25 June 1999).

[45] MEED (12 January 2001).

labor issues and compensate stevedoring contractors operating in the port. The government hired advisors to re-privatize the terminal and possibly the entire port by the end of 2002.

- **Jordan:** Aqaba, the country's only port, is state-owned but a furnish-own-operate concession has been awarded for a new industrial jetty. The government is financing the actual construction for $ 25 million and awarded that contract to the Korean contractor Hyundai in February 1999. Five international bidders for the concession were prequalified in December 1999. The 50 meter jetty is supposed to handle mineral products and is part of a broader effort to mobilize private funds to develop phosphate and other mineral exports. In the same year, a Finnish-Jordanian joint venture agreed to invest $ 100 million in a fertilizer plant in Aqaba, supported by a $ 30 million loan from the EIB. It is to process the raw material and thus permit the country to export higher value-added products. A third component in this cluster of projects is the BOT concession for the Aqaba railway, which was supposed to provide improved hinterland connections but ran into difficulties due to the loss of a large client (see section 4.3). As part of its plan to develop a free zone in Aqaba (see section 3.4), the government is considering further privatization projects in the port.

- **Israel:** The country has two large Mediterranean ports – the northern port of Haifa (17 million tons, mainly container and grain traffic) and the southern port of Ashdod (16 million tons, mainly general and bulk cargo). In the face of congestion and further traffic growth, an ambitious expansion plan for Ashdod is under implementation. A total of $ 500 million are to be invested in a new terminal close to the existing facilities. For $ 250 million, the government is supplying the basic infrastructure. "The other $ 250 million consists of gantry cranes, railways, equipment and other infrastructure that will be built privately under a build-operate-transfer concession."[46] The new Hayovel port should be able to handle 500,000 million TEU and 2.5 million tons of general cargo per annum.[47]

- **Turkey:** In May 1999, the Turkish government agreed on a 46-year BOT scheme for a 1 million TEU container port at Derince, 80 km east of Istanbul. Two years later, however, the deal had not yet been closed. The private joint venture is 60 percent-owned by P&O, which already has an international network of 27 terminals and should provide management expertise. The balance is held by the local construction company Enka, which is to build the terminal. The facility is estimated to cost more than $ 200 million and would be Turkey's first large modern container terminal. Other than East Port Said, which is positioning itself as a transshipment hub, Derince will mainly handle direct imports and exports. Unlike its Egyptian counterpart, which is strategically sited at the entrance of the Suez Canal, Derince is not located on key international trade routes. Instead, it has a trade-generating hinterland (the industrial region of Izmit) and good road and rail connections.[48] Three smaller private ports already exist in Turkey. Gemport (operational since 1992) and Sedef (1993) are each handling less than 100,000 TEU per annum; the throughput of Kumport (1996) was around 200,000 TEU.[49]

- **Morocco:** Privatization of port operations is generally less advanced in the Maghreb than in the Mashrek. In Morocco, the first private concession after the nationalization of private ports in the wake of the country's independence, was the coal terminal of Jorf Lasfar. A specialized terminal and railway bring imported coal to the region's large private power plant. Under a 20-year concession, the Jorf Lasfar Energy Company finances extensions and maintenance, while paying normal port dues and a yearly concession fee to ODEP. The only other significant concession project that has been under negotiation is that of a new container terminal in

[46] Journal of Commerce Online (6 June 2000).
[47] Israeli Ports and Railways Authority. 1999. *Sea of Challenges – Overview of Israeli Ports Development Plan.*
[48] P&O press release (4 May 1999).
[49] Drewry Shipping Consultants. 2000. *Mediterranean Container Ports and Shipping.*

Tanger-Atlantique. The transshipment hub with a total capacity of between 500,000 and 1,000,000 TEU and an investment volume of $ 300 to 400 million was originally supposed to open in 2004. In early 1998, two of the five prequalifiers declined to bid, and in April 1999 the government signed a negotiating memorandum with Bouygues of France. A full concession contract, however, was never agreed upon. The bidding process was criticized for being non-transparent and the commercial viability of the project was questioned because of the port's limited hinterland. In July 2001, Bouygues submitted a revised proposal. In early 2002, rumors surfaced that the port would not be built on the Atlantic, but at a more favorable location on the Mediterranean coast, with deep-water access and close to a planned coastal highway leading to the Algerian border.[50] It remains to be seen if this project will ever be implemented.

Diagram 3.3 The Range of Privatization Techniques

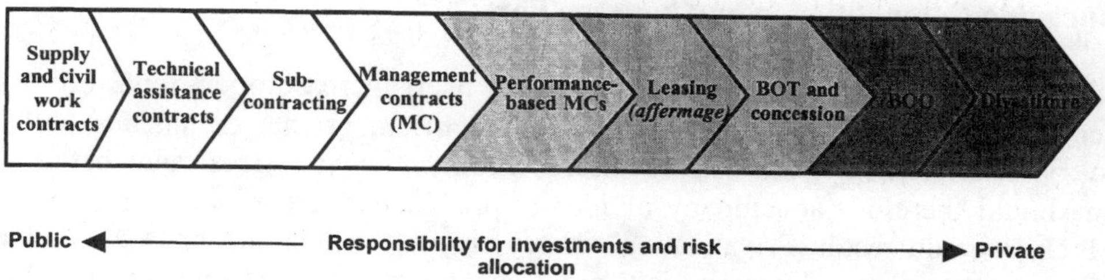

Source: Pierre Guislain.

"Private involvement can take many forms, depending on the intended degree of risk to be transferred from the public to the private sector. The spectrum runs from management contracts with performance-related fees for leasing (responsibilities for operations and maintenance but not for major investments) to full concessions (responsibility for investment but with an obligation to return assets to the government) to actual sale of public assets. At one extreme the government cedes the least control but retains the most risk, while at the other the government hands over all control (except what it retains through regulatory mechanisms) and the private investor or operator assumes most risk."[51]

As these examples show, the optimal delineation of public and private investments and responsibilities, as well the allocation of risks and revenues within these public-private partnerships, can vary greatly. Contract parameters include the length of the concession period; the magnitude and structure of concession fees; the regulatory regime for port charges and service standards; and the possible inclusion of existing facilities in addition to the construction of new ones.[52] The optimal design of a concession will be a function both of the specific circumstances of the project (e.g. expected traffic levels, competition from other ports, total investments required) and the negotiations between the involved parties. While the private sector should normally take on as much commercial risk and investment responsibility as possible, some government involvement might be required (e.g. the provision of basic infrastructure and access connections to land transport).[53] The careful design of the concession contract, a transparent and competitive international tender, and a stable regulatory regime are all important prerequisites for success.

---

[50] Al Hayat (20 February 2002).

[51] Smith, Graham, Nemat Shafik, Pierre Guislain and James Reichert. 1997. *Getting Connected – Private Participation in Infrastructure in the Middle East and North Africa*. World Bank.

[52] The *concession period* should be long enough to permit the amortization of investments required by the concessionaire (depreciation period of assets). Periodical re-tendering of concessions increases competition over time and allows the government to modify the concession arrangements as circumstances change.

[53] A basic rule for the *allocation of risk* is that the contracting party which is best positioned to reduce specific risks should bear them (e.g. the government in case of political risk, private companies in the case of commercial risk).

As mentioned above, private participation in southern Mediterranean port operations has thus far been limited to new container and bulk facilities. The primary motive for private sector participation has been fiscal constraints and less the wish to increase sector efficiency. Precedents for the privatization of existing facilities, or for facilities serving other trades than containers, are hard to come by. Malta could become the first MP to privatize its major port for an estimated $ 100 million.[54] Cyprus also invited expression of interests for a concession to redevelop the Larnaca port in late 2001. On the northern shore of the Mediterranean, this process is much more advanced. Italy, for instance, has more than ten privately operated container terminals, while Spain has at least five.[55] Given the range of privatization instruments at their disposal, MP governments should start to transfer existing ports to private operators. This would not only help to raise revenue, but more importantly, mobilize investments and increase the efficiency of existing ports.

3.6 Encouraging Competition in and between Ports

Introducing private participation in ports will in itself increase operational efficiency, but unless it is complemented by the introduction of competition, private companies will have no incentives to pass efficiency gains on to users through lower prices and better services. Liberalization should therefore accompany or ideally precede privatization. If the reverse is the case, policy lock-in could result. Privatization creates property rights and once assets have been transferred to the private sector, liberalization might encounter legal obstacles or vested interests. Moreover, private investors will pay lower prices for assets if the regulatory framework is still in flux (i.e. they will demand a premium for regulatory risk). In many cases, particularly in port services, competition can be easily introduced by simply removing legal constraints. In others, however, pro-competitive regulation will be required to successfully trigger competitive dynamics. Competitive tendering of concessions is one mechanism to introduce competition in monopolistic port activities. Intermodal competition, particularly between maritime and air transport, also exists for certain user groups, cargo categories, and hinterlands (see section 1.5).

A tool for the introduction of competition in large ports is their sub-division into different concessions with similar traffic capacity. As discussed in box 3.5, this model was successfully applied in Argentina when the government reformed the maritime sector in the early 1990s. While the port of Buenos Aires is unusually large, some of the bigger ports in the Maghreb and Mashrek countries could conceivably be split up into competing entities. Possible candidates might be the Egyptian twin-port of Alexandria and Dekheila, which are currently both under the control of the Alexandria Port Authority. Other ports where this option could be considered are Casablanca as well as the Tunisian ports of Radès and La Goulette, which are currently operated as one entity (i.e. the same public stevedoring monopoly, the same port authority). Due to fixed costs for equipment and other scale economies, port operators need to exceed a certain size threshold to become profitable (e.g. about 100,000 TEU/year for container handling). An alternative for the introduction of competition in smaller ports can be the tool port operating model (see section 3.3), where the port authority retains ownership over large equipment and rents it to competing operators.

Another potential form of competition is that between different ports. As long as the hinterlands that ports serve overlap, shippers and consignees can chose between them. For competition between ports to take hold, maritime sector reforms should ensure that ports with overlapping hinterlands are operated by different entities. Policy makers can also stimulate inter-port competition by

[54] Financial Times (19 November 2001) and Reuters Business Briefing (16 May 2001).

[55] Drewry Shipping Consultants. 2000. *Mediterranean Container Ports and Shipping.*

extending their hinterlands (and the overlaps between them) through the development of land-based transport or the creation of more efficient modal interfaces. Competition between ports is particularly effective for container and RoRo traffic (which can flexibly and easily transfer to land-based modes and thus reach extended hinterlands), as well as for container transshipment.[56]

Box 3.5 Port Reforms in Argentina

Inefficiencies and high costs in maritime transport prompted the Argentinean government to "deregulate, decentralize, and concession the sector and organize competition within it [...]. Between 1990 and 1993, the government abolished most of the restrictive regulations governing working practices at ports and on vessels. [...] Argentine ship-owners were allowed to temporarily register their ships under foreign flags and thus benefit from lower requirements on crew size. Contracting arrangements with stevedoring companies were freed up, pilotage and towage services were deregulated and operators allowed to establish their own tariffs. Foreign ships were allowed to practice cabotage. And other labor agreements and norms that were hampering productivity in port operations were abolished." The administration of ports was decentralized. All major ports "were transferred to the provinces, subject to the creation of port administration entities. Conceived as nonprofit organizations charged with owning and maintaining the port's infrastructure and common use areas [...] these entities are governed by shippers and representatives of provincial and local governments. They are required to lease the port terminals as concessions and will receive fees from the concessionaire for the use of the infrastructure. Any profits have to be invested in the port."

The government estimates that the overall cost savings resulting from port deregulation and privatization amount to $ 156 million per year. "Decentralization has led to the closure of the small, unprofitable ports transferred to the provinces, with large net savings. Most of the savings have come from improved labor productivity, however. [...] The combination of deregulation, competition, and privatization has led to dramatic reductions in port charges and in barge and ocean shipping tariffs. Charges for shipping containers between Argentina and Northern Europe declined by 30 to 70 percent in less than two years. [...] Maritime tariffs have fallen by up to 40 to 50 percent for cargo movements that were previously reserved for Argentine flag ships. [...] Most of the benefits achieved would not have been realized without coordinating all the agencies involved in the business of ports – including the police and customs. This integrated policy approach has meant significantly lower transaction costs than occurred under the uncoordinated monitoring and policing by multiple agencies before the reform. Much of the credit for this approach goes to the strong reform team of the undersecretary of ports. Still pending is the organization of an independent national port authority to act as regulator and as monitor of the concessions."

An interesting aspect of the Argentinean reform model was the mechanism used for the introduction of competition in the port of Buenos Aires, one of the largest in Latin America. After the bulk liquid port Dock Sud was transferred to the province, the general cargo area, Puerto Nuevo, which remained under national jurisdiction, was sub-divided into six terminals. Each of them was concessioned out to the private sector for 18-25 years, going to the bidder offering the highest annual fee. Contracts include annual investment targets, with cofinancing from the port authority. While every concessionaire has exclusivity rights for loading and unloading services at its terminal, dynamic competition between the six 'ports within the port' guaranteed rapid increases in operating efficiency and the passing on of cost savings to users. Between 1991 and 1995, cargo handled increased by half from four to six million tons; containers handled from 300,000 to 540,000 tons; and productivity from 800 to 3,000 tons per worker and year. The average dwell time for full containers declined from 2.5 to 1.5 days; the cost of container imports from $ 450 to $ 120/ton; and port tariffs for exports from $ 6.7 to $ 3.0/ton and for imports from $ 2.1 to $ 1.5/ton.

Source: Carbajo, José and Antonio Estache. 1996. "Competing Private Ports – Lessons from Argentina". World Bank Viewpoint Series 100.

[56] One of the cases where competition in or between ports is less of an issue are *private-use industrial ports*. Algeria's extensive oil exports, for example, are loaded to tankers in three purpose-build terminals. Both the ports and the oil company are publicly owned, but by different entities. The phosphate mined in Morocco and Jordan is brought to world markets through special bulk terminals. In Tunisia, the national oil company Trapsa owns the port of Skhira. Single commodity terminals should generally be concessioned to the main industrial operator.

In Egypt, for instance, Port Said (currently handling mainly hinterland traffic) could compete for transshipment traffic with Damietta (the main transshipment hub) as well as with the new BOT container port in East Port Said that is currently under construction. Thanks to similar capacity and geographic proximity, Port Said and Alexandria should be well placed to compete with each other for gateway traffic. In fact, all key ports of the country – Damietta, Alexandria, Port Said, and Suez – are in equal distance from the Nile delta, where 90 percent of Egypt's population lives. However, since all four ports are owned by the government and do not operate on a commercial basis, this balance of power is not translated into dynamic competition. One of the prerequisites for competition between ports is their ability to set port charges. In several countries of the region, including Egypt, port dues are not only set by decree but are also at the same level for all ports, regardless of actual costs.

In cases where port hinterlands extend across national borders, ports from neighboring countries may compete productively. Governments play an important role in promoting such competition by removing administrative bottlenecks at land borders to allow ports to extend their hinterlands into neighboring countries. Efficient land-based infrastructure and transport services will also be needed. An example of such competition is Rotterdam and Antwerp. Europe's two largest ports are located about 90 kilometers away from each other across the Dutch-Belgian border. Both are key entry points into the borderless EU Single Market and compete to the benefit of their users and their host economies. With a turnover of more than € 40 billion, the port of Rotterdam accounts for about 10 percent of Dutch GDP.[57] Another example of such dynamics is the port of Barcelona, which is expanding aggressively to compete with other Spanish ports – but also with northern European ports such as Amsterdam and Rotterdam. Spain will be adopting the European rail gauge by 2004 and the port is currently building a new rail terminal to take advantage of its expanded hinterland. A logistics zone already "manages warehouses and offices for 50 companies" and is supposed to triple in size from 67 to 259 hectares. The port increased overall cargo throughput by 60 percent and container throughput by 180 percent over the past decade; it intends to mobilize another € 1.8 billion of public and private investments by 2012; and it plans to again double the amount of goods handled by 2015.[58]

In the Maghreb and Mashrek countries there are several pairs of ports with potentially overlapping hinterlands. Two of Algeria's three key ports for general cargo are close to the border. Oran in West Algeria is about 200 kilometers from the port of Nador, a potential Moroccan competitor. Annaba in the east of the country is less than 100 kilometers from the Tunisian border and about 250 kilometers from the ports of Tunis. Gabès, in southern Tunisia, is approximately 300 kilometers from Tripoli. Haifa, which handles 46 percent of all maritime freight in Israel, is only 50 kilometers from the Lebanese border. Syria's Lattakia and Lebanon's Beirut ports are both within a 100 kilometer-radius of a common border. Aqaba in Jordan and Eilat in Israel are virtually door-to-door on the Red Sea.

The main obstacle for inter-port competition and a cross-country optimization of logistics flows within the region are of a political nature. There are a number of cases where new infrastructure is required to extend port hinterlands (see box 1.8 and section 4.1). However, several land borders such as the ones between Morocco and Algeria or between Israel and Lebanon have been closed for years. In other cases, customs procedures, tariffs, and other administrative hurdles often discourage transit traffic that would be desirable from an economic point of view. An extreme example is a Syrian law that prohibits imports and exports to the country to be processed by non-Syrian ports.[59]

[57] Financial Times Deutschland (23 August 2001).

[58] Financial Times (12 March 2002).

[59] The enforcement mechanism for this law is the letter of credit (see section 2.7). The L/C for all goods imported into Syria has a blacklist of conditions, including the prohibition of transshipment through foreign ports. Upon completion of a transaction, the buyer presents the L/C and bill of lading to the bank, which verifies that all

The creation of the Euro-Mediterranean free-trade area will remove many of these obstacles. Governments would be well advised to accelerate these reforms and prepare their domestic ports for the resulting opportunities and for increasing competition.

Box 3.6 Competing Gateways to the Middle East

Large parts of Syria, Jordan and especially Iraq are far from the sea and often much closer to a foreign rather than to a domestic port. The Damascus area, where about a third of Syria's 15 million inhabitants live, is much closer to the ports of Beirut and Haifa than to the domestic coastline. The nearest port for Amman, and thus for the majority of Jordan's population and industry, is not Aqaba but Haifa and Ashdod in Israel. Transportation costs for Mediterranean traffic to and from Jordan would "drop significantly once handled via Mediterranean ports and Israel, rather than through the Suez Canal and around the Sinai Peninsula to Aqaba, some 300 kilometers from Jordan's capital and economic center, Amman. A recent study of the economic impact of constructing a deep-sea port in Gaza estimated that using such a port would reduce the costs of transporting merchandise into Jordan by $ 11.7 per ton of general and containerized cargo and by $ 2.8 per ton of bulk cargo ($ 7.7 per ton on a weighted average basis)."[60] At the same time, the port of Aqaba has a competitive advantage for east-of-Suez trade to and from Israel. Israeli traders already export around three million tons of goods through the Jordanian port, while using it for about one million tons of imports.[61] Transit traffic already accounts for 60 percent of Aqaba's throughput. Policies to encourage such trades include a recent reduction of port tariffs and an upgrading of hinterland connections. In 1999, the Amman-Aqaba highway, for instance, became a dual carriageway along its entire length.[62]

In the context of the Oslo peace process, the government of Israel prepared studies on several infrastructure projects that would extend the hinterland of its Mediterranean and Red Sea ports. These include the completion and overhaul of railway connections from Haifa to Jordan and Syria, a bridge and road link from Haifa to Jordan, and the extension of the Israeli railway network to the Red Sea ports of Eilat and Aqaba.[63] Israel's two main ports of Haifa and Ashdod are already large by regional standards (19 and 16 million tons in 2000) and further expansion is underway.[64] The new Hayonel terminal in Ashdod will have an initial capacity of 500,000 TEU and 2.5 million tons of general cargo per year.[65]

However, the potentially biggest prize for the competing ports of Syria, Lebanon, Israel, Jordan (and possibly a new port in Gaza) is Iraq. Syria plans to build a highway from Lattakia, 100 kilometers inland, to Ariha to improve the port's hinterland connections.[66] Before the civil war, Beirut was an important entry point for maritime traffic to Syria and Iraq. In an effort to regain that function, a new container terminal is being constructed. Despite new infrastructure and higher efficiency than Syrian ports, a Syrian law prohibits cargo going to and from the Syria to be processed through foreign ports. During the Iraq-Iran war, Aqaba took over the function as the main access route into Iraq. However, for the ports of the Levant (particularly for west-of-Suez shipments) and the Red Sea (mainly for east-of-Suez traffic), large parts of Iraq can be considered contested hinterland. Once the UN embargo on that country is lifted, those ports that offer competitive services, low costs, efficient hinterland connections, and convenient access to global shipping routes will become the key gateways to the Middle East.

---

conditions have been met before releasing payment to the seller. The certificate of origin, a legal document accompanying all internationally traded goods, further facilitates the enforcement of the law.

[60] Tovias, Alfred. 1997. *Options for Mashrek-Israeli Regionalism.* Centre for European Policy Studies Research Report No. 67. The study cited is: Hirsch, S. and S. Katznelson and D. Sasson. 1993. *The Economics and Politics of a Free Economic Zone and Port in the Gaza Region*. Israel Institute of Business Research.

[61] MEED (29 October 1999).

[62] Ports Corporation Aqaba. 2000. *The Port of Aqaba – Handbook and Directory 1999/2000.*

[63] Government of Israel. 1996. *Programs for Regional Cooperation 1997* (draft, November 1996).

[64] Eurostat (MED-Trans database).

[65] MEED (26 May 2000).

[66] MEED (8 December 2000).

In summary, few of the above-mentioned conditions for competition are met in the southern Mediterranean region. The shipping market is small by international standards and competition in port services will be difficult to achieve in many secondary ports. With most ports publicly owned and not commercialized, port operators have little incentive to compete. In several of the MPs, charges are not only determined by the government, but are also set at the same level for all ports. Only a handful of private port concessions have been awarded throughout the region and thus competition through new entry of private port operators is the exception. With poor hinterland connections and many land borders closed for security concerns or political reasons, cross-border competition between ports is limited. This contrasts with the EU, where cross-border port competition is working well and where. Thanks to the abolition of controls at land borders, extended hinterland connections, commercial port management, and effective price competition, few European ports can rely on a captive market.

3.7 Port Services: Introducing Private Participation and Competition

Physical port infrastructure, whose ownership and operational structures have been discussed in the two previous sections, serves as the platform on which a multitude of transport services is provided. For inbound cargo, the sequence of services starts with the entry of the vessel into the port area, continues with the unloading, storage, and processing of goods, and ends with their transfer to land-based modes. These services can be broadly categorized into services to vessels (or sea-side services) and services to cargo (or land-side services). As discussed above, the role of the public sector in landlord ports should be confined to the creation of a transparent regulatory framework to ensure fair market access and competition between private operators. The port authority should be the public counterpart for private companies.

The introduction of competition and private participation in most of these services is a relatively straightforward matter. In some cases, the provision of services by competing private operators can be achieved by simply removing legal barriers to entry and ensuring their physical access to the port area. In cases where the provision of services involves the use of heavy equipment and specialized infrastructure (particularly container handling), service provision is more closely linked to issues of infrastructure investment and port operations (see section 3.5). As elaborated upon in box 3.7, the Commission has prepared a draft directive on market access for port services. It is intended to ensure fair and transparent competition and should accelerate the trend towards the landlord port model, which can be observed across Europe.

The main port services and the respective scope for private participation and competition are outlined below. The main cost driver in cargo movements through ports is handling charges, and increasing efficiency of this service should be a priority. Depending on cargo type and traffic levels, different mechanisms can be used to introduce competition and private participation.

- Container handling includes the transfer of containers to and from the vessel, stacking them for storage, and moving them to and from trucks or railway chasses. In modern container terminals, cargo handling requires specialized heavy equipment (e.g. container gantry cranes, grain silos, oil pipelines) and thus involves high fixed costs. The full integration of all ship-to-gate operations under unified management is required for efficient service provision. The combined concessioning of terminal infrastructure and stevedoring is thus the norm. The design and regulation of such concessions should ensure that the monopoly is not abused. There should also be restrictions to cross-ownership in potentially competing ports.

- General cargo handling requires different equipment and involves fewer scale economies. Hence, there is less justification for vertical integration between infrastructure investments and management on the one hand and service provision on the other hand. The two should be unbundled and general cargo stevedoring should be open to competing private companies, with some minimum requirements regarding capitalization and performance. In small to medium multipurpose ports (i.e. below around 500,000 tons of general cargo per annum), the tool port formula may be the preferable operating model. The port authority or a regulated private company would retain ownership over the equipment, while renting it out to competing private companies. An alternative is to have competing private stevedores rent equipment through a company they jointly own (equipment pool).

- To provide warehousing and storage services (often in conjunction with stevedoring services), private companies should be permitted to lease existing storage facilities or available space to construct their own warehouses. The lease period should be sufficient to permit a recuperation of investments. The allocation of space and the conditions of the lease should be guided by the goal to maximize competition and efficiency. In most large and medium ports, effective competition between providers of storage services is feasible. Again, certain performance standards should be set by the port authority as the regulator.

- On shore, shipping lines are usually represented by shipping agents and brokerage firms. These deal with customs, immigration, and port authorities on their behalf. On the cargo side, consignees use freight forwarders to deal with shipping line representatives as well as port and customs administrations. The provision of services by such intermediaries within the port area should be fully open to private participation and competition. Legal monopolies and provision of these services by public entities just leads to rent seeking and high costs for users. Requirements to use a different agent within ports than outside also undermine the ability to optimize the overall logistics chain. All regulations that unduly obstructs the operation of these intermediaries should be removed.

- Bunkering – the provision of fuel, water, power, and waste management to vessels – should be left to competing private companies. The most important of these is the provision of fuel, which is usually delivered by barges.[67] In some of these countries, service port authorities or other state-owned companies even operate shipbuilding and ship repair facilities. Egypt, for example, still had six publicly-owned shipyards in the late 1990s. The largest one, in Alexandria, has 6,000 employees and generates significant losses. All such activities should be privatized or simply discontinued if they are unprofitable.

- Ocean vessels may need towage for maneuvering in locks and exact positioning within the port and quay area by small tug boats. These tug services can be provided under a concession by private companies that own the boats they use. It is important that the port authority sets and enforces safety and quality standards for this activity. In order to navigate ships within the port area and through access channels, pilots may have to come on board to assist the captain. While pilotage has become a private enterprise in most European ports (under strict control with regard to the qualifications of pilots), monopoly situations have been allowed to develop, resulting in unacceptably high pilotage fees and often blanket obligations to use pilots even when the ship's master would suffice. This service should be closely coordinated with the scheduling (berth allocation) services provided by the harbormaster. For safety and efficiency reasons, port security and health services should remain the responsibility of the port authority.

[67] Most ships have sufficient storage facilities on board and thus have some flexibility to choose on which stop to fill their bunkers. Hence, there is a fair amount of competition between ports for bunkering services. Some ports with high bunker volumes and strategic locations close to main shipping lines have developed important bunkering facilities (e.g. Singapore, Canary Islands).

- While certain conditions might make it legitimate to limit the access of trucks to the port area, any such limitations should be transparent and non-discriminatory. Trucking as a service should be open to competing private companies and allow shippers and consignees to choose the carrier they consider most appropriate. This will not only render movements of cargo within the port more efficient, but will be particularly important to ensure intermodal connectivity. Monopolistic trucking on port premises also limits competition on the rest of the journey.

- For physical goods to flow smoothly, the banking services provided in ports and the administrative formalities that accompany cargo transactions have to work efficiently. Ports are the place where goods usually cross a border, transfer between modes, and change owners. As goods move through the maritime leg of a multimodal chain, they change hands several times. Parties involved include the shipping line, the shipping agent, the consignee (or his representative), the shipper (or his representative), the warehouse, and customs. Since these physical movements are associated with transfers of ownership, they also involves multiple transfers of titles, money, and insurance documents. The transfer and clearance of goods through ports can involve up to 50 documents.[68] According to another estimate for containers, a "typical large container ship can carry up to 6,000 TEU and generate 40,000 documents."[69] Port reforms should therefore go hand-in-hand with the streamlining of border-related procedures and institutions (see section 1.8). The installation of modern IT systems, which permit the exchange of information between the various parties involved in maritime trade, can also have dramatic effects on port efficiency (see section 1.7).

Providing port services requires another critical input besides infrastructure and equipment: labor. In most ports, rigid labor rules, poor labor relations, and overstaffing are important sources of low productivity and high costs. The reduction of the workforce "in a socially acceptable way must be a prominent concern of public authorities. [...] The process of port labor reform requires governments to eliminate provisions from existing labor regimes, collective agreements and work practices, which limit or restrict the supply or demand for labor, its freedom of entry and exit, and constrain productivity."[70] Severance packages and early retirement schemes, as well as retraining to help workers find new employment are called for. The constructive participation of labor representatives in the reform process from the outset will facilitate the development of transition strategies. Labor issues should either be addressed prior to privatization or otherwise provisions should be put in place to allow the new owners to make the necessary adjustments.

Nevertheless, the costs of labor adjustment should not be an argument against sector reforms. First, these costs are not caused by reforms but only made visible by them, whereas they were previously hidden by government subsidies and the inflated prices paid by customers. "Market-based employment systems introduced by the private sector initially usually reveal the existence of superfluous staff in public-sector ports, and a state hiring policy that pays no attention to commercial aspects."[71] Second, structural adjustment requires the re-allocation of resources such as labor and capital towards more productive uses; any such re-allocation implies transition costs. The long-term economic and social benefits of reforms, however, tend to outweigh the transitory costs, especially in a dynamic growth sector like maritime transport. While a phased approach is advisable, it can easily be used as a justification for unnecessary delays that prolong costly inefficiencies. The 'gradualism' or 'transition cost' arguments against reforms are often used by vested interest groups to defend privileges and economic rents that arise from market distortions.

[68] Abilio Marques of the Administration of the Port of Lisbon (May 2001).
[69] Economist (6 April 2002). The same article states that a container transport chain can involve 30-40 documents.
[70] Juhel, Marc. 1998. *Globalization, Privatization, and Restructuring of Ports*. World Bank Institute
[71] Juhel, Marc. 1998. *Globalization, Privatization, and Restructuring of Ports*. World Bank Institute.

After all, the costs of overstaffing and rigid labor regimes are a hidden transfer from port users and taxpayers to port employees.

The two case studies on port reforms in Colombia and Argentina illustrate that the long-term benefits of port reforms tend to outweigh the short-term transition costs. But there are plenty of other examples. "Compensation paid to workers laid off in Chilean ports as a result of the deregulation of dock labor in 1981, amounted to a total of $ 30 million. Payments per worker averaged $ 14,300 [...] By 1982 the increased productivity had generated savings of $ 40 million, and these economies benefited port operators as well as exporters, importers and carriers. [...] The Government of New Zealand paid $ 28 million to compensate workers made redundant, and by the end of 1990 the direct savings to port customers in that country amounted to $ 56 million. For every job lost in New Zealand's docks, the Government estimated that 10 were generated in other sectors by eliminating cost and productivity bottlenecks caused by the ports."[72]

Box 3.7 The Liberalization of Port Services in the European Union

Whereas the Commission has introduced competition in air transport primarily through sector-specific regulation, it has mainly relied on a case-by-case application of competition law for the liberalization of the port sector (see section 4.6). In February 2001, however, it produced the communication on Reinforcing Quality Services in Sea Ports: A Key for European Transport (a policy document) as well as the draft directive, On Market Access to Port Services (a complementary piece of legislation). The draft directive defines a set of principles that EU member states would have to transpose into national law. It aims to create a level playing field between different ports and service providers, while allowing for a degree of flexibility to take account of "the diversity of ports with regards to size, status and function and maritime safety and environmental protection requirements." The following excerpts outline key elements of the draft directive:

- "Member States shall take the necessary measures to ensure that providers of port services have access to the market for the provision of port services." They may maintain licensing regimes, but "the conditions for granting authorization must be transparent, non-discriminatory, objective, relevant and proportional" (e.g. professional qualifications, financial credentials, insurance coverage).
- "The number of authorizations can only be limited for reasons of constraints relating to available space or capacity or, for technical-nautical services, maritime traffic related safety. These constraints must be justified and Member States must carry out a transparent, objective and non-discriminatory selection [...] Key aspects of the selection procedure will be harmonized."
- "Member States shall take the necessary measures to allow self-handling. [...] conditions and criteria for self-handlers must not be stricter than those set for providers of port services."
- "Where the managing body of the port [e.g. a public ports authority] provides [...] port services in competition with other service providers, it must be treated like any other competitor. This requires that the managing body must not be involved in the selection procedure [...] must not discriminate [...] and must, in particular, separate its port services accounts from the accounts of its other activities. This principle reflects general competition principles and standards of transparency."
- "Member States will have to ensure full transparency of all procedures in relations to the provision of port services, as well as the availability of appeal procedures, including judicial review. This is the principle of good governance."

The communication and draft directive also call for time limitations to operating concessions and the transparent tendering of port contracts. Ports account for 70 percent of external EU trade and according to Transport Commissioner Loyola de Palacio, the objective of the directive is to "establish clear rules on access to the port services market [...] in the interest of operators, [port] authorities and consumers."

Source: European Commission (1991).

[72] UN Economic Commission for Latin America. 1999. *Port Modernization: A Pyramid of Interrelated Challenges.*

3.8 Port Services: Reform Trends in the Maghreb and Mashrek

Many MPs have started to introduce competition and private participation in port services but reforms still have some way to go, as the following examples show:

- **Lebanon:** While Lebanon is arguably the country in the region where competition and private participation in port services are most advanced, the regulatory framework for private participation remains patchy. So far, private sector participation is de facto rather than de jure. After the end of the civil war, private companies were permitted to provide services in the port of Beirut to ensure a quick resumption of port activities. The private sector now carries out all container and most general cargo handling as well as all towage and pilotage services. The public port company, on the other hand, provides all storage facilities and some handling of general cargo. In some services, cartel-like structures reduce competition. The government is considering privatizing the remaining services and turning the port company into a port authority with a clear regulatory mandate.

- **Egypt:** Egypt has initiated the liberalization and privatization of port services. In 1997, two important articles of law 12/1964 were scrapped. Article 6 had obliged all public agencies and state-owned companies to use only public service providers. Article 7 prohibited private service provision for a range of maritime activities, "including stevedoring, ship supply, repair and maintenance, storage and cargo handling." Restrictions on private shipping agents, however, remained.[73] Licenses for port services were first issued in June 1998 and eight agents are now permitted to provide certain stevedoring services in Damietta, two of them being state-owned. In Alexandria more than a dozen private stevedoring companies operate in the port area. Nonetheless, competition in key port services continues to be hampered by quasi-monopolies and insufficient separation of regulatory and commercial functions. The Damietta Container Handling Company and Port Said Container Handling Company, for example, are both controlled by their respective port authorities. State-owned freight forwarder Martrans long enjoyed a legal monopoly on freight forwarding in all ports and a reputation for high costs and low quality. As far as state ownership is concerned, about a dozen maritime transport companies (stevedoring, ship building and repairs, warehousing, etc.) with a total of more than 20,000 employees remain in the portfolio of a holding company and await privatization.

- **Jordan:** Competition and private participation in Jordan's port Aqaba are still at an early stage. Ship chandlery has been liberalized. To increase efficiency and lower costs, port regulations were overhauled, loading and unloading procedures simplified, stevedoring hours increased to 24 hours per day, port tariffs reduced, and import controls streamlined.[74]

- **Algeria:** Currently, the country's ten ports are organized as service ports with the status of autonomous public enterprises that have monopolies for service provision. A new 1998 sector law, which provides for the introduction of competition and private participation in port services (except for pilotage and towage), has not yet been enacted. A number of private companies have expressed interest in service provision but licenses are still to be granted.[75]

- **Tunisia:** OMMP is the operator ashore as well as the port authority in all Tunisian ports except for the oil port of Skhira, where the oil companies are in charge. Private stevedores exist in secondary ports, but play a limited role as they depend on OMMP for the supply of major equipment. Following the country's independence, several private stevedoring companies were merged into the Société Tunisienne d'Acconage et de Manutention (STAM), a joint stock

[73] Egyptian Business Monthly (January 1998) and American Chamber of Commerce Egypt (*www.amcham.org.eg*).
[74] Ports Corporation Aqaba. 2000. *The Port of Aqaba – Handbook and Directory 1999/2000.*
[75] Maghreb Weekly Monitor, 77th issue (4 April 2000).

company. STAM has a monopoly in stevedoring and warehousing in the three ports of Tunis (Tunis, La Goulette, Radès). Private sector participation is limited to some small stevedores in secondary ports (Bizerte, Sousse, Sfax, and Gabès). A total of six private companies handle cargo in the different ports. "Sfax is the port where competition is the most real, which favors higher productivity and lower costs. Sousse is another good performer with three operators. [...] Cargo handling tariffs charged in Tunis and La Goulette [are] 30 to 50 percent higher than in other ports where some measure of competition is possible."[76]

- **Morocco:** ODEP, set up in 1984, is a state-owned company that has a legal monopoly for most port services. In some ports, on-board handling may be carried out by private operators, while shore handling remains ODEP's monopoly. This artificial split drives a wedge between activities that should be seamlessly integrated and thus lowers productivity. Although ODEP's mandate was mainly confined to commercial activities, decree 432-26 of 04/02/93 added the regulatory function of the harbor master. In 1994, ODEP's functions were further expanded when it was put in charge of the construction of the new fishing port in Dakhla as well as dredging. The productivity of Moroccan ports approximately doubled in the decade since ODEP's creation, thanks to new investments and a shift of cargo towards containers and RoRo. These gains, however, were not passed on to users through lower tariffs and most productivity indicators remain considerably below international benchmarks. A 1997 World Bank study found that ODEP's fees were 25 to 30 percent higher than they should have been under a competitive regime.[77] The awkward organization of harbor master services and the low productivity and complex administrative set-up of ODEP increase the cost to shipping lines. The dismantling of ODEP's monopoly, a separation of regulatory and commercial functions, and the privatization of the latter should be core elements of future reforms.

As an integral part of port reforms, most of the MPs will have to address labor issues. Overstaffing is partly a result of labor-saving technological progress (e.g. containerization, modern handling equipment) and partly a result of rigid labor laws. In Egypt it was estimated that around 40 percent of the 24,000 employees of the public maritime sector holding company (mainly stevedoring and shipyards) were potentially redundant. Together with excess personnel of the port authorities, the sector is estimated to have surplus staff of up to 20,000.[78] In Israel, the situation used to be similar, but in recent years the number of port workers was gradually reduced, leading to a dramatic increase in productivity. "In 1975, 5,079 workers handled 9 million tons of cargo: in comparison, 2,324 workers handled more than 30 million tons annually in mid-1998. The manpower cutbacks were met by staunch opposition from the workers, especially during the seventies, and strained labor relations at the ports."[79] In most other MPs, overstaffing remains a problem. In Tunisia, for example, a 1949 decree that regulates the terms and conditions for the employment of dock labor has long been a main sources of low productivity. "Labor inputs could be cut in half without overstaffed gangs" and labor costs be lowered by $ 4 million per year.[80] The law was formally abolished in 1999, but many of the restrictions actually remained in place. Reform efforts, however, have met with stiff political resistance. In most EU countries, workforce reductions and the modernization of labor rules were also an integral part or port reform. In Italy, for instance, a competition case ruling by the Commission dismantled a legal monopoly by the dock workers' union and triggered broader sector restructuring (see section 4.6).

---

[76] World Bank. 2000. *Tunisia – Private Sector Assessment Update.*

[77] Loir, Michel and Pierre Guislain. 1997. *Royaume de Maroc: Participation du Secteur Privé dans les Infrastructures*. World Bank.

[78] World Bank. 1997. *Egypt – Ports Sector Note* (draft, January 1997).

[79] Etzioni, Amir. 1999. *Reforming Israel's Seaports*. Institute for Advanced Strategic and Policy Studies.

[80] World Bank. 2000. *Tunisia – Private Sector Assessment Update.*

Shipping

In most of the Maghreb and Mashrek countries, ports are currently the critical bottlenecks in maritime transport chains and should therefore be the prime target of policy reforms. For goods to flow smoothly from their origin to their destination, however, the sea-leg and the land-leg of these maritime chains also need to operate efficiently. In addition to the port reforms discussed so far, comprehensive maritime sector reforms will also involve policies related to shipping services (see the following two sections) and hinterland connections (see sections 4.1 to 4.3).

3.9 Policy Issues in the Shipping Market

Maritime transport is not a homogenous industry, but can be broken down into different market segments such as general cargo, dry bulk, gas, and liquid bulk. General cargo in turn can be either containerized or non-containerized. These distinctions are important for several reasons. Different cargo categories all require specialized vessels and terminals, and thus separate sets of infrastructure. The market structure (demand and supply dynamics, ownership patterns, etc.) and the degree of competition varies greatly. Moreover, the regulatory frameworks for these sub-sectors differ, and so do the policy priorities and reform needs in the southern Mediterranean countries.

Vessels for bulk cargo are usually purpose-built to carry specific unpacked products such as dry bulk (e.g. grain, phosphate, coal), petroleum (e.g. crude oil or refined products), liquefied natural gas, or liquid chemicals. Scheduled services are rare and charter is the norm. In contrast to the bulk sector, the liner shipping sector provides scheduled services for general cargo between advertised ports on a common carrier basis, whereby any customer has access to capacity at a given price. Only a small portion of general cargo is carried by non-scheduled ships (tramps). Different vessel types can engage in liner traffic, including general cargo, reefers (refrigerated vessels), multipurpose ships, and RoRo (where trucks and trailers are directly driven on board). RoRo permits for efficient modal transfer in maritime-land chains and plays an important role in certain trades (see box 1.6).

Nowadays, however, most liner trade is in containers and performed by specialized container vessels. Given the importance and specific nature of this market segment, it is discussed further in section 3.11. Since per-unit operating costs decrease with vessel size and the size of the route network, the liner sector – and particularly the one for container shipment – is subject to significant scale economies. The consolidation of traffic on high volume arteries between hub ports permits the use of larger mother vessels (cost advantage) and a higher frequency of services (time advantage). Connecting services from the port of origin and to the final port of destination along feeder routes are provided by smaller vessels.

An important cargo segment of maritime traffic in the southern Mediterranean, and especially in the Maghreb, is RoRo traffic. Most of the trucks carried by special RoRo vessels transport general cargo and containers. The advantage of RoRo is that it requires minimal port facilities (high flexibility, low investments) and implies fast and smooth modal transfer. This technology is well-suited for unitized multimodal traffic – especially through smaller ports and on journeys where the sea-leg is relatively short as compared to the land-legs. This explains why RoRo plays a particularly important role for traffic between southern Europe and the Maghreb as well as for traffic with the two island economies of Cyprus and Malta.

The traditional mechanism to unlock the network and scale economies inherent to the liner trade are liner conferences and alliances. There are currently more than 300 such international cartels of carriers and shipping lines, carrying approximately half of the international general cargo, with a declining tendency. Liner conferences come in a wide variety of forms: membership can vary from 2 to 40 companies and conferences can cover one route or several. Their defining characteristic is the fixing of freight rates for cargoes carried on the respective routes. Based on the assumption that the economic benefits outweigh the costs, these cartels have traditionally enjoyed block-exemptions from competition policy in most OECD countries. These exemptions, however, are narrowly defined and competition authorities have repeatedly intervened to prevent illegal anticompetitive behavior (see section 4.6 for details). In recent years, the importance of conferences has been declining considerably, largely due to a consolidation of carriers. Three-quarters of liner trades in many developed countries are carried by container vessels and consolidation has been particularly pronounced in this market segment (see section 3.11).

While the liberalization and privatization of ports should be the main priority in maritime sector reforms for most MPs, a number of policy issues arise in shipping. To maximize the efficiency and responsiveness of trade flows, it is critical that ports are well served by shipping lines and closely integrated in international route networks. To avoid the costs associated with unutilized vessel capacity, it is critical that carriers can discharge and load cargo wherever they want and that they can plan the routings of their vessels to meet commercial objectives, not regulatory constraints. For these reasons, any legal or administrative provisions that restrict market access by vessels and shipping lines should be removed. These can include bilateral cargo access regulations for liner traffic (quite rare nowadays); unilateral cargo reservations stipulating that a certain share of traffic be reserved for national flag carriers; restrictions to cabotage; requirements for international companies to enter into joint ventures with domestic carriers; restrictions on the use of shipping agents; or limitations on the right of establishment.[81]

An illustration of the economic costs imposed by restrictions to market access is Argentina where "maritime tariffs have fallen by up to 40 percent for cargo movements that were previously reserved for Argentine flag ships," after the liberalization of shipping services. Within the EU Single Market all such restrictions have been removed. A 1986 regulation made the principle of freedom to provide services applicable to maritime transport, both between EU member states and between them and non-EU countries.[82] The OECD Code of Current Invisible Operations (CLIO) and its Common Principles of Shipping Policy stipulate that the shipping policy of its members (which make up the majority of world trade) is based on the principle of free circulation of shipping in international trade and on free and fair competition. They stipulate that OECD countries remove discriminatory restrictions not only on maritime freight, but also on port services and ship repairs.

The removal of artificial restrictions to free market access is a necessary but not always sufficient condition for effective competition. Anti-competitive behavior by market participants might be

[81] *Cabotage and cross-trading* permits vessels to operate within one or between two foreign markets. Due to the limited amount of domestic traffic in the Arab MPs, cabotage restrictions are of less relevance than restrictions to cross-trading. Within the EU, remaining restrictions to cabotage and cross-trading were removed under Council Regulation (EEC) 3577/92. Bilateral traffic agreements between governments are much less common and of much more marginal importance in maritime traffic than in air traffic, where bilateral Air Service Agreements (ASAs) are a major determinant of market access and competition.

[82] European Commission. 1986. *Council Regulation (EEC) 4055/86*. There used to be some bilateral cargo access regulations for maritime traffic between France on the one hand and Tunisia and Morocco on the other hand. With the creation of the European Single Market in 1992, however, EU countries were prohibited from discrimination against operators from other EU member countries and France had to abolish these agreements.

another issue that policy makers have to address. On low-traffic routes (very common in the region), carriers may abuse their market power to set excessive fares. Another problem for policy makers are liner conferences that use their cartel to prevent competition from non-conference carriers through measures such as predatory pricing, capacity restrictions, or exclusivity arrangements with port operators. The EU's approach to competition issues in the shipping markets is discussed in greater detail in the case study on competition policy in section 4.6. In Eastern Europe, Latvia and Bulgaria have already revised their own maritime laws in accordance with EU and OECD rules. Although conferences are rare in the Mediterranean, the Maghreb and Mashrek countries should generally consider adopting stricter cross-sectoral competition laws.[83]

Box 3.8 Safety and Environmental Regulation for Maritime Transport

In addition to the economic regulation discussed in this chapter, safety and environmental regulation are also an important part of maritime sector policies (e.g. technical standards for vessels or the manning and training of crews). This is also the case in other modes, particularly in air and road transport. Such regulation is needed since the discharging of hazardous waste, oil spills, or collisions can impose high external costs. Many sub-standard vessels operate under flags of convenience, that is, they are registered in countries with low labor, safety and environmental requirements. Since vessels frequently move between jurisdictions or through extraterritorial waters, there are three layers of standards and their enforcement. The first is that of the flag-state. Due to the existence of flags of convenience, however, global minimum standards (the second layer) are set through a series of international conventions under the framework of the International Maritime Organization (IMO), a UN body with 156 member states.[84] Until 2002, for example, the International Ship Management (ISM) Code progressively improved the quality of shipping globally. Most developed countries impose a third regulatory layer with higher standards or stricter enforcement for all vessels entering their territorial waters and ports. Private certification companies, such as Lloyds Register or Bureau Veritas certify technical compliance with IMO and other international rules. On behalf of its member states, for instance, the EU introduced a Port State Control (PSC) System in 1993, which is based on several international conventions. "With ISM and PSC combined, the EU now has a rigorous system to facilitate the inspection of any ship entering an EU port and its detention if defects are found (until they are rectified)."[85] The Euro-Mediterranean partners should explore options for closer cooperation on safety and environmental regulation, such as the adoption of common standards, the exchange of information, or the association of MPs to European institutions in the sector.

The privatization of state-owned fleets is another item of the reform agenda. There is no economic justification for state involvement in an industry characterized by large scale economies and international consolidation. It rather imposes economic costs due to poor management (e.g. deficient marketing and cost control) and policy intervention (e.g. employment creation schemes, continuation of loss-making activities at the tax payers' expense). In the EU, all former state-owned shipping companies have either disappeared or are withering away.[86] Although state ownership of carriers is much less of a policy issue in maritime than in air transport, several of the MPs maintain shipping lines. Lebanon has no publicly-owned commercial fleet. The public and loss-making Egyptian Navigation Company owned 28 ships in 1998 (including general cargo and RoRo vessels), but is scheduled for privatization. Algeria still had three carriers for passengers, oil

[83] In the case of Morocco, for instance, conferences exist with ports in France, Holland, and Scandinavia.

[84] For more information see IMO web-site (*www.imo.org*). Other international regulations with relevance to the sector come from the UN Conference on Trade and Development, UNCTAD (*www.unctad.org*), the International Labor Organization, ILO (*www.ilo.org*) and the UN Commission on International Trade Law, UNCITRAL (*www.uncitral.org*). On these issues, see also box 1.12.

[85] Oxford Analytica (16 June 1997).

[86] Some of the last to be sold were France's Compagnie Generale Maritime and Italy's Lloyd Triestino. Government protection had shielded them against market forces for too long. By the time of privatization, most of these companies were so uncompetitive that they were either absorbed by private companies or went bankrupt.

transport, and general cargo transport with a total of several dozen vessels. In Tunisia, two state-owned shipping lines were liquidated in the mid 1990s.[87] The privatization of the remaining Companie Tunisienne de Navigation (COTUNAV) has been discussed for several years, but the government has not yet taken a decision to that effect. After staff reduction, the elimination of loss-making routes, and heavy investments in fleet-renewal, losses for Companie Tunisienne de Navigation have been reduced significantly. In Morocco, which has two public shipping companies for liner traffic (Comanav) and bulk chemicals (Morphoceau), a recent report by the Inspection Générale des Finances on Comanav illustrates the potential drawbacks of state ownership.[88] Poor management of both the fleet and human resources, as well as excessive perks for managers, were strongly criticized. Continuous losses eventually required a recapitalization of the company. One of the irregularities that raised the suspicion of substantial corruption was the purchase of two expensive container vessels, despite the existence of a cheaper offer. Two 1994 and 1999 audits of Comanav found "dysfunctionalities at all levels of the organization," but problems continued to fester without intervention from the treasury, which holds 69 percent of the equity. This case is not unusual for mismanagement under state ownership, but rarely are such deficiencies as openly exposed by a government watchdog.

There are at least two ways in which port policies can improve the sea-side links of ports. Efficient ports will encourage large international shipping lines to include ports in their route networks. High and unpredictable vessel turn-around times arising from port inefficiencies disrupt sensitive schedules, delay cargo to subsequent stops, and impose significant costs by increasing the times that vessels and crews sit idle. High port dues or restrictions on cabotage can also deter shipping lines. The shipping company Delmas Vieljeux, for example, stopped to service Moroccan ports with its large container vessels, since delays caused by inefficient services were costing tens of thousands of dollars.[89] In 1998, CMA, one of Damietta's most important customers, switched its transshipment operations from Egypt to Malta, citing operational difficulties. Another way in which port policies can affect shipping patterns, especially in container transshipment, is through privatization. Concessioning of terminals to one of the global container lines that have successfully diversified into terminal operations, or to some of the international port operators with strong links to shipping lines, facilitates the integration of the port into international route networks. For example, PSA Corporation, which operates the Port of Singapore, uses its good reputation and existing links with shipping lines to build a global port network, including the new Yemeni container port of Aden. APM Terminals, a subsidiary of the shipping line Maersk, is a key member of the consortia building the new container terminals at East Port Said and at Salalah (Oman). A joint venture of P&O Ports with a local construction group was granted a concession for Derince in Turkey.

3.10 Containerization and Transshipment

As discussed in sections 1.5 and 3.2, a large and increasing percentage of general cargo is being transported in containers and the majority of liner traffic already consists of container vessels. The total capacity of the world container fleet almost tripled over the past decade from 1.25 million TEU in 1988 to 3.56 million TEU in 1998. Global container traffic increased from 79.8 to 147.4 million TEU between 1989 and 1996. This translates into an average annual rate of more than 9

[87] Tunisian Ministry of Transport. 2000. *Evolution du Transport Maritime en Tunisie 1999-2000*.

[88] La Vie Economique (18 January 2002).

[89] Paelinck, Honoré. 1999. *Maroc – Facilitation du Transport*. World Bank (not published). An 18-hour delay is estimated to cost $ 27.5 per container and the largest vessels carry up to 6,000 TEUs. A one-day delay of a ship loaded with 1,000 TEU will thus cost up to $ 30,000.

percent, compared to 2 percent in the bulk market.[90] Container traffic is also the fastest growing segment of maritime transport in the Mediterranean region. Total container traffic handled by all (North and South) Mediterranean ports grew by an annual average of 13 percent between 1990 and 1998. Container transshipment grew even faster, by close to 20 percent per annum and now accounts for about one-third of Mediterranean container traffic.[91] This is partly due to the fact that important global shipping routes transit the Mediterranean (e.g. between the Far East and Europe).

However, these high growth rates were from a low base and several of the Maghreb and Mashrek countries are still lagging behind with regard to the rate of containerization in general cargo. In 1997, the containerization rate of Egypt's general cargo was 27 percent for imports and 36 percent in exports. In 1998, Algeria's average containerization rate for trade was a mere 16 percent; Tunisia's has been estimated at 37 percent.[92] These figures compare with international averages of around 50 to 60 percent and even much higher percentages for most developed economies.[93] Another indicator for the penetration of containers is TEU per $ million of GDP. In 1998 Portugal, for instance, had a ratio of 17.3 and Israel's was as high as 30.5, while Algeria (5.5), Morocco (7.3), Syria (7.4), and Tunisia (8.9) were all much lower. The notable exception among the Arab MPs was Lebanon with 26 TEU/$m of GDP.[94] As discussed in chapter 1, a high rate of containerization is not only important for the efficiency of maritime transport but also for that of the overall multimodal system (low costs of modal transfers). Policy makers can help to increase the rate of containerization by concessioning container terminals to private operators, improving the sea-side integration of ports into the global route networks, and streamlining customs.

Table 3.3 Container Traffic by Country

Country	Throughput (98 TEU)	Growth (97-98 %)	TEU/ $m GDP
Algeria	187,500	4	6
Egypt	1,587,400	14	19
Jordan	n.a.	n.a.	n.a.
Lebanon	300,000	8	26
Morocco	236,658	14	7
Syria	155,000	3	7
Tunisia	145,500	10	9
Total	**2,612,058**	**12**	**17**
Israel	1,181,000	6	31
Turkey	1,306,569	5	8

Source: Drewry Shipping Consultants (2000).

The consolidation of carriers in container shipping is well advanced and still increasing. Seventy-three percent of the world's container fleet is being operated by only 20 global shipping companies.[95] Global players like Maersk (which bought Sea-Land), Evergreen, NOL/APL, or Cosco are not only increasingly dominating the liner trades in containers but are also vertical integrating into stevedoring and the operation of container terminals through specialized subsidiaries.[96] As in all of these other parts of the logistics industry, the sources of the scale

[90] OECD. 1999. *Discussion Document on Regulatory Reform in International Maritime Transport.*

[91] Drewry Shipping Consultants. 2000. *Mediterranean Container Ports and Shipping.*

[92] World Bank. 2000. *Tunisia – Private Sector Assessment Update.*

[93] Cross-country comparisons of containerization rates (as percentage of general cargo) are complicated by the fact that not all general cargo lends itself to containerization and that the composition of general cargo can vary significantly (e.g. heavy general cargo items like machinery or raw sheet-iron are usually not containerized but can constitute a significant percentage of total cargo in terms of weight).

[94] Drewry Shipping Consultants. 2000. *Mediterranean Container Ports and Shipping.* The penetration indicator TEU/$m relative to GDP can be inflated by transit traffic (e.g. transshipment in Egypt).

[95] OECD. 1999. *Discussion Document on Regulatory Reform in International Maritime Transport.*

[96] Some of the shipping lines, which have diversified into port operations, have a dedicated terminal strategy, whereby they use the entire terminal only to serve their own vessels, but most provide services to competitors.

economies are high fixed costs of equipment and IT, the management-intensity of these industries (management expertise can be spread over a larger number of units), and network externalities.

Box 3.9 The Regional Competition for Container Transshipment

From the perspective of policy makers, one of the key features of transshipment is that it is an internationally mobile economic activity, which a country can attract through adequate policies – or deter through an antiquated sector framework and inadequate infrastructure.[97] Virtually all transshipment traffic is in containers since the low handling costs and transfer times of unitized cargo makes the transfer between vessels commercially viable. The establishment of a transshipment hub can attract significant investments, related value-added activities, and employment to a country. It can also reduce transport costs for the host country's own trade, due to economies of scale (unit costs fall as volume increases) and better connections to shipping routes (vessel frequencies and the number of destinations rise). The transshipment potential in the Mediterranean does not only stem from hub-and-spoke patterns of traffic within the region, but also from East-West traffic between Asia and Europe traversing the Suez Canal as well as for Black Sea traffic via the strait of Bosphorus. According to Drewry Shipping Consultants, "the Mediterranean transshipment market is highly concentrated […] with four countries accounting for over 90 percent of transshipment traffic. Moreover, each country only has one dominant transshipment port."[98] (See diagram 3.1.)

The competition for transshipment hubs in the Mediterranean region is in full swing. After the expansion of the port of Damietta over the past decade (90 percent of turnover is transshipment), Egypt is building a new BOT container terminal in East Port Said. A new container terminal in Beirut is also under construction, and Morocco would like to build a container port near Tangier (all three projects discussed in section 3.5). At the same time, the MPs face significant competition from existing or planned hubs on the northern shore of the Mediterranean, such as the private ports of Gioia Tauro in southern Italy and Cagliari in Sardinia, the to-be-privatized Malta Freeport, or Algeciras in Spain. On the other side of the Red Sea, the Saudi port of Jeddah as well as the new ports of Salalah (Oman) and Aden (Yemen) have started to attract significant transshipment traffic. Dubai Port Authority, which won the concession in Beirut is also developing a container terminal in Djibouti and plans to create a regional network of ports. An example of hub competition within the region is Limassol (Cyprus), whose container throughput dropped by half from 400,000 to 200,000 TEU in only two years (1996-98) after ports with better location and services took away transshipment traffic (mainly Gioia Tauro). As mentioned above, Damietta lost one of its most important customers, DMA, to Malta in 1998.[99] With all of these container terminals already operating or under construction, there could soon be excess transshipment capacity in the region. Even though transshipment hubs can bring important benefits to a country, only few and well-located ports will eventually be able to reach and maintain the critical mass needed.

Container traffic tends to be highly concentrated in a few ports. In the Mediterranean, six 'million TEU plus' ports account for 44 percent of the region's throughput.[100] The size of modern container vessels and the technical specificities of these trades mean that most older ports cannot cater to the requirements of containerized cargo. New ports – or refurbished terminals in existing ones – with

[97] Other *determinants for the location of hubs* are (i) the size of a port's cargo-generating hinterland, (ii) proximity to global shipping routes, and (iii) the reach of its feeder network (catchment area). There are also different forms of transshipment: Relay transshipment takes place between connecting deep-sea vessels and does not involve regional feeder services, as does hub-and-spoke transshipment. Examples of relay hubs are the new port in Aden or Marsaxlokk in Malta. Origin/destination traffic (as opposed to transshipment), in turn, can be broken down into deep-sea direct (long-distance with large vessels), near-sea intra-regional (smaller vessels for mid-range traffic), and short-see feeder traffic (hub-related traffic, performed at spoke ports).

[98] Drewry Shipping Consultants. 2000. *Mediterranean Container Ports and Shipping*.

[99] Unless otherwise stated, information in this paragraph from MEED (26 January 2001, 31 March 2000, 19 May 2000).

[100] Drewry Shipping Consultants. 2000. *Mediterranean Container Ports and Shipping*. The six ports were Gioia Tauro, Algeciras, Genoa, Marsaxlokk, Barcelona, and Valencia. The only Maghreb or Mashrek ports on the top 20 list of Mediterranean container ports are Damietta (No. 10), Alexandria (No. 13), Port Said (No. 14), and Beirut (No. 20). Of these, only Damietta had a throughput in excess of half a million TEU (670,000).

specialized loading equipment and sufficient water depths are needed.[101] Due to the large investments required and the complexity of managing such terminals, a small number of global players with far-flung port networks is emerging. The five largest container port operators, with their respective numbers of terminals and annual volume of containers handled are: Hutchinson Ports (29 ports, 25 million TEU); PSA Corporation (11 ports, 20 million TEU); APM Terminals (28 ports, 13 million TEU), P&O Ports (27 ports, 8 million TEU); and Eurogate (9 ports, 8 million TEU).[102] Key players on the global scene include some port authorities that have developed particularly efficient operations in their home port. The Port of Dubai, for instance, won the concession for the new container terminal in Beirut and PSA heads the consortium which constructed and operates the new terminal at Aden, Yemen. A third group of are global shipping lines, like Maersk/Sea-Land, which vertically integrate into terminal operations and stevedoring. To attract the investments and state-of-the art management, container ports should be run by private port operators with international expertise. While a number of private terminals are being built in the southern Mediterranean, the Maghreb and Mashrek countries should concession not only new terminals to international operators, but also existing facilities that are in need of new investments and commercial management.

[101] The largest container vessels to date have a capacity of 7,600 TEU, but most modern ports can only handle vessels of up to about 5,000 TEU. Feeder vessels take between 300 and 1,200 containers, compared to 1,500 and above for long-haul ('mother') vessels.

[102] American Shipper.

Box 3.10 Satellite Navigation and the EU Galileo Project

Modern satellite technology facilitates the operation of transport networks in many ways. The exact positioning of aircraft and vessels through global navigation satellite systems (GNSS) permits efficient routing and safe navigation through busy waterways or crowded airspace. Satellite positioning and communication services – in combination with signal receivers and ground control centers – are required for state-of-the-art fleet management by trucking companies or the optimal use of rolling-stock by railway operators. Other services that are being introduced or under development include satellite-based road charging and traffic management systems or anti-theft devices for cars. Currently, the only two worldwide GNSS are the American Global Positioning System (GPS) and the Russian Glonass system, which were both originally developed for military purposes.

In 1994, the EU's Council of Ministers called on the Commission to develop a European satellite-based navigation system for world-wide civilian use and in compatibility with GPS and Glonass.[103] As in the case of GPS, the receipt of the basic signals is to be free of charge. The EC has opted for a public-private partnership to ensure the joint delivery of this general public service as well as additional commercial services. Enhanced-quality signals and value-added services (e.g. navigation and timing services resold by mobile phone companies as part of a package) will be available only to authorized users financed on the basis of fees. The private consortium Galileo Industries SA – owned by EADS, BAe Systems (together 50 percent), Alcatel, and Alenia Spazio (each 25 percent) – is meant to finance up to half the total investments of about € 3 billion.[104] The balance should come from the Commission and the European Space Agency (ESA), with no further subsidies expected beyond 2007.

The successfully completed concept ional phase (1999-2000) is to be followed by the development phase (2001-2004) and the deployment phase (2005-2008). As the precursor to Galileo, the *EGNOS* system (available 2003) will use the basic US and Russian signals, but enhance them with an overlay system for increased accuracy and reliability. Once Galileo is complete, 30 satellites will circle the earth on a 20-kilometer orbit to provide position coordinates and time signals with a margin of error of a few meters and a fraction of a second respectively.[105] In May 2000, the World Radiocommunication Conference agreed to set aside the frequencies required for the venture. Some EU governments, however, have voiced concern about the size of the required investment, the uncertainty of the long-term economic benefits, and a reluctance of the private sector to make firm commitments concerning its share of the cost.[106] These problems have repeatedly threatened to derail the project.

The MPs might also benefit from the services provided by Galileo. Besides the navigational and positioning services mentioned above, oil exploration and geodesity, search and rescue operations in remote areas, environmental monitoring, or the work of fishing fleets could be facilitated. To fully benefit from this, however, each country needs to ensure interoperability between the GNSS and complementary domestic systems (e.g. air and maritime codes, navigational plans, air traffic control); the construction of ground stations where necessary; and equal access of users to the system (e.g. through the provision of frequency and transparent licensing). At the multilateral level, a regional MEDA project currently under preparation should help the partners to assess bottlenecks and opportunities (e.g. the development of a seamless navigation and positioning system) as well as to develop a Euro-Mediterranean strategy for GNSS. While such policy initiatives appear to be useful, navigation does not constitute an important bottleneck in the maritime and air transport chains of the region. From a transport efficiency point of view, satellite navigation is thus not one of the priority issues.

[103] General information about the project in this box was taken from: European Commission. 2000. *Communication on Galileo*.

[104] Financial Times Deutschland (9 April 2001).

[105] Financial Times Deutschland (27 November 2000).

[106] Financial Times (8 February 2002) and Financial Times Deutschland (5 December 2001).

Chapter 4

Land-Based Transport and Other Sector Issues

Chapter 4

Land-Based Transport and Other Sector Issues

The vast majority of cross-border transport in the southern Mediterranean, especially in the Maghreb, is conducted by sea and air. These two modes have been discussed in detail in the previous chapters. This chapter will round off the analysis by looking at the policy issues associated with the land-legs of maritime and air chains (sections 4.1 to 4.3). The remaining sections are devoted to some additional aspects of transport sector policy, namely customs reforms (4.4), postal sector reform (4.5), competition policy in transport (4.6), and a case study of policies for the development of multimodal logistics clusters (4.7).

Land-Based Transport

4.1 Land-Based Modes in the Multimodal Transport System

Land-based modes only account for a small fraction of the cross-border transport flows in the southern Mediterranean, especially in the Maghreb. This is due to the closure of several borders for political reasons (e.g. between Morocco and Algeria or between Israel and Lebanon); the low volume of intra-regional trade; and the geographical separation of most Mediterranean Partners (MPs) from their main trading partners by the sea. But even though the bulk of trade is processed via ports and airports, road and rail transport are needed for door-to-door delivery. The efficiency of the land-leg is important for the overall efficiency of multimodal chains. With regard to land-based transport, the modal mix is heavily skewed towards road haulage, with a small and decreasing market share for rail freight. Policy issues related to road traffic and railroads are discussed in sections 4.2 and 4.3.

Table 4. 1 Length of Road and Rail Network

Country	Road Network (km)	Rail Network (km)
Algeria	100,992	4,219
Egypt	44,498	4,810
Jordan	7,519	386
Lebanon	6,359	0
Morocco	57,520	1,907
Syria	41,451	2,767
Tunisia	18,997	1,860
WB & G	2,055	0
Total	**279,391**	**15,949**
(Israel)	15,464	962
(Turkey)	382,000	8,607

Source: Eurostat (MED-Trans Database).

The MPs should consider identifying cross-border land corridors with large traffic volumes (see section 1.9 and box 4.1). Policy reforms and infrastructure investments should be prioritized and coordinated along a regional backbone-network of roads and railroads, with the objective of increasing traffic flow efficiency (costs, time, reliability). Specific corridor proposals that have been floated in the past include that of an east-west highway across the Maghreb, the Integrated Transport System in the Arab Mashrek by the United Nation Economic and Social Commission for

Western Asia, and the Programs for Regional Cooperation proposed by the government of Israel in the context of the Oslo peace process.[1]

Smooth hinterland connections are particularly important for ports, which handle the vast majority of trade in the southern Mediterranean.[2] Effective integration between ports and land-based transport will require a number of reforms. In some countries, foreign logistics companies are permitted to provide port-to-port services but may not offer integrated multimodal services that include a land-leg from the port to the final destination. The liberalization of trucking on port premises is another item on the reform agenda. It will increase competition and reduce the costs of trucking for the entire land-leg, since customers are unlikely to transfer cargo between trucks at the port exit. The same holds for restrictions on the activities of logistics intermediaries, particularly freight forwarders, on port premises. Finally, any regulatory reforms that encourage greater use of intermodal technology will smoothen modal transfers in ports. This can include policies to encourage higher rates of containerization; the adoption of electronic data interchange (EDI); a streamlining of customs; and the facilitation of roll-on, roll off (RoRo) traffic. Trucks using RoRo ferries are an important form of intermodal transport for trade between the Maghreb and southern Europe, especially Spain and France.

A series of reforms are needed to facilitate traffic flows at the land borders between southern Mediterranean countries. First, those frontiers that are currently closed for political reasons should be reopened. Second, the simplification of customs and other border controls for cargo, passengers, drivers, and vehicles will be needed (see sections 1.9 and 4.4). Third, mode-specific issues for rail and road traffic have to be addressed. A large number of international agreements for trade and transport facilitation at land borders exist. The MPs should ratify and implement the most important of these (see box 1.12). Besides facilitating trade, the removal of political, administrative, and tariff barriers at land borders would have an important secondary effect. It would bring ports and airports of neighboring countries into competition with each other by extending their hinterlands beyond national borders – as is already the case in the borderless EU Single Market. Examples of potential competitors are the ports of Oran (Algeria) and Nador (Morocco), or the airports of Tel Aviv (Israel) and Amman (Jordan), which are equidistant from Jerusalem. An extreme example of red tape hampering cross-border competition between ports and airports is a Syrian law prohibiting trade to be processed through foreign ports. It is mainly targeted at Lebanese ports, which are more efficient and closer to Damascus than their Syrian competitors.

Besides regulatory reform, physical integration through connecting infrastructure is needed. As discussed in box 1.8, however, most such investment decisions should be taken by the private sector. The role of policy makers should primarily be confined to the creation of an enabling regulatory framework. Modern infrastructure facilities in ports, particularly transfer equipment for containers and dedicated RoRo terminals, are still lacking in several ports of the Maghreb and Mashrek. In other cases, missing link infrastructure needs to be developed to extend land-based rail and road networks into ports.

- In Morocco, for example, the port of Nador is one of the few key ports that is not linked to the railway system, which otherwise connects all main population and industrial centers of the country. In the mid-1990s, the national railway company ONCF estimated the potential for merchandise traffic to be around 2.5 million tons per year. This figure could be even higher, if

[1] (1) ESCWA transport website (*www.escwa.org.lb/divisions/sectoral/transport.html*). (2) Government of Israel. 1996. *Programs for Regional Cooperation 1997* (draft, November 1996).

[2] Airports on the other hand tend to be located closer to the main population centers (and thus the catchment areas for trade) and are generally not as serious a multimodal bottleneck as ports.

an existing connection between the Moroccan and Algerian track-systems would be used to expand Nador's hinterland beyond the border. The Moroccan government has considered mobilizing the required investments of $ 250-300 million for the 120-kilometer link through a private concession. In 1977, ONCF started construction, but after two years public sector financing constraints led to an abortion of the project. More than 20 years later, a rudimentary track of 28 kilometers remains as testimony to the shortcomings of public-sector management in the transport sector.

- Another example of a missing link in port hinterland infrastructure is Damietta in Egypt. It is very close to the existing railway network, but until the remaining kilometers of track are laid, Damietta will continue to be at a disadvantage vis-à-vis the competing ports of Alexandria and Suez, which both have access to railroads.
- In Israel, the government is considering to extend the railway system southwards to the ports of Eilat (in Israel) and Aqaba (in Jordan), on the shores of the Red Sea. Only 15 kilometers would be needed to extend the existing line from the Mediterranean port of Ashdod to the Mt. Zin Phosphate Terminal. Israel has also studied the possibility of upgrading the roads that connect the port of Haifa with its potential Jordanian hinterland.
- In Tunisia, the port of Radès – close to the capital Tunis and the country's main container terminal – was finally connected to rail network in 2001, but for unknown reasons it was still not being used a year later.[3]

Urban and public transport, important parts of land-based transport, are not covered by this study, since they have little relevance for cross-border traffic flows. Nonetheless, there is also significant scope for institutional restructuring, liberalization, and privatization in these segments of the transport market, as some examples show. After Syria lifted a ban on private taxis, for instance, the market for intercity transport became a thriving and highly competitive business, including the high-density route between Damascus and Beirut. As part of its ongoing privatization program, Jordan has sold its public bus company; 15-year concessions for four route packages have been awarded to three local operators; and the former public entity is being transformed into a regulatory authority. In late 2000, the Egyptian government hired Canadian consultants to conduct a feasibility study for the use of a BOT scheme to renew and extend 22 kilometers of metro line in Cairo at an estimated cost of $ 240 million. In Israel, the government has started to tender up to half of the 1,400 public bus routes operated by Egged Transport Cooperative to private operators under franchises of four to six years.[4]

Inland waterways and pipelines are also part of the intermodal transport system, but of limited relevance to the Maghreb and Mashrek. A number of important oil and gas pipelines exist in the region, but since they involve few intermodal issues they remain outside the scope of this report. Egypt has the only inland waterways in this arid region. Its 3,100 kilometers of navigable waterways are more or less equally divided between canals and the Nile. The vast majority of the population lives in close proximity to the river, but this mode of transport accounts for a mere 4 percent of domestic freight.[5] There seems to remain significant potential for higher traffic volumes, especially since more than 90 percent of Egypt's trade is via the sea and can be reloaded to barges for inland transport. Introducing competition and private participation in this sector would be comparatively easy, but the process is at an early stage. In mid-2000, the private company Egytrans obtained a 20-year operating license for the port in Old Cairo. The company, which will handle container traffic by barge, plans investments of $ 30 million.

[3] World Bank. 2000. *Tunisia – Private Sector Assessment Update.*
[4] MEED (24 March 2000).
[5] Economist Intelligence Unit. 2000. *Egypt Country Profile 2000.*

Box 4.1 Trans-European Networks

In the early 1990s, the EU launched its Trans-European Network (TEN) initiative to improve physical infrastructure networks in the transport, energy, and telecommunication sectors.[6] The total financing needs for this ambitious program were estimated between € 400 and € 500 billion. Some money will come from the Commission budget and the EIB will provide long-term loans. Most of the financial burden, however, will have to be borne by the governments of those member states on whose territory investments are being made. To minimize the costs of the TEN projects to governments, the EU tries to use public-private partnerships to the extent possible.

For transport, a Council decision of December 1994 identified 14 TEN projects to upgrade existing and to complete missing links. These projects include six high-speed rail links, two conventional rail links, two highways, a rail/road bridge between Germany and Denmark, an airport, and a multimodal corridor. By 2000, three of these had been completed.[7] The Commission has recommended a revision of the TEN guidelines, which was submitted in 2001.[8] Ports should be given higher priority; intermodal issues receive greater prominence; projects should promote the provision of new services and not just physical infrastructure; and user requirements should be factored into the project design.

In 1996, the Commission launched the Transport Infrastructure Needs Assessment (TINA) with a secretariat based in Vienna, to "oversee and develop an integrated transport network in the CEE accession candidates" and to extend the TENs eastwards.[9] Through the new pre-accession instrument ISPA, the Commission helps finance environmental and transport infrastructure in the accession candidates with about € 1 billion per year (half of which for transport). This, however, is small compared to the preliminary cost estimate of € 91 billion for the completion of the TINA network by 2015. Almost 90 percent of this amount is for a backbone network of roads and railways – modes that play a limited role for cross-border traffic in the MPs.[10]

The extension of the Trans-European Network (TEN) (see box 4.1) to the countries of the southern Mediterranean has repeatedly been discussed. For a number of reasons, however, the application of the TEN concept to the MPs would require some modifications:

- As discussed throughout this publication, many pressing transport bottlenecks are policy-induced, rather than the result of lacking infrastructure. Since these are also easier and cheaper to remove, they should be the main focus of attention. Internally, the EU also tackled policy reforms first – the TEN program was only launched after the completion of the Single Market package of legislative reform, which removed most regulatory barriers to trade between EU member states. Moreover, the Commission is revising the TEN guidelines to take greater account of transport services, compared to a pure focus on physical infrastructure.
- Another reason why the TEN approach makes more sense within the EU and vis-à-vis the Central and Eastern Europe (CEE) accession candidates than in the MPs is that European countries are connected by land borders and most transport between them is land-based.[11] In the MPs, the majority of trade flows through maritime and air transport chains. Such infrastructure is less capital-intensive than the motorways and high-speed rail links that the TEN focuses on. Moreover, there is less need to coordinate infrastructure investments in ports and airports (this is mainly the responsibility of individual countries) than regarding the construction of roads and railways, where the physical infrastructure actually crosses the border.

---

[6] European Commission, DG TREN website (*www.europa.eu.int/comm/dgs/energy_transport*).
[7] European Voice (17 May 2000).
[8] European Commission. 2001. *Proposal for a Decision of European Parliament and Council Amending Decision No. 1692/96/EC on Community Guidelines for the Trans-European Transport Network.*
[9] Oxford Analytica (25 September 2000).
[10] World Bank. 2000. *Transport Sector Restructuring in the Baltic States – Proceedings of a Seminar.*
[11] In the EU, 87 percent of all passenger transport and 75 percent of freight transport is land-based. (European Commission. 1999. *Guide to the Transport Acquis.*).

- It is sometimes assumed that the TEN program could become a vehicle for the Commission to pay the costs for infrastructure projects in the MPs. The TEN program, however, is mainly a planning tool to coordinate investments by member states. It is questionable whether the highly capital-intensive investment projects supported by TEN are the ones the MPs could afford. The costs of the 1,200-kilometer section of the trans-Maghreb highway in Algeria, for example, have been estimated at around $ 5 billion.[12]

Even if the direct extension of the TENs to the MPs seems unlikely, the underlying idea – the identification of bottlenecks in international transport corridors – is highly relevant. The focus, however, should be on multimodal corridors and the countries participating in a corridor should coordinated policy reforms as well as infrastructure investments. This line of reasoning has been endorsed by two important documents approved by Euro-Mediterranean policy makers. In the Lisbon Declaration, regional transport policy makers demanded that comparisons "of alternative solutions to the given transport problem should be made, especially where operational and organizational changes (including private participation) offer viable alternatives to capital-intensive and infrastructure solutions."[13] According to a Commission communication, "'software' measures [...] should be given priority over 'hardware' measures. Many transport bottlenecks [...] have their principal causes in 'software' rather than 'hardware.'"[14]

4.2 Roads and Trucking

Throughout the EU and the southern Mediterranean, road haulage is the dominant form of land-based transport, with rail a distant second. A variety of policy issues arise in the road sector with regards to services, physical infrastructure, and border crossings. As far as the domestic liberalization of road haulage is concerned, several of the MPs have made progress in recent years. In Tunisia, the sector was privatized and liberalized in the 1990s. Tariffs were de-regulated, legal barriers to market entry removed, and government-owned trucking companies sold. Under a loan agreement with the World Bank, Morocco has recently committed itself to abolish the truck-forwarding monopoly of the Office National des Transports (ONT) and associated levies. Traditionally, ONT has "regulated and coordinated all domestic shipments by vehicles weighing more than eight tons [...]. No vehicle [could] travel without the ONT road permit ('feuille de route'), [costing] 5 percent of the value of the freight or a receipt for payment of an additional 4.5 to 5.0 percent coordination tax [...]. Beyond this 10 percent excess cost, ONT rigidities seldom allowed the loading of backhaul shipments, so vehicles returned empty most of the time."[15] It appears self-evident that any remaining regulations of that type should be abolished.

Besides the liberalization of markets, a number of other domestic policy issues arise in the road haulage sector. The objective of the fiscal regime (fuel and vehicle taxes) should be to ensure that the sector bears all economic costs, including the full cost of infrastructure (damage to roads, congestion), environmental costs (pollution, noise), and social costs (accidents). The enforcement of standards for drivers (licenses, working hours), trucks (weight, noise, pollution), fuel (restrictions on lead or diesel) and infrastructure (signs, roads) is also needed to minimize externalities, create a level playing field for competition, and harmonize the sector framework

[12] World Bank. 1999. *Algérie – Note sur la Strategie des Transports*. The cost estimate is from 1995.
[13] UN Economic Commission for Europe and European Commission. 1997. *Lisbon Declaration*. (Adopted at the Lisbon transport conference in January 1997).
[14] European Commission. 1998. *Communication on the Euro-Mediterranean Partnership in the Transport Sector*.
[15] Amiot, François and Ovadia Salama. 1996. "Logistical Constraints on International Trade in the Maghreb." World Bank Policy Research Working Paper Series 1598.

across the region. Overall, the policies that were used to reform road haulage in the EU could provide some useful guidance for similar reforms in the southern Mediterranean (see box 4.2).

Box 4.2 The Liberalization of Road Freight in the EU

After the implementation of deregulation measures, the market for road haulage services in the European Union is now highly competitive, integrated, and efficient:

- *Prices:* Council Regulation 4058/89 made prices for international operations freely negotiable and thus subject to market forces as of January 1990.
- *Market access:* Council Regulation 881/92 removed all quota restrictions for international and transit traffic across the EU after January 1993.
- *Cabotage:* As an intermediate step, Council Regulation 4059/89 established a quota of 15,000 cabotage licenses before Council Regulation 3118/93 increased this number on a yearly basis, and finally abolished all quotas by July 1998.
- *Right of establishment and the freedom to provide services:* Two of the fundamental principles governing the European Single Market are the right of establishment (i.e. to engage in FDI) and the freedom to provide services. These also apply to the road haulage sector.
- *Border controls:* Council Directive 83/643 stipulated that "the various inspections and formalities are carried out with the minimum delay necessary." Council Regulation 719/91 established the customs union between EU countries and thus removed associated controls and frictions. The Schengen Agreement (now incorporated in the Treaty) finally removed all border controls.
- *Intermodal transport:* Across the EU, airlines are allowed to transport freight under an airway bill to the final destination. Such 'air trucking' constitutes a significant share of the total air transport market in the EU (e.g. 26 percent in Germany).

A host of legislation on safety, social and environmental protection, taxation, and technical standards accompanied these deregulation measures to ensure a level playing field for competition and the minimization of external costs caused by road haulage. Selected performance indicators illustrate the beneficial effects of these reforms. Ton-kilometers worked by professional operators increased by half in France and two-fifths in Ireland between 1986 and 1990. The elimination of border controls reduced the 1,200-kilometer journey between London and Milan by about a third. A 1992 study by the Commission calculated the total costs of border controls within the EU to be in the range between € 400 and € 800 prior to reform.

Source: European Commission (1994).

There is also a need to reduce costly and time-consuming formalities at border crossings. These include immigration and license controls for drivers; checks of documentation and licensing for vehicles; the collection of various fees, taxes, and duties; as well as customs clearance for cargo (verification of type and quantity of goods, documents on origin and destination, guarantee documents for import duties, etc.). Although controls are necessary, they are often excessively disruptive to logistics flows due to the complexity of the paperwork; the number of different fees and taxes; confrontational behavior of border personnel; the duplication of checks by different authorities; and corruption. Syrian trucks carrying fruit and vegetables to Europe, for instance, must transfer their cargo to Turkish trucks at the border between the two countries, because Turkish regulation limits the length of vehicles to 13.6 meters, whereas Syrian trucks measure up to 15 meters. Smaller trucks that may cross the border are not allowed to pick up return cargo in Turkey and the Turkish authorities issue driver visas only for one trip at a time.[16] Efforts to remedy this situation are now underway. The West Bank provides an extreme example of policy-induced frictions at land borders. Until 2000, Israel prohibited trucks from crossing the frontier between Jordan and the Palestinian territories. All cargo had to be reloaded to another truck before continuing the journey.[17]

[16] World Bank. 2000. *Syria – A Preliminary Assessment of Transport Costs for Export Development* (draft).
[17] MEED (19 May 2000).

A range of administrative reforms at land borders could facilitate trade between the MPs:

- In most cases, the biggest challenge will be to restructure customs and improve the qualifications of border personnel (e.g. training, adequate salaries). The wide-spread practice to control 100 percent of vehicles is costly and time-consuming. Risk-analysis and selectivity (RAS) techniques should be introduced at all border crossings. Several studies have found "that success rates in detecting fraud and crime (including illegal immigration and smuggling of controlled goods) are far higher when RAS techniques are employed. These techniques allow most vehicles to be processed faster, while the selected vehicles can be removed from the queue to specialized buildings for thorough control."[18]
- Inter-agency cooperation at land borders is also needed to reduce the cost frictions associated with multiple controls. Specific measures should include joint clearance and the appointment of a border-crossing manager for each border crossing.
- A specific feature of land borders (as opposed to ports and airports) is that two countries maintain control posts in direct proximity to each other. Neighboring countries could considerably reduce the time and costs associated with border procedures if they organized joint border crossings and juxtaposed controls. At the German-Polish border crossing of Swiecko, for instance, authorities of both countries perform controls in the same building and use harmonized EU procedures. Moreover, bilateral customs cooperation committees can be formed to address generic issues.
- There should also be a special regime for transit traffic, with simplified documentation, streamlined clearance, and truck seals. Clearance procedures at borders would be further reduced if there were more inland customs clearance centers.
- There should be a systematic compilation of clearance statistics and official target processing times for cargo and vehicles at all border crossings. This would help to identify bottlenecks and create an incentive for authorities to reduce clearing times. Donor assistance for infrastructure investments could be tied to target processing times.
- In some cases, infrastructure deficiencies create additional bottlenecks. Investments might be needed to widen approach roads, for facilities to allow several vehicles to be processed simultaneously, or for equipment to carry out required examinations on site (i.e. without the need to send cargo samples to inland laboratories for tests).

There are several international initiatives to streamline and harmonize documentation requirements and procedures at border crossings, which the MPs should consider to adopt. Examples are the Vienna Convention on Road Traffic or the International Convention on the Harmonization of Frontier Controls of Goods (see also box 1.12).

An interesting precedent for multilateral liberalization between the EU and neighboring countries is the Interbus Agreement. In December 2000, the EU and 13 accession candidates (including Turkey) signed a treaty that liberalizes coach and bus operations between them. It provides for a harmonization of national legislation and fiscal regimes, mutual recognition of documentation, common standards for vehicles and employment conditions, and the establishment of a joint committee to oversee the implementation of the treaty. Although this market segment is of limited importance for cross-border passenger flows in the Euro-Mediterranean region, the Interbus Agreement is a model that could apply to other parts of the transport market (e.g. road haulage) for several reasons. First, the EU member states gave the Commission a mandate to negotiate the agreement with a group of foreign countries (similar to the ECAA discussed in section 2.6). Second, the treaty applies the same principles that govern the concerned market within the EU, as

[18] ECMT and OECD. 2000. *Integration of European Inland Transport Markets*.

laid out in Regulation 56/83 (EEC) and other pieces of EU legislation. Thus it amounts to an extension of parts of the Single Market beyond EU borders.[19] Third, it is multilateral in nature and replaces many bilateral agreements between contracting parties. The treaty not only liberalizes services between the EU and its neighbors, but also between neighboring countries.

Another set of policy issues arises with regards to the financing and management of the road network. In many southern Mediterranean countries, traffic growth and years of underinvestment have lead to a backlog of capacity expansions (e.g. highway construction) and insufficient operation and maintenance (O&M) of existing roads. Moreover, infrastructure bottlenecks and missing links should be removed, especially on major corridors. Governments have a number of options to finance road investments. First, they should enforce the user pays principle by levying fuel and vehicle taxes and/or road charges that take account of infrastructure use as well as external costs, such as pollution and congestion (see box 4.5 for details). Second, the government needs to enforce weight limits for trucks because heavy vehicles cause significant damage to roads. Third, they should try to mobilize private management and investment. At the minimum, they should outsource new construction and O&M activities to private contractors. In Algeria, for instance, the government has decided to hand all civil works to the private sector through competitive tenders.[20]

International experience with privately financed highways is mixed and great care must be taken during project selection and contract design.[21] One of the few successful build-operate-transfer concession (BOT) roads in the southern Mediterranean is the Cross-Israel Highway project, which reached financial closure in October 1999. A private consortium will construct 250-300 kilometers of highway at a total cost of $ 1.3 billion and operate the toll road between key metropolitan areas under a 30-year concession.[22] Much of the commercial risk, however, is borne by the government, which will cover 80 percent of the losses arising from traffic levels below the official projections.[23] In mid-2000, the Egyptian government signed a memorandum of understanding with a private consortium for a 200-kilometer toll road between Alexandria and El-Fayyoum. As a mechanism to cross-subsidize the expected construction costs of $ 200-300 million, the 75-year concession would include the right to develop a large stretch of land along the highway for tourism, agriculture, and industrial use. BOTs for two other toll roads (Cairo-Ain Sokhna and Helwan-Kurinate) are also being discussed.[24] Egypt had launched four similar schemes in 1997, but met with insufficient investor interest. It remains to be seen if any of these projects will actually be implemented. In the meantime, efforts are also underway to secure private funding for a three-kilometer road tunnel underneath the Suez Canal through a BOT scheme.[25] Morocco's efforts to find private investors for a highway section from Tetouan to Fnideq and Lebanon's attempt to use a BOT scheme for a bypass in Beirut were not successful.

---

[19] European Commission. 2000. *Proposal for a Council Decision on the Signature of the Interbus Agreement on the International Occasional Transport by Coach and Bus.*

[20] Different mechanisms can be used to outsource road planning and management. The Argentine model, for instance, is analyzed in: Liautaud, G. 2001. "Maintaining Roads – The Argentine experience with Output Based Contracts." World Bank Viewpoint Note Series 231.

[21] Detailed information on private involvement in the road sector can be found in: (1) Halperin, Ricardo and Patrick Malone. 1999. "Overview of World Experience in Private Financing in the Roads Sector." World Bank ECSIN Working Paper Series 2. (2) Estache, Antonio and Jose Carbajo. 1996. "Designing Toll Road Concessions – Lessons from Argentina." World Bank Viewpoint Note Series 99. (3) Engel, Eduardo, Ronald Fischer, and Alexander Galetovic. 1997. "Privatizing Roads – A New Method for Auctioning Highways." World Bank Viewpoint Note Series 112.

[22] MEED (12 November 1999).

[23] Der Spiegel (47/2001).

[24] Reuters Business Briefing (23 July 2001).

[25] MEED (28 April and 11 February 2000).

4.3 Rail Freight

Unlike trucks, railways cannot provide door-to-door services, but have a potential cost advantage for long-haul traffic (approximately above 500 kilometers). In the multimodal logistics system of the southern Mediterranean, railways seem well suited to carry long-distance freight between neighboring countries and to provide efficient hinterland connections for ports – especially for containerized and bulk cargo. In several MPs rail plays an important role in passenger transport (e.g. in Egypt and Morocco) and could help to relieve pressure on the congested road systems of densely populated countries such as Israel and Lebanon. The railroad networks of most MPs were built in the nineteenth and the early twentieth century, often with the involvement of private investors. Except for the Palestinian territories and Lebanon, whose railways fell into disuse during the civil war, all MPs have operating railroad networks.[26] The reform needs in the sector include the restructuring of state-owned companies, the introduction of private participation, and the facilitation of cross-border traffic. Following are several examples of recent reforms in the southern Mediterranean:

- Morocco can be considered a model for the restructuring of state-owned railway companies for other MPs. With support from the World Bank, the government launched an ambitious reform program in 1995 to turn around the loss-making Office National des Chemins de Fer (ONCF). Operations were rationalized, surplus staff reduced, and commercial management introduced. These measures proved so successful that the company made profits in each of the three years from 1998 to 2000. The next stage of reforms, to be implemented in 2002, will transform ONCF into a joint stock company that will operate the existing network under a concession agreement. An ongoing investment program to modernize tracks and rolling stock is being supported by several donors, including the World Bank, the EIB, and the African Development Bank.
- Until recently, it seemed as if Jordan would become the first country in the region to introduce private participation in the sector. Its 620 kilometers of track are mainly used to transport mined phosphate to the port of Aqaba. In 1998, the government finalized negotiations with an international consortium (including two US railways and a Japanese company) for a 25-year operation and management contract. The Aqaba Railways Corporation was supposed to lease and upgrade the existing line between Amman and the Red Sea and build two extensions – a 22-kilometer track to the Shidiyeh phosphate mine and a 16-kilometer connection to the industrial area of the port of Aqaba. Investment commitments of around $ 120 million and a lump sum transfer to the government of $ 30 million were agreed upon. Five hundred of the existing 1,300 employees were to be retained.[27] In early-2001, however, the deal collapsed for reasons that are not fully known. In Tunisia, a similar concession scheme could be considered: two-thirds of the total freight tonnage is phosphate, extracted from mines in the south of the country.[28]
- In Egypt, the government provides subsidies of about $ 350 million per year to the national railway company.[29] The German Kreditanstalt für Wiederaufbau has provided several hundred million of euros in assistance to the Egyptian National Railways (ENR) during the last couple of decades. Attempts to contract out rail-track and locomotive maintenance work have been so successful that this instrument is now widely used. Significant restructuring of ENR, tariff-adjustments – even the intensively used first-class between Cairo and Alexandria is being subsidized – and more private participation seems desirable. Private concessions or licenses on key routes (e.g. from the ports on the Mediterranean and Red Sea along the Nile river) should be considered. There might also be potential for the multimodal transfer of containers from

[26] In December 2000, the Lebanese government announced its intention to re-establish a 34-kilometer connection between Tripoli and Aboudieh in Syria as part of a broader strategy to rebuild the country's railway system.

[27] MEED (20 August 1999) and Wall Street Journal (4 March 1999).

[28] Economist Intelligence Unit. 2001. *Tunisia Country Profile 2001*.

[29] Economist Intelligence Unit. 2001. *Egypt Country Profile 2001*.

ports around the Suez Canal to land-locked parts of central Africa. This, however, would require considerable investments and private commercial management.

- The Israeli railway system has seen an impressive revival in the late 1990s thanks to an ambitious expansion program. Between 1998 and 2000, the number of passengers doubled to 13 million and investments of around $ 250 million annually are planned for the coming years. During the late Ottoman Empire, regular connections between Damascus and Haifa, as well as between Haifa and Cairo, existed and the government has studied the possibility of re-establishing these regional links.[30]

Despite these reforms, the restructuring needs of state-owned railways in the southern Mediterranean remain significant. Decades of state ownership have left a legacy of underinvestment, poor management, overstaffing, and a severely eroded competitiveness vis-à-vis road transport. To reduce excessive costs, state-owned enterprises (SOEs) need to lay off surplus staff in a socially acceptable manner (redundancy payments, early retirement, retraining) and rationalize their networks by closing loss-making routes. On the revenue side, they have to rebalance tariffs by charging full-cost prices to freight customers and by increasing the cost recovery rate in passenger transport. Institutional restructuring will involve the sale of subsidiaries and the outsourcing of non-core activities, the streamlining of organizational structures, corporatization, and the introduction of commercial management (including proper accounting practices). Better maintenance of tracks and rolling stock should increase asset utilization and thus productivity. To maintain or even increase their market share in freight services, railway companies must provide much more flexible, reliable, and user-friendly services and they must ensure better integration with other modes. Intermodal services require appropriate transfer infrastructure (rail-truck, rail-ship) and well-managed transfer operations (tight time-tables, reliable schedules, etc.). All of these restructuring measures would reduce the need for government subsidies and permit railway companies to fulfill their true potential in the multimodal logistics system of the region.

The global trend towards railroad privatization began later and is less advanced than in other transport modes. A 1999 World Bank survey reviewed the recent experience of developing countries. Between 1990 and 1997, 14 countries awarded a total of 37 contracts for the operation and maintenance of railways to private companies, mobilizing investment commitments of $ 14 billion (see diagram 4.1).[31] Mirroring a pattern found in other infrastructure sectors, the vast majority of these projects (81 percent of transactions) were in Latin America, with most of the remainder in Asia and Sub-Saharan Africa. The southern Mediterranean region was notably absent from this international trend. In most countries, the results of privatization have been positive. In Argentina, for example, traffic started to grow again after years of declining volumes, labor productivity rose four-fold, service quality improved significantly, and the public deficit was reduced by $ 600 million per year. The flip side of these reforms were the closure of loss-making routes and layoffs.[32]

---

[30] Frankfurter Allgemeine Zeitung (21 August 2000) and Government of Israel. 1996. *Programs for Regional Cooperation 1997* (draft, November 1996).

[31] Tynan, Nicola. 1999. "Private Participation in the Rail Sector – Recent Trends." World Bank Viewpoint Series 186.

[32] Details of the reforms in Argentina, Brazil, Chile, and Mexico in: Thompson, L. and Karim-Jacques Budin. 1997. "Global Trends in Railway Concessions – Delivering Positive Results." World Bank Viewpoint Note Series 134. In the United States, "freight prices have fallen an inflation-adjusted 56 percent since the 1981 liberalization," while the number of regional railroad companies increased from 200 to 550. (Financial Times, 3 July 1998).

The main privatization instrument are concessions to operate infrastructure and provide rail services.[33] In most cases, significant investments in track and rolling stock are required. The duration of the concession – ranging from one to several decades – is largely a function of the investment needs, project risks, and the profitability of the operation. Except for Bolivia and two projects in Africa, only freight services and track maintenance have been privatized, while passenger transport remained with the public operator. Argentina awarded loss-making passenger concessions on a least-subsidy basis, while defining service standards and maximum fares to be monitored by an independent regulator. To ensure the commercial viability of a railway concession, significant restructuring is normally needed. Redundancy packages for surplus staff hired under public ownership and debt restructuring usually accompany privatization transactions. Many governments also seek a strategic investment by an experienced international operator who can inject management expertise.

Diagram 4.1 Investment in Rail Projects with Private Participation in Developing Countries (cumulative)

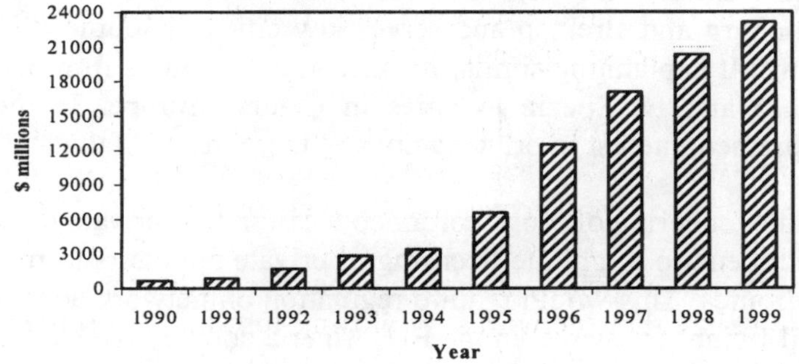

Source: World Bank (PPI Database).

Private participation can also facilitate cross-border rail traffic, as the following examples show:

- Mexico, for example, separated its network into several regional concessions and designed the system in a way that should facilitate cross-border traffic flows with the United States. The two concessions along the border were both awarded to Mexican-US consortia. Kansas City Railway, for example, operates the 'NAFTA railway' that runs from Mexico all the way to Canada.[34] In 2001, the concessionaires invested $ 300 million and have committed themselves to investments of $ 1.3 billion over a five-year period. In addition, the harmonization of technical standards for rolling stock is being addressed by the intergovernmental Land Transportation Standards Subcommittee of NAFTA.
- Ivory Coast and Burkina Faso jointly concessioned the line between the port of Abidjan and Burkina's capital, Ouagadougou, to the private company Sitarail in 1994. Although the 1,300-kilometer line faces competition from road traffic, and the alternative corridor from the port of Lomé in Togo, it continues to be important for international traffic. The governments financed the severance program for half of the original 3,500 employees that were laid off. Two state-owned "railway landlord corporations" retain ownership over the infrastructure and collect concession fees. Sitarail is responsible for the operation of passenger and freight transport and for infrastructure maintenance. It also prepares infrastructure investment programs and submits these to its regulators. After exclusivity rights for the first 7 years of the 15-year concession, infrastructure access may be granted to competing operators. In the first full year of operation after privatization, freight traffic nearly doubled to 430 million tons and the quality of freight services increased considerably.[35]

[33] Detailed information about concession results, contract design, and concession examples can be found on the World Bank web-site (*www.worldbank.org/html/fpd/transport/rail/rl_conc.htm*).
[34] Reuters Business Briefing (27 November 2001).
[35] Mitchell, Brigitta and Karim-Jacques Budin. 1999. "The Abidjan-Ouagadougou Railway Concession." World Bank Findings Series 140.

- In October 2000, two concessionaires operating railway services in Chile (Ferronor) and Argentina (Belgrano Cargas) signed an agreement to operate an international line over a distance of 900 kilometers. It will be the first regular train service between the two countries and both companies will interchange equipment and provide common billing to shippers.[36]
- A European example of private logistics companies offering cross-border rail freight in combination with port services is Eurokai. The company operates container terminals in Hamburg and Bremen and serves key cities in southern Germany and Hungary with its own trains. It is planning similar hinterland connections from its Italian container terminals of Gioia Tauro and La Spezia to cities in Central Europe. In the southern Mediterranean, Eurokai expressed interest in privatizations of the ports of Malta and Damietta.[37]

While the tendering of cross-border concession to a private consortium could be considered, a more realistic scenario might the licensing of private operators to run domestic and cross-border services on key routes. This would require regulation on network access and would be somewhat similar to the 'rail freight freeways' in the EU. Algeria adopted legislation that allows for such licensing, and similar adjustments to the legal framework are now being discussed in Morocco. In the Middle East, there also seems to be significant potential for cross-border rail projects once political obstacles are overcome (see box 3.6). Policy reforms and regional cooperation of railway companies are also needed to facilitate cross-border traffic in the southern Mediterranean. Standards for equipment, signaling, and professional qualifications should be harmonized in accordance with international agreements (UIC, EU). Border controls for cargo and personnel should be streamlined. National railroad companies should coordinate their schedules to reduce waiting times at borders. Ideally, all railway operations and non-railway procedures should be carried out at the point of origin and not at the border. If they are, there should be a joint border station to avoid a duplication of controls. MPs should improve the transmission of train operating information from the point of origin to the border crossing. All such measures should take account of ongoing initiatives to facilitate cross-border flows at the European and international level (see box 4.3).

There seems to be potential for greater cross-border rail cooperation in the two sub-regions of the southern Mediterranean: the Mashrek and the Maghreb. In 1965, Morocco, Algeria, and Tunisia signed a comprehensive agreement for technical cooperation between their railway companies (Chemins de fer trans-Maghreb, CFTM). In the years to 1989, rail traffic between these countries doubled, but has declined significantly since 1992, due to tensions between Morocco and Algeria.[38] Cross-border rail traffic is now basically non-existent between Morocco and Algeria, while cumbersome border transfers leave the traffic between Tunisia and Algeria far below its potential level. In principle, the backbone network of the Maghreb – traversing the region from East to West and well connected to key ports and population centers – could play a useful role in medium and long-haul traffic within the multimodal transport system of the region. A revival of the CFTM cooperation would be required to realize that potential. In the Mashrek, the railway systems of Egypt, Israel, and Lebanon are also compatible (Jordan's is not). If it were not for the political tensions in the region, the potential for long-haul traffic along a backbone rail route traversing these three countries could be substantial.

---

[36] PR Newswire (20 October 2000).

[37] Financial Times Deutschland (15 June 2001).

[38] Amiot, François and Ovadia Salama. 1996. "Logistical Constraints on International Trade in the Maghreb." World Bank Policy Research Working Paper Series 1598.

Box 4.3 Railway Liberalization in the EU

Europe has a well-developed railroad network, and thanks to heavy investments in high-speed rail infrastructure, the mode successfully competes in passenger transport on medium-distance routes (e.g. Paris-London). In freight transport, however, the average travel speed in the EU is 16 km/h and rail's market share in total freight has declined from 32 percent in 1970 to 14 percent in 1996.[39] This compares to 41 percent in the United States.[40] This gap reflects national fragmentation, a lack of competition, and prevalent state ownership in the EU. To reduce traffic congestion and environmental damage caused by road haulage, the Commission has initiated a number of railway reforms:

- Directive 91/440 gives railway companies access rights to tracks in other EU countries for the provision of international combined freight transport. It obliges EU countries to separate the accounts of their railway companies from those of the state. To increase the transparency of state aid, it also stipulates that accounts for infrastructure and transport services shall be separated.
- Directive 95/18 of 1995 defines the licensing regime for companies seeking the legal status as 'railway undertakings'. This is an important precondition for fair and transparent market access.
- Directive 95/19, issued at the same time, sets out the criteria for the non-discriminatory allocation of infrastructure capacity (path allocation) and the charging of fees for infrastructure use (e.g. cost-related and non-discriminatory fares).
- A 1996 White Paper (a document stating policy intentions and legislative proposals) calls for an increased role for market forces and greater commercial independence of railway undertakings. Moreover, it suggests the creation of international 'rail freight freeways' to provide smooth and integrated transport services across EU borders.
- Since 1998, three rail freight freeways have been established: 'North-South' (linking several ports in northern Europe with ports in southern Europe via Austria and Switzerland); 'Scanways' (between Denmark, Finland, Norway, and Sweden); as well as 'Belifret' (connecting the Benelux countries with France, Italy, and Spain). A fourth one, 'UK-Sopron' (between Great Britain and Hungary with onward connections to other CEE countries) is under discussion.
- Directive 2001/12/EC defines a Trans-European Rail Freight Network of 50,000 kilometers of track to be opened to competition by 2003 (cross-border routes). This shall be extended to 150,000 kilometers by 2008 (including domestic lines) and could turn out to be the most far-reaching reform to date.
- Several member states have institutionally separated infrastructure and services by creating a body for track management, fully independent from the incumbent. The Commission intends to make such unbundling obligatory and replace Directive 95/18 by stricter rules on path allocation.
- All railway operators licensed in the EU should have fair and non-discriminatory access to these freeways, but excessive infrastructure charges discourage potential users. To prevent such anticompetitive behavior, the Commission proposes strict rules on the calculation of user fees.
- Some member states are already granting network access to private rail operators. In Italy, ten companies are licensed to provide such services.[41] In Germany, the chemical firm BASF obtained a rail license in 1996. By 1999 it transported one million tons of cargo, cutting costs by 20 percent, and is planning a joint venture with logistics companies to provide third-party rail services.[42] In 1998, Deutsche Post and UPS set up Express Shuttle to operate trains between their sorting depots.[43] In 2001, the furniture retailer Ikea created a rail subsidiary to supply its superstores across Europe.[44]
- A lack of technical harmonization (electricity voltage, track gauges, crew training) and cumbersome procedures at borders (e.g. transfer and verification of information on wagons and loads) cause significant delays and make rail uncompetitive. The Commission wants to establish a European Railway Agency to harmonize safety and technical standards across the EU.[45]

[39] Financial Times (24 November 2000).
[40] The Wall Street Journal (29 March 1999).
[41] Financial Times (2 August 2001).
[42] Frankfurter Allgemeine Zeitung (4 January 2000).
[43] European Voice (16-22 April 1998).
[44] Financial Times Deutschland (9 March 2001).
[45] European Voice (24 January 2002).

Other Sector Issues

Chapters 2 and 3, as well as the previous sections, analyzed mode-specific issues. The following four sections will discuss some additional aspects of transport sector policy that should not be forgotten. These include customs reform, postal service reform, competition policy, and strategies for the development of multimodal logistics clusters.

4.4 Customs Reform: The Example of Lebanon

Lebanon's customs have traditionally been a major logistics bottleneck and source of economic inefficiency.[46] Procedures were cumbersome, non-transparent, and time-consuming (most of the seven to twelve days needed for container delivery were due to customs delays). Such deficiencies not only imposed unnecessary economic costs but also created a fertile breeding ground for corruption. In order to address these problems and to ensure that the 45 percent of public revenues coming from customs duties are collected effectively, the Lebanese government opted for a radical overhaul of the existing system.

One of the three components of a UNDP and World Bank-sponsored Fiscal Reform Project, launched in 1995, is geared towards customs reforms.[47] The objectives were to streamline and automate customs clearance, to make the entire system as transparent as possible, and to move to a non-confrontational relationship between customs agents and their clients. For this to be achieved, processes had to be re-engineered and made computerizable, institutional structures streamlined and strengthened, and information technology installed. Whereas customs clearance used to involve 13 stages, it was reduced to 5 basic steps: (i) entry of declaration; (ii) acceptance of declaration; (iii) inspection of goods (verification of declared information); (iv) assessment of information thus gained (automatic calculation of taxes); and (v) payment.

The first stage of the project, which started in early 1995, focused on tariff reforms. The structure of the tariff regime was simplified both horizontally (number of duty categories) and vertically (number of duty rates), while clearance procedures were aligned with international standards.[48] A single-page administrative document (SAD) replaced 26 much more complex and outdated forms. In fact, it was the first time that this UN and EU standard was translated into Arabic. These and other reforms made the clearance process computerizable and the Najm computer system was rolled out. It was first introduced at the Port of Beirut in September 1997, at Beirut International Airport in August 1998, and was installed in all customs offices by mid-2000. Najm is an adaptation of UNCTAD's Automated System for Customs Data (Asycuda) and it is compatible with EU systems. The new computer software permits a constant monitoring of the days required for clearance. As an important side benefit, it also yields more accurate and real-time trade statistics.

---

[46] The information in this section is based on discussions with UNDP staff. Some of this information can also be found in: Al Khouri, Riad. 2000. "Trade Policies in Jordan, Lebanon, and Saudi Arabia." In Bernard Hoekman and Hanaa Kheir-El-Din, eds., *Trade Policy Developments in the Middle East and North Africa*. Mediterranean Development Forum and the World Bank Institute.

[47] The project components correspond to the three directorates of the Ministry of Finance: cadastre, customs, and finance. Executing agency of the customs component has been UNDP, with UNCTAD in charge of IT-related work.

[48] On January 1, 1996, Lebanon adopted the Harmonized System (HS) of tariffs – a six-digit coding, which is the de facto international nomenclature for classifying goods.

The introduction of information technology was complemented through staff training and a restructuring of work procedures. Another innovation that is already being applied is the relocation of customs clearance to the shop floors of some of the main importers and exporters, such as the privatized LibanPost. Being in charge of final clearance, the Ministry of Finance's customs department executes the trade-related regulations of all other ministries. To inform users of their rights and responsibilities and to further streamline the inspection process, the customs administration summarized all border regulations in an index and made it available to its clients. Efforts are now under way to perform all checks at one time.

Besides reducing the need for paper-work, the key advantages of Najm are its information storage, processing, and retrieval capacities. Thanks to the database, regular importers and exporters can build up a track record of past compliance, which permits customs officials to assess individual client risk. This allows for much more selective testing of those companies with high risk or an insufficient track record and helps to build trust.[49] Since inspections are costly and time-consuming, such active risk management benefits both the authorities and their clients. Although the project was still ongoing, the benefits of reforms were already clearly visible after a year and a half, as demonstrated by diagram 4.2. The green line ratio of shipments (those cleared without inspection) quadrupled from 10 to 40 percent between October 1997 and March 1999. Nonetheless, the average rate of tariff collection remained constant. During the same period, the average days needed for clearance declined from six to four days, as a result of more selective testing. These results, yielding the 'scissors effect' shown by the diagram, are in line with the experience of other countries that have implemented similar reforms.

Diagram 4.2 Customs Performance Indicators

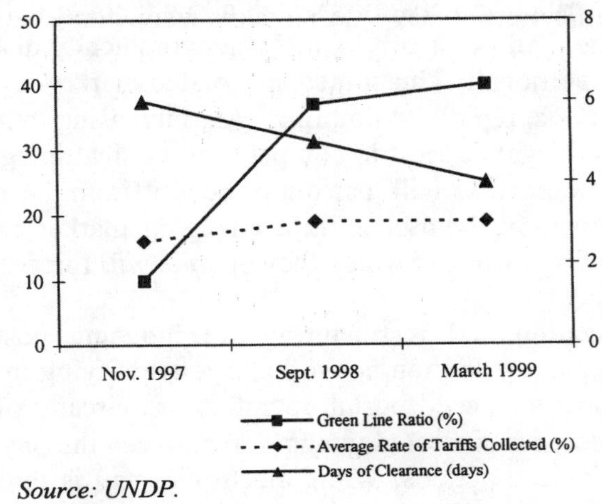

Source: UNDP.

The final stage of reforms, launched in early 1999, is the transition towards EDI. The first step in this transition is the introduction of Najm Online Operations (NOOR), which gives importers and exporters access to what was initially a purely intra-governmental network. In fact, it was the first time that the Lebanese government interfaced electronically with taxpayers. The final stage of EDI will be the creation of Value Added Networks (VAN). Such a system allows the various participants in the clearing process (and related transactions) to interact electronically and in a real-time manner using a single platform – including shipping agents and brokers, customs and port authorities, banks and insurance companies, as well as importers and exporters. The development of such a system, however, will no longer be the task of the authorities. A number of private sector VAN providers are already operating and a common standard should emerge through competition between these systems. To stimulate this process and to ensure compatibility between the VANs and NOOR, NOOR software will be distributed free of charge to software companies.

One of the last items to be addressed was reform of customs legislation. The anachronistic law, which had not been updated since 1934, inhibited efforts to liberalize procedures and created

[49] Before, companies had no 'history' and the relationship between customs and clients was transaction-based. With greater access to information, the relationship can become 'entity-based'. A committee meets regularly to evaluate clients and to categorize them to determine future treatment.

opportunities for corruption. The notion of containers, for instance, did not exist when the law was drafted and strictly speaking containers had to be unstuffed for clearance. This is time-consuming and labor-intensive. By permitting customs officials to impose such costs on importers at their discretion, the law gave them leverage to extract bribes. The new law 4461/2000 streamlined procedures and eliminated unnecessary steps, such as the certification of invoices by consulates.

4.5 Postal Service Reform and Transport Logistics

The global postal service industry has an annual turnover of $ 207 billion, a network of 700,000 post offices, and a total of six million employees.[50] Due to liberalization and technological change, the sector is currently in the midst of a metamorphosis. The main competitive advantages of postal operators vis-à-vis other logistics service providers (see section 1.6) are far-flung office and distribution networks, which allow them to deliver not only logistics but also communications, banking, and other services to a geographically dispersed customer base. Although postal services have traditionally constituted an isolated market-segment, this compartmentalization of the logistics industry is rapidly crumbling. An increasing number of countries are removing government-imposed legal barriers to competition, vertical integration, and cross-border consolidation. Whether postal companies will lose out or benefit from these changes will depend on how fast they manage to re-position themselves in a changing market environment – and how fast an overhaul of the policy framework in which they operate will force them to do so.

Privatization and restructuring are inducing postal companies to leverage their main assets (elaborate distribution networks) by diversifying into other logistics and communications services. The most advanced postal operators are already offering comprehensive logistics solutions. This requires a sophisticated integration between the physical handling of goods, information flows, and financial transactions. While electronic mail is threatening to erode revenues from letter services, delivery of purchases over the internet is expected to become an important source of traffic. Reverse logistics, where the post offices picks up a faulty product from a customer's home (and delivers a replacement) on behalf of the manufacturer, is another innovation. In such transactions, the post office's role is not only to ensure physical transport but also to act as "a trusted third party in certifying payments and delivery."[51] Hybrid mail, whereby companies send electronic documents to post offices for printing and distribution, is a further recent development. Another facet of the complex redefinition of the postal business currently taking place is the expansion of post offices from savings bank services (traditionally part of postal systems in most countries) into much broader financial services.

Liberalization in the EU

In the EU, the Commission is pressing for increased competition in the € 80 billion ($ 71 bn) postal market.[52] After the liberalization of telecommunication, power, and gas across the European Union, postal services are one of the last utility-type network industries to be transformed by market forces.[53] Express mail and large parts of the parcel business have long been competitive and are

[50] Financial Times (20 November 2000).
[51] Financial Times (20 November 2000).
[52] Financial Times (11 May 2000).
[53] *Network industries* are markets in which the delivery of goods and services requires the establishment of complex physical networks, such as electricity grids, gas distribution networks, or railway systems. Since the fixed costs tend to be too high to make the operation of more than one such networks economically viable, these markets constitute a natural monopoly. Because of this and other features, network industries require specific

pitching courier service providers against postal companies.[54] A 1997 EU postal directive obliged the 15 member states to further liberalize postal services. In February 1999, the transport of packages above 350 grams was opened to competition. A further reduction of the weight limit to 100 grams is expected and eventually, domestic standard letters could be the only market segment where EU countries may still grant exclusivity rights to their postal companies.[55] In the meantime, several EU countries have gone beyond the minimum EU standards for market opening. Sweden and Finland, for instance, scrapped their domestic postal monopolies in the early 1990s.[56] Britain plans to phase out the monopoly by 2006.[57] Other countries, like Spain, permit competition for deliveries within the same city or, like the Netherlands or Germany, have unilaterally reduced the weight limits that delineate the legal monopoly. Six countries have fully liberalized direct mail.[58] As Klaus Zumwinkel, the CEO of Deutsche Post puts it: "The fact that we jumped into the cold water earlier will help us to be stronger later."[59]

While some member states are trying to delay further liberalization, the Commission is using competition policy to accelerate market opening. According to EU competition and state aid rules and the postal directive, member states can only grant exclusivty rights to postal companies to the extend required to fund universal service provision (i.e. country-wide services at uniform tariffs and quality standards). While the maximum scope of the monopoly is defined by the weight limit, the principle of proportionality requires that it must not be larger than necessary to achieve this public-interest objective. At the same time, market distortions must be minimized. In particular, any cross-subsidization between monopolistic and competitive services is illegal. Member states must also ensure regulation of their postal monopolies by an independent body and all postal companies have to keep separate accounts for monopolistic services to facilitate effective regulation. A number of violations against these rules have been under investigation. In a precedent-setting case, the Commission levied a € 24 million fine against Deutsche Post for cross-subsidizing its parcel services and obliged the company to create an independent subsidiary to prevent such abuses in the future.[60] Further antitrust cases against the German operator are pending concerning illegal state aid and the disruption of international mail through surcharges on incoming mail. Simultaneously, the German regulator is reviewing the company's high charges for standard letters. The EC has launched similar state aid and competition investigations against the Dutch and Italian operators.

To ensure high-quality universal services, the EC's directive on postal services has set minimum standards for two key performance indicators: 85 percent of EU mail has to be delivered within 3 days (J+3 or speed target) and 97 percent within 5 days (J+5 or reliability target). To ensure compliance, the International Post Corporation (IPC), an association of 21 postal operators, has hired an independent company to carry out a regular cross-country benchmarking exercise. Since 1994, one million test letters are sent in the course of each year, delivery times are recorded, and results for each operator published twice a year. To a large extent thanks to the peer pressure induced by benchmarking, the J+3 average has increased from 79 percent in 1994 to 94 percent in 2000; 99 percent of all letters meet the reliability target, and average delivery times have been

---

policies to ensure market access and competition (e.g. network access regulation or the unbundling of network ownership and operations from the provision of services through the network).

[54] Express mail has a number of defining characteristics, including guaranteed delivery at a fixed date, as well as collection from point of origin and direct delivery to the addressee (see also section 1.6).

[55] Financial Times (16 October 2001).

[56] Financial Times (11 May 2000).

[57] Financial Times (31 January 2002).

[58] The Economist (13 May 2000).

[59] Financial Times (15 September 2000). European business associations and companies have launched the Fair and Free Post Initiative to lobby for a full liberalization of EU postal markets by 2007 (*www.freefairpost.com*).

[60] Financial Times Deutschland (21 March 2001).

reduced by a third to 2.2 days (see diagram 4.3). In a separate move, the Commission has also called upon the European postal companies to revise their terminal dues, the mutual charging framework for cross-border mail, in order to better reflect real costs. User groups are criticizing the cartel-like structure of the current system for artificially maintaining high charges.

Diagram 4.3 Performance Benchmarking in the the EU Postal Services – Quality Improvements (1994-2000)

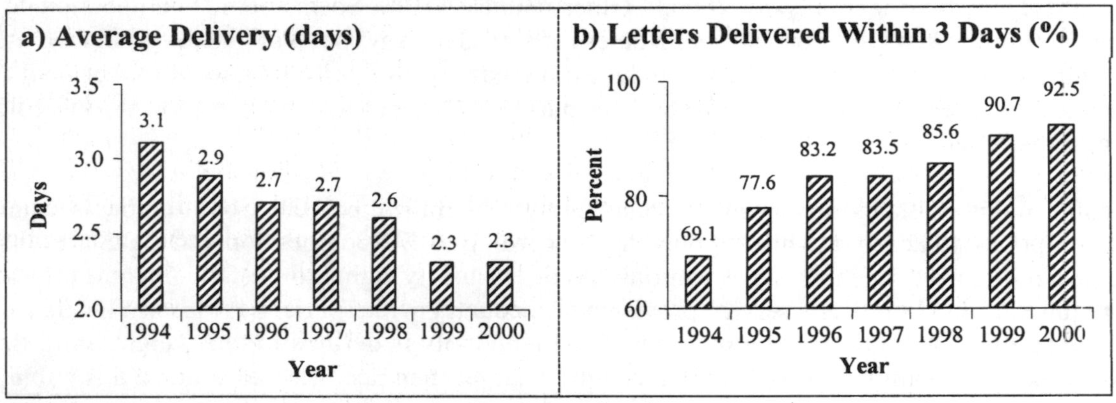

Source: International Post Corporation (2001).

Sector Restructuring and Consolidation in the EU

Across the EU, liberalization of the sector is being accompanied by restructuring and privatization of postal companies at the level of the member states.[61] The Dutch TNT Post Group became the world's first listed postal company when it joined the Amsterdam and New York stock exchanges in 1998. In November 2000, the German government followed suit by floating 29 percent of Deutsche Post for € 6.6 billion. In what became the second largest initial public offering (IPO) in German history, the company was valued at € 23.4 billion. A decade of intensive restructuring and expansion had preceded the IPO. First, postal services were split from telecommunication and banking activities and then transformed into a joint stock company. Regulatory functions were separated from operations and remained with the postal ministry until it was dissolved in 1998 and replaced by an independent regulator. The company's balance sheet was thoroughly restructured, mainly with regard to pension-related obligations. The payroll was reduced by one-third from 380,000 in 1990 to 240,000 in 2000, turnover increased from DM 19 billion in 1990 to about DM 60 billion in 2000, and earnings rose from a loss of DM 624 million (1990) to a profit of about DM 2.2 billion (1999).[62] The successful restructuring of Deutsche Post, the EU's largest postal company, exemplifies the continent-wide transformation of postal operators from inefficient state-owned monopolies to competitive companies run along commercial lines. This trend is most advanced in Holland, Germany, the Nordic countries and the United Kingdom, but also well under way in Italy and some other EU member states. In late 1999, Finland and Belgium launched far-

[61] The industry federation *PostEurop*, based in Brussels, has 42 postal companies as members and is a useful point of contact for information concerning the sector (*www.posteurop.org*). It was created to provide a more commercial forum and representation than that provided by the *Universal Postal Union* (UPU). The structure of the UPU, a UN institution where member countries are represented by government officials, dates from the days where all postal services were being provided by state-owned monopolies.

[62] Financial Times (1 December 1999, 15 September 2000) and Die Woche (3 December 1999). It should be noted that the East German postal service with 80,000 employees were integrated after German reunification in 1990.

reaching restructuring programs of their postal operators and in December 2000, the Greek government opened negotiations with four international companies about the sale of a strategic 25 percent stake in Hellenic Post Office (Elta).[63]

Two other recent developments (besides liberalization, restructuring, and privatization) are the diversification of postal companies into related logistics services and cross-border sector consolidation. The Dutch and German postal companies have progressed farthest in their efforts to become global players and full-blown logistics suppliers. In the past three years, Deutsche Post has made more than 30 international acquisitions for a total of € 10 billion. These included the Swiss-based logistics group Danzas, the Dutch transport group Nedlloyd, Air Express International of the United States, and a 50 percent stake in the global express carrier DHL. In early 2000, 28 percent of Deutsche Post's sales came from abroad, up from a mere 2 percent in 1998.[64] In 1996, Dutch KPN acquired the global express and logistics service operator TNT for € 1.7 billion and renamed it TNT Post Group.[65] Other international acquisitions have followed since. "The UK post office has bought a dozen delivery companies in Europe and the US in just 18 months, while the French post office [La Poste] recently announced an alliance with FedEx, the US express delivery service. Earlier this year [2000] TNT Post Group and the UK and Singapore postal services signed a joint venture accord that will create the world's largest global business mailing company, serving more than 200 countries worldwide."[66] Cross-border consolidation is bringing incumbents into competition with each other. In Germany, for instance, La Poste has taken over DPD and British Post has acquired German Parcel – both fierce competitors of Deutsche Post.[67] Another unexpected competitor emerged in 2001, when eight newspaper publishers decided to connect their regional distribution networks to provide nation-wide mail services.[68]

Postal companies are increasingly competing against express carriers and other players, vying to be among the small group of integrated logistic providers that should eventually dominate EU markets. "To date, with the exception of Deutsche Post, most of the recent post office acquisitions have involved the express, parcel or direct mail distribution sectors. However, as the boundary lines between those activities and other distribution-related operations become ever more blurred, it looks increasingly likely that some postal organizations will become significant international logistics providers."[69] Such diversification brings postal companies into direct competition with integrators, express carriers, and other providers of logistics services. Following recent acquisitions, about a quarter of Deutsche Post's turnover in 2000 came from its logistics division, up from almost zero in 1998. However, the company is still struggling to integrate its recent acquisitions and to transform itself into a fully-integrated logistics provider.[70]

Postal Reform in the Southern Mediterranean

In the southern Mediterranean, postal service reforms are at an early stage. In Lebanon, where postal services ceased operating during the civil war, the government awarded a management contract to a private consortium, led by Canada Post. In October 1998, the new operator, LibanPost, took over

[63] Financial Times (31 January 2000, 7 December 1999, 14 December 2000).
[64] Financial Times (20 November 2000).
[65] European Voice (16 April 1998).
[66] Financial Times (20 November 2000).
[67] Financial Times (28 December 2000).
[68] Frankfurter Allgemeine Zeitung (31 August 2001).
[69] Financial Times (17 June 1999).
[70] Financial Times (17 May 2001). DP now has three main units: post, express, and logistics (latter is in turn sub-divided into heavy goods, world-wide logistics, value-added services).

more than 300 public-sector employees, started rehabilitating 200-250 post offices, and launched an investment program of $ 50-90 million. The contract fee to the government should be gradually increased from 5 percent of revenues in the first year to 40 percent in the twelfth and final year of the contract. While courier services are open to competition (DHL reduced its prices by 10 percent when LibanPost entered the market), the government has committed itself to the exclusive use of LibanPost and the company has been granted a monopoly for letters up to two kilograms in return for a universal service obligation. The government remains in charge of printing stamps and regulating prices. Although the contract was awarded through international competitive bidding (four bidders), the process was criticized for being non-transparent and cumbersome (e.g. negotiations took two and a half years). Since the privatization, a poorly-developed regulatory regime, political interference, and the withdrawal of two consortium partners have plagued the sector. Nonetheless, postal services in Lebanon were re-established and since 1998 mail volumes quadrupled to 19 million letters per year.[71]

Even though the Lebanese reforms provide some useful lessons for other countries, the civil war legacy (e.g. years without an operational postal service, no country-wide system of addresses) makes it a somewhat special case. However, some other countries in the region have also launched initiatives to reform their postal sector. Algeria is separating postal services from telecommunications and plans to create an independent regulator for both sectors. In Jordan, the government has decided to privatize and liberalize the postal services. On the basis of a consultant report, a sector strategy is being drafted. In Morocco, the government has already separated postal from telecommunication services. Recent activities aim for the gradual liberalization of the sector, without sacrificing public service obligations, and at significant improvements in the operations of the postal network. In April 2001, the Egyptian government launched a tender for the construction and operation of a postal network in ten governorates.[72] It also intends to overhaul the regulatory framework and restructure the postal operator.

Table 4.2 Postal Sector Indicators (2000)

Country	Letters/ Inhabitant	Post Offices	Employees	Domestic Letters/ Employee	Operational Balance
Algeria	21	3,245	20,115	27,537	positive
Egypt	3	7,513	38,331	3,393	positive
Jordan	n.a.	626	2,849	n.a.	negative
Lebanon	2	358	495	6,599	negative
Morocco	9	1,569	8,745	25,838	positive
Syria	1	1,135	2,729	6,137	positive
Tunisia	7	973	9,140	n.a.	negative
Total/Av	**7.17**	**2,203**	**11,772**	**13,901**	
Israel	104	702	4,300	141,162	positive
Turkey	15	5,605	36,057	26,807	positive
France	450	17,000	236,224	109,046	positive

Source: UPU (Tunisia: 1998 figures).

Despite these positive developments, most postal services in eight Arab MPs continue to be relatively inefficient state-owned monopolies, starved of private investments and modern management. In line with global and EU trends, the agenda for postal reforms in the southern Mediterranean should include:

[71] The Economist (5 January 2002).

[72] MEED (6 April 2001).

- the separation of regulatory and operational functions and the creation of a transparent and stable regulatory framework (e.g. quality and price regulation for monopolistic activities, regulatory independence);
- a clear definition of universal service obligations for the operator and the identification of the best financing model for their provision (e.g. subsidies or limited exclusivity);
- the gradual introduction of competition;
- the commercialization and corporatization of the postal company;
- its restructuring (staff reductions, balance-sheet clean-up, commercial management); and
- eventual privatization.

The sooner the MP governments tackle this reform agenda, the sooner their postal service operators will be able to modernize and re-position themselves. The World Bank and the European Commission are already advising several countries in the region on postal sector reform, including Algeria, Egypt, Morocco, Lebanon, and Saudi Arabia.

4.6 Competition and State Aid Policy in the Transport Sector

Reflecting the importance of competition for a dynamic market economy, all OECD countries and an increasing number of developing countries use competition laws to protect consumers from cartels, restrictive practices, and the abuse of market power by companies. Competition (or antitrust) rules complement other policy instruments that stimulate competition, including deregulation (removing government-imposed constraints to competition), sector-specific regulation (to address instances of market failure), free trade (cross-border competition), and privatization. Sector-specific regulation addresses structural obstacles to competition in a sector (e.g. rules for airport slot allocation, the unbundling of port services from infrastructure provision, network access in for private rail operators). In contrast, the cross-sectoral and more general nature of competition law provides for a flexible framework to tackle anti-competitive behavior on a case-by-case basis.[73]

In addition to national competition authorities in member states, the European Commission as the guardian of the Single Market, enforces EU competition and state aid laws. They are enshrined in Articles 81, 82, and 87 of the Treaty of Rome, elaborated upon in implementation regulations, and continue to evolve as a result of precedent-setting decisions by the European Commission, the European Court of First Instance, and the European Court of Justice (the appeals courts for Commission decisions).[74] The Commission scrutinizes cartels, mergers, price fixing, market sharing agreements, predatory pricing, restrictions of market access, and other cases of anti-competitive behavior. It also monitors subsidies by national EU governments that distort cross-border competition. It frequently prohibits or grants conditional approval for transfers to private or public enterprises in whatever form (e.g. subsidies, guarantees, tax breaks). Its considerable powers of investigation, combined with the international reputation for independence and strict

[73] For a general overview over these and related policy issues, see: OECD and World Bank. 1999. *A Framework for the Design and Implementation of Competition Law and Policy.*

[74] "*Article 81* [formerly Article 85 of the Treaty of Rome] prohibits agreements between firms which prevent, restrict or distort competition unless those agreements can be shown to promote technical or economic progress and that consumers enjoy a fair share of the resultant benefits. *Article 82* [formerly Article 86] prohibits the abuse of a dominant position. The rules are restricted to situations where trade between [EU] member states may be affected." (CAA UK. 1998. *The Single European Aviation Market.*) *Article 87* (formerly Article 92 of the Treaty of Rome) prohibits state aid in whatever form, if it distorts competition by favoring certain firms at the expense of others. There are well-defined derogations, such as regional aid.

enforcement that it has built, deter private companies and EU governments from interfering with the competitive dynamics of the EU Single Market. In exceptional cases where benefits outweigh the costs, clearly defined individual or block exemptions to competition laws can be granted.[75] Block exemptions are limited in time and reviewed periodically prior to their renewal.

EU Competition Cases in Maritime and Air Transport

Maritime and air transport are subject to EU competition and state aid laws, just like any other sector.[76] While the Commission's main instrument for the introduction of competition in aviation has been liberalization through a series of sector-specific directives and regulations (see chapter 2), the primary instrument in maritime transport has so far been the application of EU competition laws. An interesting example of the complementarity and substitutability between sector-specific regulation and cross-sectoral competition policy are discriminatory airport charges. After an EU directive on airport charges was blocked by some member states, the Commission decided to use its powers as the EU competition authority to roll back the practice of discriminatory charges through the application of competition law in a number of precedent-setting cases (see also section 2.10).

In air transport, several recent cases concerned state aid, alliances, and predatory pricing.[77] State aid to Sabena (1991 to 1995), for instance, was permitted on the condition that the Belgian government ceased to grant the airline preferential treatment regarding slot allocation, groundhandling, and airport charges. In the case of Iberia, state funds approved in 1992 could only be used for the implementation of a comprehensive restructuring plan that included staff reductions and fleet modernization. An alliance between Lufthansa and SAS was approved in August 1995, on the basis that the airlines cede slots and thus facilitate the entry of competitors on six major routes. The EC also scrutinized the proposed merger between British Airway and American Airlines. It made the approval conditional on a transfer of 267 weekly slots at Heathrow to reduce the carriers' dominant position at this important trans-Atlantic hub (the two airlines hold 61 percent of the slots used for London-US flights).[78] In June 1995, following a complaint by British Midland, the Commission ruled that discriminatory discounts for airport charges gave an unfair advantage to Sabena. In November 1996, Alitalia was fined for the abuse of a dominant position related to slot allocation. The low fine of 1 percent of revenues (it could have been up to 10 percent) was due to Alitalia's decision to give up its role in slot allocation. In mid-2001, Scandinavian Airlines Systems (SAS) and Maersk Air were fined € 53 million for collusion. SAS had secretly paid its competitor for ceasing operations on the Copenhagen-Stockholm route.[79] Around the same time, the EC was reviewing one of the two remaining block exemptions for the air transport sector (the other one permits consultations on slot allocation), which allows IATA airlines to coordinate fares for the

[75] According to *Article 90 (2)*, such exemptions are subject to the principle of *proportionality*, "designed to ensure the best match between the duty to provide general interest services and the way in which the services are actually provided, so that the means used are in proportion to the ends pursued. [...] It also makes for the best possible interaction between market efficiency and general interest requirements, by ensuring that the means used to satisfy the requirements do not unduly interfere with the smooth running of the single European market [...]" (excerpt from the web-site of DG Competition).

[76] General competition rules became applicable to air transport through Council Regulations (EEC) 3975/87 and 3976/87. In maritime transport they became applicable through Council Regulation (EEC) 4056/86.

[77] The EC's 1994 "guidelines for state aid in the air transport sector" stipulate, among other things that "The aid must form part of an overall restructuring program and must be of limited duration [...]. The restructuring program must be self-contained, that is to say no further aid will be requested [...]. The aid is a one-off payment, on the principle 'one-time, last-time'. [...] The government must play no part in managing the airline, which must be run on commercial principles." (Quotes from web-site of DG TREN).

[78] Financial Times (4 August 2001). Because of these conditions, BA and AA opted for a looser alliance.

[79] Financial Times (19 July 2001).

purpose of interlining (through-ticketing on journeys involving flights of different airlines). Critics claim that this has facilitated price-fixing and cartellization and is one reason why EU fares are higher than those in the US, where interlining is no longer permitted.[80]

Box 4.4 Prices and Subsidies in the Transport Sector

Just like prices in any market, transport prices influence the decisions and behavior of suppliers, investors, and consumers. They are an important instrument for economic resource allocation and the pursuit of sector efficiency. Several pricing principles govern the EU Single Market and are enshrined in the EU's competition and state aid rules, as well as other parts of the acquis communautaire. First, where competition is feasible, prices should be determined by market mechanisms. Price competition induces companies to cut costs and to pass on efficiency improvements to their customers. Second, in monopolistic market segments (e.g. airports, rail services), a degree of regulation is generally needed to prevent monopolistic pricing. Such regulation should be transparent and well-targeted. Third, economic efficiency requires that prices reflect economic costs (e.g. full cost recovery of transport companies and pollution taxes to take account of environmental costs). Prices should neither be artificially low as a result of open or hidden subsidies, nor excessively high because of monopoly rents. Distortions to price competition between modes should be removed. Fourth, price increases resulting from scarcity (e.g. airport or port capacity) should provide signals to investors as to where new infrastructure is needed, and at the same time permit them to generate a fair return on their investments. Scarcity pricing will also ensure that scarce resources (e.g. airport slots) will go to those market participants that have the greatest use for them and the greatest willingness to pay.

Throughout the southern Mediterranean, price reform should be an integral part of transport sector reform. Liberalization should introduce the market mechanisms needed for price competition and efficient pricing. In many MPs, prices for some transport services are still below cost-recovery levels, while others are inflated through monopoly rents. Tariff rebalancing and the regulation of monopolistic activities are therefore needed. General price subsidies (which often favor higher income groups) should be replaced by more targeted and less distortive assistance to the poor. Finally, price distortions and excess costs resulting from bureaucratic customs procedures and para-tariff measures should be tackled.

Sources: European Commission (1998e) and (1995c).

In maritime transport, a total of six cases have thus far clarified the limitations of a block exemption granted to liner conferences.[81] In December 1992, for instance, the EC imposed a € 10.1 million fine on the members of the CEWAL conference for the use of 'fighting ships' (sailing at the same times as competitors and offering dumping prices) as well as anti-competitive rebate structures to deter competition on routes between northern European ports and Zaire. In September 1998, 15 of the world's largest shipping lines, participating in the Trans-Atlantic Conference Agreement (TACA), received record fines of € 273 million. They had given competitors financial incentives to join the conference in order to restrict competition and they had extended their collusive behavior beyond price-fixing for sea-based transport (covered by block exemptions under certain conditions)

[80] Currently, 39 European IATA members still "set fares for each of the 6,950 routes in the EU three times a year." The block exemption was extended in 2001; three years earlier, the Commission had abolished a similar exemption for air cargo, after coming to the conclusion that freight tariffs coordinated through IATA were considerably higher than market prices. (Financial Times, 29 November 2000). In any case, airline alliances and code-sharing agreements have largely "superseded the former practice of interlining." (AEA Yearbook 1999).

[81] This well-defined block exemption is granted on the assumption that the economic costs of liner conferences are outweighed by their public benefits (reliability, frequency, and price stability). However, strict conditions and limitations apply to ensure that this balance does not tilt. "Article 3 of *EC Council Regulation 4056/86* grants exemption to members of a liner conference in respect to the fixing of a uniform price and any other agreed conditions with respect to the provision of scheduled maritime transport services. [...] Any agreements between conferences and non-conferences do not benefit from the block exemption and the Commission scrutinizes these agreements with great attention. This is because the Commission considers that the counter balance of the block exemption granted to conferences is that they remain subject to effective competition from non-conference liners." (OECD. 1999. *Discussion Document on Regulatory Reform in International Maritime Transport*).

to price-fixing on inland transport and freight forwarding, as well as to the fixing of terms and conditions of service contracts (not covered by the block exemption). They had thus managed to impose price increases of more than 80 percent on Europe-US trade between 1993 and 1995.[82]

While the Commission's mandate has yet to be extended to include competition on air transport routes outside the EU, it already has such a mandate regarding maritime transport. In an April 1992 case against four liner conferences and eleven shipowners' committees covering trade between France and eleven West and Central African countries, the Commission punished the companies, in part, for lobbying the foreign authorities for exclusivity rights geared at restricting competition on bilateral routes. In an independent but parallel development, the World Bank helped several of the respective African governments liberalize their maritime sectors. While the Commission had objections to the cartel because of the costs it imposed on European importers and exporters, the World Bank was concerned about the economic costs that the restrictions on maritime competition were having on the African economies. In the five years after the Commission ruling, freight rates on these routes fell by 50 percent.[83]

There have also been several cases related to infrastructure access and other abuses of monopolistic positions in ports. In 1992, Sea-Link had to modify ferry schedules that discriminated against its competitors in the port of Holyhead (which it operates). In 1993, Denmark was obliged to give Stena Lines access to the port of Rødby or permission to construct a new terminal next to the existing port. In 1997, the Italian port of Genoa had to modify discriminatory tariff structures for pilotage services. In response to pressure from the Commission and the European Court of Justice, Italian legislation granting monopoly rights to docker unions, was dismantled in the early 1990s and in fact triggered broader port reforms. The Commission also ruled on a number of cases on infrastructure access in airports.

Competition Policy in the Southern Mediterranean

The Commission's work in the area of competition and state aid laws are of relevance to the Mediterranean Partners for a variety of reasons. First, the above examples illustrate the range of competition issues that can arise in the transport sector and which policy makers should take into account when designing sector frameworks. Second, they show the need to complement sector-specific regulation with cross-sectoral competition policy. Third, EU competition and state aid laws will gradually become applicable to the MPs, as a result of the Association Agreements (AAs). Any Maghreb and Mashrek country wishing to accede to the European Civil Aviation Area (ECAA) would also have to fully adhere to the principles of EU competition laws in aviation. Moreover, the Euro-Mediterranean AAs contain provisions on competition and state aid. In the case of Jordan, for instance, Article 53 of the Agreement stipulates that:

> "1. The following are incompatible with the proper functioning of the Agreement [...]: (a) all agreements between undertakings [...] which have as their object or effect the prevention, restriction or distortion of competition; (b) abuse [...] of a dominant position [...]; (c) any public aid which distorts or threatens to distort competition by favoring certain undertakings [...] 2. Any practice contrary to this Article shall be assessed on the basis of the criteria resulting from the application of the rules contained in Articles 85, 86 and 92 [now Articles 81,82, and 87] of the Treaty establishing the European Community [...].[84] 3. The Association Council shall, within five years of the entry into force of the

[82] Financial Times (17 September 1998).

[83] OECD. 1999. *Discussion Document on Regulatory Reform in International Maritime Transport*. Other factors contributed to a fall in rates, notably liberalization in these countries, supported by the World Bank.

[84] Both Egypt and Israel rejected this subclause to prevent EU competition law from determining whether anti-

Agreement, adopt by decision the necessary rules for the implementation of paragraphs 1 and 2. Until these rules are applied, the provisions of the Agreement on interpretation and application of Articles VI, XVI and XXIII of the GATT shall be applied [...]. 4. (b) Each Party shall ensure transparency in the area of public aid, inter alia by reporting annually to the other Party on the total amount and the distribution of the aid given and by providing, upon request, information on aid schemes. Upon request by one Party, the other Party shall provide information on particular individual cases of public aid."

The competition and state aid provisions will become effective upon the enactment of the implementing regulations. These are to be drawn up jointly by the EU and the Mediterranean Partner, within five years from the entry into force of the respective Association Agreement. They will necessitate policy adjustments within the MPs, either in the form of sector-specific regulation or through the introduction of cross-sectoral competition laws, in order to deal with anti-competitive cases that affect trade between the EU and its Mediterranean Partners. Several countries in the southern Mediterranean are adopting competition laws, but virtually none of them have clear rules on state aid. Competition laws were passed in Algeria (1995), Tunisia (1991 and 1995), and Jordan (1997) while still being drafted in Egypt and Morocco.

Box 4.5 Donor Coordination in the Transport Sector

A multitude of donor institutions support economic adjustment in the southern Mediterranean – including the European Commission, the World Bank, the EIB, the International Monetary Fund, a dozen national donors from EU countries, the Arab Fund, the African Development Bank, the United States Agency for International Development (USAID), UNCTAD, and the United Nations Commission on International Trade Law (UNCITRAL) (see box 1.2 and box 1.12). The World Bank, for instance, has ongoing transport projects in Algeria and Tunisia and has been assisting Lebanon, Jordan, and Morocco in their sector reforms. Donor coordination is needed to avoid duplication, exploit synergies, ensure that donors focus on areas where they have comparative advantages, and minimize the burden on limited absorption capacity in recipient countries. Although everyone agrees that better donor coordination is needed, it is still quite rare in practice. This is due to institutional jealousies, bureaucratic constraints, a fear of some recipient countries that donors might 'team up against them', and the sheer complexity of coordination.

A number of mechanisms could enhance donor coordination in the transport sector. First, MP governments should play a more active role in orchestrating the interventions of their various partners – after all, it is these countries that would benefit most. Second, the Commission should try to draw other donors into the activities of the Euro-Mediterranean Transport Forum and the regional MEDA project (see box 1.2). These are the only real multilateral instruments currently available for transport reforms in the region and, if properly used, they could become the focal point for policy dialogue and donor coordination in the sector. Third, a common sector strategy is needed to ensure that all parties know what needs to be done.

An interesting precedent could be the CEE enlargement countries, where the ultimate goal of EU accession provides both a clear vision and a detailed road map for reforms. The Commission's main priority is to help the countries to adopt the acquis communautaire, while other donors provide technical assistance for the regulatory and institutional reforms this entails. The World Bank, for instance has prepared dozens of studies related to the accession process and all of its projects in the region take account of accession requirements. While their mandates might differ (e.g. development in the case of the World Bank, EU enlargement in the case of the Commission), most parties regard EU accession as the most effective vehicle to achieve their respective objectives. The objective of membership gives the CEE governments the determination to implement reforms that might be difficult in the short term. Even though EU accession is an unrealistic scenario for the majority of the MPs, this report argues that a common vision and a joint strategy can also be defined for the transport sector of the Euro-Mediterranean region. The vision could be the development of a common transport space in order to facilitate trade in the emerging free-trade area. Devising a strategy to achieve this goal requires identifying the frictions that persist in the multimodal system across the region and to agree on means to remove them. This report is a first attempt to develop such a common strategy.

---

competitive practices that may affect trade between the EU and Egypt or Israel actually took place.

4.7 Policies for a Multimodal Logistics Cluster: Panama and Suez Canal Compared

The contrast between the Panama Canal and the Suez Canal demonstrate how significant economic benefits can be derived from a multimodal approach to transport policy. Both canals are global transport corridors and were built at around the same time. In 1999, the Panama Canal recorded 13,653 ocean-going transits and the Suez Canal reported 13,490. One hundred forty-four international shipping routes and 4 percent of the world's trade pass through the Panama Canal. It is estimated that about 7 percent of sea-transported world trade is passing through the Suez Canal.[85] Both waterways are strategically located at the center of their respective regions and thus have the potential to function as distribution hubs.[86] Despite these similarities, however, the performance of the areas around the two canals has diverged considerably. Policies conducive to the transport sector turned the Panama Canal zone into a dynamic logistics cluster, whereas the area around the Suez Canal was long a quiet backwater. If recent reforms in Egypt gather momentum, the country might eventually be able to fully exploit its strategic location.

The Panama Canal and Transport Policies in Panama

The Panama Canal was built by the United States at the beginning of the twentieth century and handed over to Panama at the end of 1999. Thanks to coherent transport policies, Panama is leveraging its geographical position to turn the country into a regional transport hub. "As part of its plan to increase services exports, the government has articulated a 'national maritime strategy' organized around the concept of a multimodal transport system involving the canal, ports and airports, the railway, and the trans-isthmian road links. In addition to facilitating the transportation of cargo, the plan would make Panama a center for ship and container repair, oil bunkering and other shipping services."[87] In 1998, "a National Maritime Authority was created to oversee and coordinate strategy for what has until now been a fragmented sector."[88] Even before the creation of this authority, Panama unlocked synergies between different modes by simultaneously implementing reforms throughout the transport sector.

Liberalization and the introduction of private participation have been at the core of sector policy. All four ports north and south of the Panama Canal are now privately operated and competing with each other. Between 1995 and 1998, the existing harbors of Cristobal and Balboa were privatized and expanded by their new owners. Further investments in capacity expansion are ongoing, especially in Balboa. In parallel, two new BOT ports around Colon on the Atlantic coast were concessioned to foreign companies. Since 1995, $ 600 million of private capital has been invested in the four facilities.[89] Thanks to competition between these ports, services have improved, rates have dropped, and traffic has increased. Between 2000 and 2020, tonnage transiting the canal is expected to double.[90] Handling 1.4 million twenty-foot equivalent unit containers (TEU) per year, Colon has become Latin America's largest container port before Buenos Aires – and traffic is still growing rapidly. Seventy-five percent of container throughput is accounted for by transshipment.[91]

[85] Economist Intelligence Unit. 2002. *Egypt Country Profile 2002.*
[86] Financial Times (12 October 2000).
[87] Economist Intelligence Unit. 1998. *Panama Country Profile 1997-98.*
[88] Economist Intelligence Unit. 1998. *Panama Country Report II/1998.*
[89] Financial Times (12 October 2000), Oxford Analytica Brief (29/8/97), The Journal of Commerce (30/6/1998) and Sommer, Dirk. 1999. "Private Participation in Port Facilities." World Bank Viewpoint Note Series 193.
[90] Financial Times (3 December 1999).
[91] Reuters Business Briefing (27 November 2001).

Private participation in transport infrastructure, however, has not been confined to ports. After obtaining a toll-road concession, a Mexican company was to invest $ 230 million in a private highway along the Panama Canal.[92] In the late 1990s, a private consortium purchased the derelict trans-Isthmus railroad from the government. Panama Canal Railway Co. is investing $ 75 million to upgrade 75 kilometers of track parallel to the waterway and $ 10 million for intermodal infrastructure and transfer equipment – in order to serve all four ports on both ends of the Canal. The government received a lump sum payment from the concessionaire and will collect 5 percent (eventually 10 percent) of annual revenues. Containers shipped between the free ports of Colon and Balboa will not be subject to customs.[93] At the reopening of the railway in October 2001, contracts for the handling of 100,000 TEU per year had been signed. Throughput should increase to 500,000 TEU at the end of phase one and is expected to eventually reach one million TEU after further investments.[94] The concession period is 25 years, with the option of a 25-year extension. While the toll road and the railway are expected to be in intermodal competition with each other, they are both complementary to the Canal itself. Given draft and size limits, many container vessels either have to unload some of their cargo or cannot pass the canal at all.[95]

The poor efficiency and maintenance track record of both the railway and the ports under public ownership was a key motive for turning them over to private operators.[96] Before privatization, only three to four trains were crossing the isthmus each week at an average speed of 8 km/h. Private investments and management are expected to increase this to about 100 km/h and thus cut transit times to 1.3 hours, compared to 12 hours that ships need to traverse the canal.[97] Together, these various private sector investment projects are the cornerstone of a strategy to transform Panama into a container transshipment hub. So far, the results have been impressive. Container movements increased by 33.5 percent between 1997 and 1998 and the country has started to take away business from Kingston in Jamaica.[98] At the same time, prices fell. Containers to Hong Kong, for instance, became 50 percent cheaper between 1995 and 1998, partly as a consequence of the Asian crisis.

Private participation and competition are also being introduced in air transport. The flag carrier Air Panama was sold and the country signed an open skies agreement with the United States. At the end of 1999, the United States returned the Howard Air-Force Base to Panama. It is in close proximity to Panama City and the Canal Zone, and at the end of 2001 the government was searching for a private investor that would build a regional air cargo hub.[99] In conjunction, these various reforms are to turn Panama into an intermodal maritime-air transport hub, similar to Dubai in the Gulf.

Even the Panama Canal Authority itself is being restructured and commercialized. For the hand over of the Canal from the United States to Panama in 1999, the constitution of Panama was amended to ensure that the state-owned Panama Canal Authority would remain shielded from political interference. A new management is currently restructuring the organization along commercial lines. Examples are the outsourcing of non-core activities and the creation of 41 separate business units, whose profitability can now be scrutinized thanks to the introduction of a

---

[92] Journal of Commerce (June 8, 1998).

[93] Although containers will be transported across Panama, they will be sealed and (for customs purposes) treated as if they were not entering the country ('in-bond').

[94] Reuters Business Briefing (27 November 2001).

[95] The largest ships that can transit the canal are referred to as 'Panamax' vessels. The latest generation, however, have to transfer their cargo via land to ships waiting on the other side. An expansion of the Canal is being discussed.

[96] Oxford Analytica (29 August 1997). Until 1977, the railroad belonged to a private US company. (Project Finance, February 2000).

[97] The Journal of Commerce (8 June 1998 and 16 December 1999).

[98] The Journal of Commerce (30 June 1998) and Oxford Analytica (29 August 1998).

[99] Reuters Business Briefing (30 May 2001).

modern financial accounting system. The authority has become much more customer focused. It has reduced waiting times and accidents and just awarded a concession for a new visitors center and restaurant. "Like China and Hong Kong, Panama and the canal have opted for the concept of one country, two systems. Panama is a third world country while the canal remains a first world operation. Corruption allegations swirl around Panama's congress and president daily but none has yet been leveled at the canal."[100] The canal's arms-length relationship with the government has been a reason for its success since it reduced political interference and induced the government to concentrate on attracting related value adding activities, instead of merely relying on a constant revenue stream from transit tolls.

Panama's logistics strategy, however, goes beyond transport sector policies in the narrow sense. To foster a whole cluster of transport-related services, concessions are being awarded along the canal for chandleries, ship repair yards, cargo services, warehousing, and bunkering. There are also plans to provide more attractive facilities to the 300 cruise ships transiting the canal each year and thus tap additional sources of revenue. Most important for the ancillary business of the canal, however is the Colon Free Zone, created in 1948 at the entrance of the Canal. It is the second largest Free Zone in the world after Hong Kong, contributes 12 percent to Panama's GDP, and accommodates 1,600 businesses handling $ 5.5 billion in imports and $ 6.2 billion in re-exports (transshipment).[101] With trade liberalization spreading throughout the Americas, the zone's key advantage is no longer its duty-free status but its position as a regional warehousing center and distribution hub.[102] Container loads are broken down and forwarded to buyers in the quantities they demand and with much smaller lead-times than if ordered from the factory directly. A wide range of specialized transport and logistics service providers, including legal and financial firms, are attracted by, and in turn reinforce the advantages of the favorable policy environment and the state-of-the-art private infrastructure.

The Suez Canal and Transport Policies in Egypt

Even though the Suez Canal has a higher transit volume than the Panama Canal, Egypt derives more narrow economic benefits from it. Whereas the number of ocean-going transits is almost identical for the two canals, the cargo tonnage was significantly higher in the Suez Canal (360 million tons) than in Panama (223 million tons). In 1999, toll revenues of $ 1.8 billion in Egypt were more than three times as high as in Panama ($ 0.6 billion).[103] This reflects the different strategies of the two countries. The Panama Canal operates as a non-profit entity (fees are set at a level that permits cost-recovery) and the country reaps the economic benefits associated with the value-added services and infrastructure investments that the canal attracts. In Egypt, the main economic benefit derived from the canal is the fees. According to industry sources, transit costs per container are about twice as high in the Suez Canal. Although the tolls are an important source of foreign revenue, Egypt is not fully leveraging its strategic location as the 'gate-keeper' of the canal. To date, there has also been little private investment in complementary infrastructure. A dynamic value-adding logistics industry, which could serve both Egypt and its neighbors, has yet to emerge. Moreover, toll revenues have gradually declined in recent years.[104]

---

[100] Financial Times (22 March 2002).

[101] It should be noted that Panama's population and GNP is considerably smaller than that of Egypt.

[102] Financial Times (9 October 1998).

[103] Economist Intelligence Unit. 2000. *Country Profile Egypt 2000* and *Country Profile Panama 2000.* Tonnage figures are from 1997.

[104] This decline has been caused by a number of factors. One is the depth of the canal, which cannot accommodate very large vessels. Another is the tendency of shipping lines to avoid the Suez Canal and to go around the Cape of Good Hope on the southern tip of Africa instead to save costs. Moreover, an increasing part of oil and gas trade is via pipelines. Finally, a cyclical factor contributing to the decline, was the Asian Crisis.

A key obstacle for the development of a logistics hub around the Suez Canal has long been the lack of an enabling policy framework. Public ownership and monopolistic structures throughout the transport sector, years of underinvestment due to government budget constraints, heavy administration, and cumbersome customs clearance, as well as the absence of an overall strategy for the liberalization and privatization of the transport sector, deterred private investment and made it difficult for competitive dynamics to unfold. In 1998, the World Bank estimated that the total economic costs of maritime sector inefficiencies alone amounted to more than $ 1 billion per year. Private sector sources cite the Suez Canal Authority as one of the most bureaucratic public entities in the country. A striking example for public sector inefficiency is the port of Damietta. Although the container terminal was opened in 1985, it only handled its first deep-sea containership in January 1990 – a five-year delay caused mainly by poor marketing and planning.[105]

The railway, which connects Port Suez, Port Said, and Damietta, is state-owned and barely used for cargo transfers due to poor management and under-investments. Most traffic between ports on the two sides of the canal is transported by a public toll road between Suez and Port Said. The idea of using railroads to transport containers from the ports near the canal to land-locked parts of central Africa has been floated and might be an interesting way to unlock intermodal synergies. This, however, would require considerable investments and a significant improvement in the operational efficiency of Egyptian National Railways. The SUMED pipeline for oil products runs from Port Suez to Alexandria. Tankers discharge their cargo in the Red Sea, from where it is pumped to the Mediterranean and reloaded onto another ship. Although oil from the Gulf is a key trade for the canal, competition with the pipeline is limited because it is mainly ships too large to transit the canal that use the pipeline. SUMED is 50 percent owned by the Egyptian government (the balance being held by governments of different Gulf countries). In fact, the Suez Canal Authority, which also owns Port Said, Port Suez and Port Ismaliya, is trying to reach an agreement with SUMA to "bar any tanker small enough to traverse the canal from transporting oil through the pipeline."[106] Important obstacles for the development of a multimodal air-maritime transport hub are the state ownership and quasi-monopoly of the flag carrier Egypt Air, as well as restrictive bilateral air service agreements that reduce the flexibility of airlines to develop their route networks (see section 2.6). In summary, most critical infrastructure continues to be state-owned. Cartel-like structures and cross-ownership between the respective entities prevent competition and reduce efficiency.

As part of broader efforts to modernize the economy, however, the government of Egypt has begun to tackle transport sector reforms. New port infrastructure in Damietta and Ministerial Decree No. 40 of 1990, which grants significant discounts for port dues and other charges for transshipment, helped boost Egypt's role as a cargo hub. In 1998, container transshipment in the country (mostly in Damietta) amounted to 695,000 TEU, or 11 percent of total transshipment in the Mediterranean.[107] Given Egypt's prime location, however, the potential for transshipment seems to be much larger. In January 1998, the government changed the law relating to the Suez Canal Authority and placed it under the direct authority of the Prime Minister, in an effort to improve its operations.[108] At the same time, a new maritime sector law and two related decrees were issued, ending a 30-year state maritime monopoly and permitting private participation in the sector (e.g. shipping agents, forwarders). Since July 1998, for instance, agents have been able to obtain licenses for certain

[105] Containerization International (April 1999).
[106] United States Energy Information Administration (February 1999) In 1998, the SUMA pipeline transported 2.4 million barrels/day and the Suez Canal 0.7 million barrels per day.
[107] Drewry Shipping Consultants. 2000. *Mediterranean Container Ports and Shipping.*
[108] MEED (30 January 1998).

stevedoring activities.[109] In addition, several stevedores and other transport companies, particularly in the maritime sector, have long been on the privatization list, but are yet to be sold.

Around the Suez Canal, private companies are developing two new ports and a free zone. The BOT container port in East Port Said, which is under construction, could become the main hub-port for the eastern Mediterranean. In August 1999, following an international tender, the government signed a 30-year concession agreement with a consortium led by ECT International of the Netherlands and Maersk of Denmark.[110] The private venture, Suez Canal Container Handling Company, will invest $ 480 million to equip the port with an annual capacity of one million TEU, which might increase to three million TEU in a second phase. The government is providing the basic port infrastructure, including dredging and breakwater work for $ 211 million. The port is expected to become operational in 2001 and will compete with the existing ports in Damietta and Port Said. As part of the contract, however, the government has committed itself to limiting the capacity of these two competitors to 1.2 and 0.6 million TEU respectively. The government plans to develop a free zone around the port. More advanced is the 2,400-hectare Suez Development Zone, a free zone for industrial and trading activities, which is being developed at the southern end of the canal. The government has sold the land to private developers and is providing the trunk infrastructure. The private partners will build all infrastructure within the zone and resell plots to industrial investors. In late 1999, they hired a US company to develop a master plan and expected total investments of more than $ 1 billion within the zone.[111] A new port is under construction as part of the overall scheme. The government is providing the basic infrastructure, including quay walls ($ 60 million) and dredging ($ 105 million). A private consortium, Sokhna Port Development Company, will operate the port. It includes Stevedoring Services of America (25 percent) and the local partner OCI, which is also one of the main investors in the development zone.

Despite these encouraging developments, key segments of the Egyptian transport sector have yet to be reformed. Egypt continues to have some of the highest freight costs in the region (see table 1.2). The toll road, railways, and SUMA pipeline could all be privatized and intermodal competition between them encouraged. Except for a few smaller BOT airports in tourist resorts, competition and private participation in air transport still have a long way to go. In the port sector state ownership (including six shipyards), cross-shareholdings (e.g. between ports authorities and stevedores), and monopolies remain wide-spread. The corporatization of the Suez Canal Authority, or at least its organization along commercial lines, should also be considered (the canal was originally built as a private concession, but subsequently nationalized). Again, the restructuring of Panama Canal Authority could provide useful guidance. Despite some improvements, inefficient customs services continue to be an important logistics bottleneck. Other trade-related formalities, such as product standards, create additional frictions (see section 1.7). Broader reforms of the legal, regulatory, and institutional framework for all transport modes still need to be tackled. In Panama, the government withdrew from all commercial and most investment activities, created a competitive and transparent framework for the sector, and then relied on private initiative and competitive dynamics to unfold. Another contrast between the two countries is that the free zone in Panama is specializing in logistics and other services, whereas Egypt puts the main emphasis on industrial projects. If Egypt wants to fully leverage its strategic position on the Suez Canal, it should build on its recent transport sector reforms and develop a strategy for the development of a logistics cluster.

[109] Containerization International (April 1999). Legislation referred to are law 1/1998 and decrees 30-31/1998.
[110] Financial Times (20 August 1999).
[111] MEED (20 August 1999).

Box 4.6 The Benefits of Good Advice and Transparent Procedures

Both sector reforms and individual privatization transactions involve complex technical, legal, and financial issues. It is thus critical that governments receive the best possible advice. Assistance from second-rate consultants is not only money wasted, but usually leads to suboptimal policy decisions. Given the high economic costs of such mistakes, it generally pays to hire top-notch advisors, even if they charge comparatively high fees. Following a number of disappointing privatization results in Egypt, for instance, the government issued a policy statement in July 1998 declaring that international advisors would be involved in all future asset disposals. The willingness to pay a fair price for good advice, however, is not enough in itself. It is also important to carefully select consultants, to closely monitor their performance, and to provide them with the right incentives. Finally, tender processes for privatizations, concessions, or procurement contracts should be transparent and well-managed. This involves carefully prepared tender documents, international competitive bidding, a transparent selection procedure, careful bid evaluation, and speedy contract negotiations. All this will lower transaction costs, increase competition between bidders, and enhance a country's reputation in the international investor community. The Public Private Infrastructure Facility (PPIAF), a multi-donor initiative managed by the World Bank. – published a comprehensive handbook to help governments handle such transactions: *Toolkit – A Guide for Hiring and Managing Advisors or Private Participation in Infrastructure, PPIAF (2001),* (*www.ppiaf.org*).

BIBLIOGRAPHY

BIBLIOGRAPHY

Websites

Airport Council International, ACI (*www.airports.org*).

Arab Air Carriers Organization, AACO (*www.aaco.org*).

Arab Chambers (*www.arabchamber.com*).

Arab World Online (*www.awo.net*).

Association of European Airlines, AEA (*www.aea.be*).

Baltic Ports Organization, BPO (*www.bpo.sai.se*).

Bolero (*www.boleroltd.com*).

Eurocontrol (*www.eurocontrol.be*).

European Civil Aviation Conference, ECAC (*www.ecac-ceac.org*).

European Commission (*www.europa.eu.int/comm/index_en.htm*).

European Commission, Directorate General External Relations, DG Relex, Euro-Med web-site (*europa.eu.int/comm/external_relations/med_mideast/intro/*).

European Commission, Directorate General for Energy and Transport, DG TREN (*www.europa.eu.int/comm/dgs/energy_transport/index_en.html*).

European Commission, DG TREN, air transport (*www.europa.eu.int/comm/transport/themes/air/*).

European Commission, DG TREN, land-based transport (*www.europa.eu.int/comm/transport/themes/land*).

European Commission, EuropAid (*www.europa.eu.int/comm/dgs/europeaid/index.htm*).

European Commission, Directorate General for Competition, DG Competition (*www.europa.eu.int/comm/dgs/competition/index_en.htm*).

European Commission, Directorate General for Taxation and Customs Union, Customs Union website (*www.europa.eu.int/comm/taxation_customs/customs/customs.htm*).

European Conference of Ministers of Transport (*www.oecd.org/cem*).

Free and Fair Post Initiative (*www.freefairpost.com*).

Holland International Distribution Council, HIDC (*www.hidc.nl*).

International Air Transport Association, IATA (*www.iata.org*).

International Chamber of Commerce, ICC (*www.iccwbo.org*).

ICC Transport Homepage (*www.iccwbo.org/home/menue_transport.asp*).

International Civil Aviation Organization, ICAO (*www.icao.int*).

International Express Carriers Conference, IECC (*www.iecc.ch*).

International Federation of Freight Forwarders Associations, FIATA (*www.fiata.org*).

International Maritime Organization, IMO (*www.imo.org*).

Middle East Economic Digest, MEED (*www.meed.com*).

Organisation for Economic Co-operation and Development, OECD (*www.oecd.org*).

Port of Antwerp (*www.portofantwerp.be*).

PostEurope (*www.posteurop.org*).

Swedish Maritime Administration (*www.sjofartsverket.se*).

TINA Secretariat (*www.tinasecretariat.at*).

United Nations Commission on International Trade Law, UNCITRAL (*www.uncitral.org*).

United Nations Conference on Trade and Development, UNCTAD (*www.unctad.org*).

United States Bureau of Transport Statistics (*www.bst.gov*).

World Bank (*www.worldbank.org*).

World Bank, Port Reform Toolkit (*www.worldbank.org/html/fpd/transport/ports/toolkit.htm*).

World Bank, Global Facilitation Partnership (*wbln0018.worldbank.org/twu/gfp.nsf/*).

World Bank, Middle East and North Africa Region (*wbln0018.worldbank.org/mna/mena.nsf*).

World Bank, Transport Sector Website (*www.worldbank.org/html/fpd/transport/*).

World Bank, railway information (*www.worldbank.org/html/fpd/transport/rail/rl_conc.htm*).

World Bank, Viewpoint Notes (*www.worldbank.org/html/fpd/notes/*).

World Customs Organization, WCO (*www.wco.org*).

World Tourism Organization (*www.world-tourism.org*).

World Trade Organization, WTO (*www.wto.org*).

Documents

Advani, Asheesh.1999. *Passenger-Friendly Airports: Another Reason for Airport Privatization*. Los Angeles: Reason Foundation.

Al Khouri, Riad. 2000. "Trade Policies in Jordan, Lebanon, and Saudi Arabia." In Bernard Hoekman and Hanaa Kheir-El-Din, eds., *Trade Policy Developments in the Middle East and North Africa*. Washington, D.C.: Mediterranean Development Forum and World Bank Institute.

Amiot, Francois, and Ovadia Salama. 1996. "Logistical Constraints on International Trade in the Maghreb." World Bank Policy Research Working Paper Series 1598. Washington, D.C.: World Bank.

Association of European Airlines 1998. *Yearbook 1998*. Brussels.

——.1999. *Yearbook 1999*. Brussels.

——.2000. *Yearbook 2000*. Brussels.

Burr, K. 1998. In Organisation for Economic Co-operation and Development, Trilog. *Conference Proceedings: Public Policy Issues in Global Freight Logistics*. Paris: OECD.

Carbajo, José, and Antonio Estache. 1996. "Competing Private Ports – Lessons from Argentina". World Bank Viewpoint Series 100.

Drewry Shipping Consultants. 2000. *Mediterranean Container Ports and Shipping*. London.

Economist Intelligence Unit 1998a. *Panama Country Profile 1997-98*. London.

——. 1998b. *Panama Country Profile II/1998*. London.

——. 2000a. *Egypt Country Profile 2000*. London.

——. 2000b. *Panama Country Profile 2000*. London.

——. 2001a. *Egypt Country Profile 2001*. London.

——. 2001b. *Morocco Country Profile 2001*. London.

——. 2001c. *Tunisia Country Profile 2001*. London.

——. 2002. *Egypt Country Profile 2002*. London.

Engel, Eduardo, Ronald Fischer, and Alexander Galetovic. 1997. "Privatizing Roads – A New Method for Auctioning Highways." World Bank Viewpoint Note Series 112. Washington, D.C.

Estache, Antonio, and José Carbajo. 1996. "Designing Toll Road Concessions – Lessons from Argentina." World Bank Viewpoint Note Series 99. Washington, D.C.

Estache, Antonio, and Ginés de Rus. 2000. *Privatization and Regulation of Transport Infrastructure – Guidelines for Policymakers and Regulators*. Washington, D.C.: World Bank Institute.

Etzioni, Amir. 1999. *Reforming Israel's Seaports*. Jerusalem: Institute for Advanced Strategic and Political Studies.

European Commission. 1991a. *Council Directive* (91/440/EEC) *of 29 July 1991 on the Development of the Community's Railways.* Brussels.

——. 1991b. *Reinforcing Quality Services in Sea Ports: A Key for European Transport.* Brussels. COM (2001) 35 final.

——. 1993. *Council Regulation (EEC) 95/93 of 18 January 1993 on Common Rules for the Allocation of Slots at Community Airports*. Brussels.

——. 1994. *Road Freight Transport in the Single European Market.* Brussels.

——. 1995a. *Council Directive* (95/18/EC) *of 19 June 1995 on the Licensing of Railway Undertakings*. Brussels.

——. 1995b. *Council Directive* (95/19/EC) *of 19 June 1995 on the Allocation of Railway Infrastructure Capacity and the Charging of Infrastructure Fees.* Brussels.

——. 1995c. *Towards Fair and Efficient Pricing in Transport: Policy Options for Internalizing the External Costs of Transport in the European Union*. Brussels. Green Paper COM (95) 691 final.

——. 1996a. *Council Decision 1692/96/EC of 23 July 1996 on Community Guidelines for the Development of the Trans-European Network*. Brussels.

——. 1996b. *Council Directive 96/67/EC of 15 October 1996 on Access to the Groundhandling Market at Community Airports*. Brussels.

——. 1996c. *White Paper on A Strategy for Revitalizing the Community's Railways*. Brussels. COM (1996) 421 final.

——. 1997a. *Communication on Intermodality and Intermodal Freight Transport in the European Union*. Brussels. COM (97) 243 final.

——. 1997b. *Community Competition Law in the Transport Sector – Recent Landmarks 1991-1997.* Brussels.

——. 1998a. *Communication Concerning the Euro-Mediterranean Partnership in the Transport Sector*. Brussels. COM (1998) 7 final.

——. 1998b. *Communication on the Euro-Mediterranean Partnership in the Transport Secto*r. Brussels.

——. 1998c. *Communication on Trans-European Transport Network – 1998 Report on the Implementation of the Guidelines and Priorities for the Future*. Brussels. COM (1998) 614 final.

——. 1998d. *Trans-European Transport Network – 1998 Report*. Brussels. COM (1998) 614 final.

——. 1998e. *White Paper on Fair Payment for Infrastructure Use: A Phased Approach to a Common Infrastructure Charging Framework in the EU.* Brussels. COM (1998) 466 final.

——. 1999a. *Communication on the Creation of the Single European Sky*. Brussels. COM (1999) 614.

——. 1999b. *Guide to the Transport Acquis*. Brussels.

——. 1999c. *Communication on the European Airline Industry: From Single Market to World-Wide Challenges*. Brussels. COM (1999) 182 final.

——. 2000a. *Single European Sky – Report of the High Level Group*. Brussels.

——. 2000b. *Proposal for a Regulation of the European Parliament and of the Council on establishing common rules in the field of Civil Aviation and creating a European Aviation Safety Agency*. Brussels. COM (2000) 598.

——. 2000c. *Communication on Galileo*. Brussels. COM (2000) 750 final.

——. 2000d. *Proposal for a Council Decision on the Signature of the Interbus Agreement on the International Occasional Transport by Coach and Bus*. Brussels. COM (2000) 799 final.

——. 2001a. *Communication on Enhancing Euro-Mediterranean Cooperation on Transport and Energy*. Brussels.

——. 2001b. *Proposal for a Decision of the European Parliament and of the Council Amending Decision No. 1692/96/EC on Community Guidelines for the Development of the Trans-European Transport Network*. Brussels.

——. 2001c. *White Paper on European Transport Policies for 2010: Time to Decide*. Brussels. COM (2001) 370.

European Commission and Eurostat. 2000. *Euro-Mediterranean Statistics*. Luxembourg.

European Conference of Ministers of Trade and Organization for Economic Cooperation and Development. 2000a. *Transport Benchmarking – Methodologies, Applications, and Data Needs*. Paris: OECD.

——. 2000b. *Integration of European Inland Transport Markets*. Paris: ECMT/OECD.

Eurostat. 1999. *EU Direct Investment Yearbook 1999*. Luxembourg.

——. 1999. *Tourism in the Mediterranean Partner Countires 4/1999*. Luxembourg.

——. 1999. *Transport Trends in the Mediterranean Countries*. Luxembourg.

——. 2000. *Euro-Mediterranean Statistics 2/2000*. Luxembourg.

——. 2001. *Euro-Mediterranean Statistics 1/2001*. Luxembourg.

——. 2001. *Tourism Trends in the Mediterranean Countries*. Luxembourg.

——. *MED-Trans Database*. Luxembourg.

Gannon, Colin, and Zmarak Shalizi. 1995. "The Use of Sectoral and Project Performance Indicators in Bank-Financed Transport Operations." World Bank Working Paper Series 16121. Washington, D.C.

Gaviria, Juan. 1998. "Port Privatization and Competition in Colombia". World Bank Viewpoint Note Series 167.

Guislain, Pierre. 1997. *The Privatization Challenge – A Strategic, Legal and Institutional Analysis of International Experience*. Washington, D.C.

Gwilliam, K. 1998. *Public Policy Issues in Global Freight Logistics – Conference Proceedings of the OECD Trilog Plenary Symposium*. Paris.

Halperin, Ricardo, and Patrick Malone. 1999. "Overview of World Experience in Private Financing in the Road Sector." World Bank ECSIN Working Paper Series 2, Washington, D.C.

Handoussa, Heba, and Jean-Louis Reiffers. 2001. *The Evolution and Structure of Trade and Investment Between the EU and its Mediterranean Partners*. FEMISE Research Network.

Hirsch, Seev, Shauli Katznelson, and David Sasson. 1993. *The Economics and Politics of a Free Economic Zone and Port in the Gaza Region*. Tel Aviv: Institute of Business Research.

Holland International Distribution Council. 1998. *World Wide Logistics – The Future of Supply Chain Services*. Ed. Phillip Hastings.

International Air Transport Association. 1996. *Regulatory Developments in 1996*. Geneva.

——. 1997. *Regulatory Developments in 1997*. Geneva.

——. 1999a. *Annual Report 1999*. Geneva.

——. 1999b. *Regulatory Developments in 1999*. Geneva.

——. 2001. *World Air Transport Statistics 2001*. Geneva.

——. 2002. *Passenger Forecast 2001-2005 – Special Interim Edition*. Geneva.

International Monetary Fund. 1998. *Direction of Trade Statistics Yearbook 1998*. Washington, D.C.

International Post Corporation. 2001. *Improving the Quality of International Mail – First Half Year Results 2001*. Brussels.

Israel, Government of. 1996. "Programs for Regional Cooperation 1997". (draft). Tel Aviv.

Israel, Ports and Railways Authority. 1999. *Sea of Challenges – Overview of Israeli Ports Development Plan*. MEED (26 May 2000). Tel Aviv.

Juhel, Marc. 1998. *Globalization, Privatization, and Restructuring of Ports*. Washington, D.C.: World Bank.

Kaninski, Batolomiej, and Francis Ng. 2001. *Trade and Production Fragmentation – Central European Economies in EU Networks of Production and Marketing*. Washington, D.C.: World Bank.

Kerf, Michel, David Gray, Thimoty Irwin, Celine Levesque, Robert Taylor, and Michael Klein. 1998. *Concessions for Infrastructure – A Guide to their Design and Award*. Washington, D.C.: World Bank.

Kheir-El-Din, Hanaa. 2000. "Enforcement of Product Standards as Barriers to Trade: The Case of Egypt." In Bernard Hoekman and Hanaa Kheir-El-Din, eds., *Trade Policy Developments in the Middle East and North Africa*. Washington, D.C.: Mediterranean Development Forum and the World Bank Institute.

Kopicki, Ron, and Louis Thompson. 1997. *Best Methods of Railway Restructuring and Privatization*. Washington, D.C.: World Bank.

Lakshmanan, T.R, and William Anderson. 2001. "Transport and Trade in the North American Free Trade Agreement." In *Integration of Transport and Trade Facilitation*. Washington, D.C.

Liautaud, Gerard. 2001. "Maintaining Roads – The Argentine Experience with Output Based Contracts." World Bank Viewpoint Note Series 231. Washington, D.C.

Loir, Michel, and Pierre Guislain. 1997. *Royaume de Maroc: Participation du Secteur Privé dans les Infrastructures*. Washington, D.C.: World Bank.

Magold, Martin. 2001. *Transport Facilitation in Europe* (not published). United Nations Economic Commission for Europe. Geneva..

Mission of Mexico to the EU. 2000. *The Mexico-EU Free-Trade Agreement*. Brussels: Mission of Mexico to the EU.

Mitchell, Brigitta, and Karim-Jacques Budin. 1999. "The Abidjan-Ouagadougou Railway Concession." World Bank Findings Series 140. Washington, D.C.

Organisation for Economic Co-operation and Development. 1996. *Integrated Advanced Logistics for Freight Transport*. Paris.

——. 1997. *The Future of International Air Transport Policy*. Paris.

——. 1999a. *Discussion Document on Regulatory Reform in International Maritime Transport*. Paris.

——. 1999b. *Regulatory Reform in International Air Cargo Transportation*. Paris.

——. 1999c. *The Nature of Competition in the Airline Industry and Airline Alliances and Mergers*. Paris.

——. 2001. *The Development Dimensions of Trade*. Paris.

——, World Bank, and US Department of Transportation. 1998. *Public Policy Issues in Global Freight Logistics – Conference Proceedings of the OECD TRILOG Plenary Symposium*. Washington, D.C.

Ollivier, Gerald, and Pedro Taborga. 1999. "Development of Trade Support Services." World Bank ECSIN Working Paper Series 12. Washington, D.C.

Paelinck, Honoré. 1999. "*Maroc – Facilitation du Transport*". World Bank. Brussels.

Petri, Peter. 1997. "Trade Strategies for the Southern Mediterranean." OECD Technical Paper Series 127. Paris.

Piazolo, Daniel. 2001. *The Integration Process Between Eastern and Western Europe*. Kiel Institute of World Economic Studies Series 310. Berlin: Springer.

Ports Corporation Aqaba. 2000. *The Port of Aqaba – Handbook and Directory 1999/2000*. Aqaba.

Raven, John. 2000. *Trade and Transport Facilitation – An Audit Methodology*. Washington, D.C.: World Bank and International Express Carriers Conference.

——. 2001. *Trade and Transport Facilitation – A Toolkit for Audit, Analysis, and Remedial Action*. World Bank Discussion Paper Series 427. Washington, D.C.

Ruster, Jeff. 1997. "A Retrospective on the Mexican Toll Road Program (1989-94)." World Bank Viewpoint Series 125. Washington, D.C.

Sample, K. 1998. In Organisation for Economic Cooperation and Development Trilog. *Conference Proceedings: Public Policy Issues in Global Freight Logistics*. Washington, D.C.: World Bank and OECD.

Silva, Gisele. 1999. "Private Participation in the Airport Sector – Recent Trends." World Bank Viewpoint Note Series 202. Washington, D.C.

Smith, Graham, Nemat Shafik, Pierre Guislain, and James Reicher. 1997. *Getting Connected – Private Participation in Infrastructure in the Middle East and North Africa*. Washington, D.C.: World Bank.

Sommer, Dirk. 1999. "Private Participation in Port Facilities – Recent Trends." World Bank Viewpoint Note Series 193. Washington, D.C.

Swedish Maritime Administration. 2000. *Baltic Maritime Outlook 2000.* Stockholm.

Thompson, Louis, and Karim-Jacques Budin. 1997. "Global Trends in Railway Concessions – Delivering Positive Results." World Bank Viewpoint Note Series 134. Washington, D.C.

Tovias, Alfred. 1997. *Options for Mashrek-Israeli Regionalism in the Context of the Euro-Mediterranean Partnership*. Centre for European Policy Studies Research Report No. 67. Brussels.

Trujillo, Lourdes, and Gustavo Nombela. 2000. "Seaports." In Estache, Antonio and Ginés de Rus, eds., *Privatization and Regulation of Transport Infrastructure*. Washington, D.C.: World Bank Institute.

Tunisia, Ministry of Transport. 2000. *Evolution du Transport Maritime en Tunisie 1999-2000*. Tunis.

Tynan, Nicola. 1999. "Private Participation in the Rail Sector – Recent Trends." World Bank Viewpoint Note Series 186. Washington, D.C.

United Nations Conference on Trade and Development. 1998. *Review of Maritime Transport 1998.* Geneva.

United Nations Economic Commission for Europe, Transport Division. 1999. *International Agreements and Conventions in the Field of Transport* (not published). Geneva.

United Nations Economic Commission for Latin America. 1999. *Port Modernization: A Pyramid of Interrelated Challenges.* Santiago de Chile.

United Kingdom, Civil Aviation Authority. 1998. *The Single European Aviation Market – The First Five Years*. Cheltenham, England: Westward Digital Limited.

United Nations Economic Commission for Europe and European Commission. 1997. *Lisbon Declaration*. Geneva.

University of Texas at Austin. 1998. *Multimodal/Intermodal Transportation in the United States, Western Europe, and Latin America – Government Plans, Policies, and Programs*. Austin.

Willoughby, Christopher, and Phil Anderson.1999. "Eastern European and Central Asian Railways: Trends, Prospects, and Challenges." World Bank ECSIN Working Paper Series 10. Washington, D.C.

——. 1994. *World Development Report 1994 – Infrastructure for Development*. New York: Oxford University Press.

——. 1995a. *Airport Infrastructure – The Emerging Role of the Private Sector*. Washington, D.C.

——. 1995b. *Claiming the Future – Choosing Prosperity in the Middle East and North Africa*. Washington, D.C.

——. 1995c. *Claiming the Future*. Washington, D.C.

——. 1996. *Logistical Constraints on International Trade in the Maghreb*. Washington, D.C.

——. 1997a. *Brazil – Multimodal Freight Transport: Selected Regulatory Issues* (not published). Washington, D.C.

——. 1997b. *Morocco: Private Participation in Infrastructure – Synthesis*. Washington, D.C.

——. 1997c. *Tunisie – Étude sur la Stratégie des Transports*. Washington, D.C.

——. 1998a. *Egypt – Ports Sector Note* (not published). Washington, D.C.

——, and OECD. 1998b. *A Framework for the Design and Implementation of Competition Law and Policy*. Paris: OECD.

——. 1999a. *Algérie – Note sur la Strategie des Transports* (not published). Washington, D.C.

——. 1999b. *World Bank Debt Tables 1999*. Washington, D.C.

——. 1999c. *World Development Indicators 1999*. Washington, D.C.

——. 2000a. "Questionnaires to Assess Services Trade Policy and Performance". World Bank Research Program on Trade in Services. Washington, D.C.

——. 2000b. "Staff Appraisal Report: Klaipeda Port Project". Washington, D.C.

——. 2000c. "Syria – A Preliminary Assessment of Transport Costs for Export Development". Washington, D.C.

——. 2000d. *Transport Sector Restructuring in the Baltic States – Proceedings of a Seminar*. Riga: World Bank and Latvian Ministry of Transport and Communications.

——. 2000e. "Tunisia – Private Sector Assessment Update". Washington, D.C.

——. 2001a. "Egypt Country Assistance Strategy". Washington, D.C.

——. 2001b. *World Development Indicators 2001*. Washington, D.C.

——. *PPI Database*. Washington, D.C.

World Trade Organization. 1998a. "Air Transport Services". Geneva.

——. 1998b. "Maritime Transport Services". Geneva.

——. 1998c. "Land Transport Services". Geneva.

Zarrouk, Jamal. 2000. "Para-Tariff Measures in Arab Countries." In Bernard Hoekman and Hanaa Kheir-El-Din, eds., *Trade Policy Developments in the Middle East and North Africa*. Washington, D.C.: Mediterranean Development Forum and the World Bank Institute.